KU-263-586

ACC. No: 03149016

TALES OF
TWO CITIES

Also by Jonathan Conlin

Civilisation

The Nation's Mantelpiece:
A History of the National Gallery

The Pleasure Garden, from
Vauxhall to Coney Island (ed.)

JONATHAN CONLIN

TALES OF
TWO CITIES

Paris, London and the
Birth of the Modern City

Atlantic Books
London

942.1
CON

Published in Great Britain in 2013 by Atlantic Books,
an imprint of Atlantic Books Ltd.

Copyright © Jonathan Conlin, 2013

The moral right of Jonathan Conlin to be identified as the author of this work
has been asserted by him in accordance with the Copyright, Designs and
Patents Act of 1988.

All rights reserved. No part of this publication may be reproduced, stored
in a retrieval system, or transmitted in any form or by any means, electronic,
mechanical, photocopying, recording, or otherwise, without the prior
permission of both the copyright owner and the above publisher of this book.

Every effort has been made to trace or contact all copyright holders.
The publishers will be pleased to make good any omissions or rectify
any mistakes brought to their attention at the earliest opportunity.

10 9 8 7 6 5 4 3 2 1

A CIP catalogue record for this book is available from the British Library.

Hardback ISBN: 978-1-84887-026-0
Ebook ISBN: 978-1-78239-019-0
Paperback ISBN: 978-1-84887-025-3

Printed in Great Britain by TJ International Ltd, Padstow, Cornwall

Atlantic Books
An Imprint of Atlantic Books Ltd
Ormond House
26–27 Boswell Street
London
WC1N 3JZ

www.atlantic-books.co.uk

Contents

The city, however, does not tell its past, but contains it like the lines of a hand, written in the corners of the streets, the gratings of the windows, the banisters of the steps, the poles of the flags, every segment marked in turn with scratches, indentations, scrolls.

Italo Calvino, *Invisible Cities*

FIG. 1: Thomas Rowlandson, *The Paris Diligence.*

Rough Crossings

The Doll in the Diligence

Somewhere north of Abbeville, spring 1778

'Hold it in your lap, please, don't let it drop.'

'Don't worry, I'm holding her tight.'

That was it, then. The two women were sitting to his right. He could tell he had a gentleman to his left by his snores, which even the hardest jolts had not interrupted. But until now he hadn't been able to work out who was sitting next to him on the other side. Given the way everyone was squeezed together, he presumed there were another three passengers on the seat opposite him, and another by the opposite door on the right. But they remained silent, so he had only the pressure of clothing and knees to go on. What with the ladies' long dresses and the travelling cloaks, it was almost impossible to determine where one person stopped and another began. He felt like a mouse trapped inside a lady's workbox that was being shaken violently.

It was still dark when he had entered this London-bound coach at Abbeville. He had been the last of the eight passengers to board, and the window curtains were drawn. As was usual, the coach had left the Bureau

1

de la Diligence de Londres in the Rue Notre Dame des Victoires the day before, one of three noon departures a week. Leaving Paris via the Porte Saint-Denis, it had passed through Clermont-en-Beauvaisis, stopping for dinner at Amiens. It had then continued to Abbeville, where he had snatched a few hours' sleep before this early morning departure. He had his trusty copy of *The Spectator* in his pocket, but, like sleep, reading on the journey was clearly impossible. But then, he had read it so many times that he almost had it committed to memory.

And anyway, he was determined to be an attentive traveller. Hadn't he agreed to send reports back to a friend in Paris who edited a weekly newspaper? Once in England, he would observe the customs of the country with the eye of reason, taking time to study them closely and consider their advantages and disadvantages, rather than jumping to conclusions or simply parroting the prejudices of his fellow Frenchmen. He knew he had a lot to learn. He wasn't going to be like those aristocrats who visited London simply because it was fashionable, whose insights went little beyond noting that London, like Paris, has courtesans, gardens and theatres, and that you can get drunk on champagne there just as you can at home.

But how much longer was this journey going to take? Today they would dine at Montreuil-sur-Mer (which wasn't on the sea), spending the second night at Boulogne, where he had to decide whether to board ship for Dover or press on by road to Calais, where the Channel crossing was shorter. He cursed whomever had invented this moving building, the diligence [Fig. 1]. Compared to the carriages in which he had travelled around Paris, this infernal machine was archaic. None of those leaf-springs that made a ride in a *berline* so smooth. No fine carriage work here. Instead the massive cabin of wood and wicker swung on chains from the huge chassis, rocking violently every time the enormous wooden wheels hit a rock or a hole in the poorly surfaced road. And now, to make things worse, these two ladies were nervously fussing over – well, what?

A lapdog? Some equally spoiled brat of a child? Either way, they were in for some yapping or mewling, he knew it. He wondered idly whether it would rouse the man on his left, deaf to the world. Not that he could blame the child. Terrible, how fashionable ladies wrapped up their children in rich garments that restricted their movements and even stunted their growth. They weren't so foolish in England, he knew; there children of even the highest rank wore plain cotton clothes, which allowed them to move and play freely. Yes, those English certainly had a lot to teach us, he mused, pleased at the thought that he was already making useful observations on national customs, even though he had barely got under way.

The creaking, jolting and snoring continued for several hours. Gradually the sky lightened somewhat. Somewhere over there in the gloaming one of his fellow passengers awoke. Entirely forgetting that he was in the London diligence rather than tucked up at home, he made to rub the sleep out of his eyes. Lifting his arms, his elbows poked both of his neighbours in the face, setting off a wave of expletives and apologies in a babble of French and English, both good and bad:

Ouch!

Sir . . .

Ah!

Monsieur, je vous demande excuse!

Mind what you're about!

Madam, I beg your pardon.

Several of his fellow passengers were clutching or holding personal items in their laps – things too precious to leave in their trunks – which were piled in the luggage compartment over the front axle, where they were open to the prying gaze of every tiresome customs official. In the excitement these things slid to the floor, from where they were almost irretrievable.

It was now light enough for him to make out from his plain dress that the gentleman opposite and to the right was a Huguenot. He had been clinging on to a heavy breviary, probably because it would have pushed his trunk over the weight limit (there was a one-bag limit on the diligence, and you had to pay for every extra pound). On its journey to the floor it collided with the heavily swaddled creature on the lady's lap, striking it roughly where the head would have been. The woman shrieked. It must be a child, after all. Keeping his head, he reached across his neighbour, pulled up the curtains, lowered the windows and shouted to the coachman to stop. As the diligence juddered to a halt, everyone's eyes were drawn to the bundle. It had even captured the attention of the snoring man. The ladies began carefully removing some of the bundle's outer garments. Not a peep from the child. Had it been knocked unconscious?

He leaned over to take a look. Why, it wasn't a child at all! It was one of those fashion dolls that they sent each month from Paris to London! A large doll dressed in scaled-down versions of the latest fashions, sent to London to be studied by the city's dressmakers. This precious mannequin had been destined to become the idol of all those foolish followers of fashion who convened in London. Much was at stake, therefore, as the ladies inspected every aspect of the doll's attire to determine what damage it had sustained. He chuckled to himself as he imagined all the fine ladies of London going into fits on hearing the news that this accident in the London diligence had condemned them to wearing the same gowns two months running. Perhaps the English weren't so enlightened after all, he mused, as the doll was rewrapped, apparently none the worse for its adventure, and the diligence lurched on towards Calais.[1]

This account is based on a description taken from a 1778 issue of *Le Babillard*, a French periodical edited by James Rutlidge. The grandson of an Irish Catholic who had emigrated to Dunkirk in 1715, Rutlidge was determined to foster improved communication between London and Paris, England and France. As Rutlidge himself noted, his was the latest in a spate of French periodicals modelled on English ones, above all *The Spectator* and *The Tatler* (*Le Babillard* is French for a 'tatler', or talkative person).[2] Such periodicals reflected a new curiosity among the French about their neighbours, perhaps a willingness to improve relations, to question familiar national stereotypes. 'We feel that there may be something to be gained, for all of us, by acting thus,' Rutlidge wrote, 'and bit by bit we are learning to see the whole world as one vast school, where the only true masters acknowledged as such by reason are experience and propriety.'[3]

Our traveller was taking part in an experiment Rutlidge had announced in the twenty-fifth issue of *Le Babillard*. He had sent one young Parisian to report on what he observed in London, and a second young man, a Londoner, to do the same in Paris. Each was to write to him with their impressions and adventures. The study would, he promised, ensure that any prejudices that lurked on one side or the other would cancel each other out, allowing the voice of reason to come through loud and clear. Though travel was certainly involved, these letters were not to be travelogues. 'My intention is not that they admire a new sky, picturesque sites or grand buildings,' Rutlidge insisted.[4]

Whether or not these intrepid voyagers existed outside Rutlidge's imagination, their anecdotes certainly had a basis in fact. The fashion doll travelled between Paris and London regularly, even during wartime (when it had to take a detour via Ostend, rather than travelling direct, via Calais). The *modiste* or dressmaker whose shriek temporarily interrupts the diligence's journey, Madame Alari, was a real-life *modiste* who kept a shop near Hyde Park. Her companion is described as an Englishwoman returning from a three-month stay in Paris, where she had been sent by her employer to learn the art of dressing *à la Polonaise*.[5] We know from surviving indentures that London milliners and dressmakers did indeed send their staff to Paris to receive training in the latest fashions.[6]

Rutlidge's traveller certainly had grounds to be concerned that Anglo-French prejudices might influence how the two capitals were viewed as cities. Even Londoners who had spent time in Paris, like the journalist and radical politician John Wilkes, viewed Parisians as 'dancing slaves'.[7] Though starved and oppressed by their king, somehow they remained cheerful and fashionable. And deep down, Londoners knew they were badly dressed and tried their utmost to ape Parisian fashions. Late eighteenth-century prints and plays devoted to 'the Frenchman in London' and 'the Englishman in Paris' [Fig. 2] contrasted the bluff yet uncouth Londoner with the fashionable but effete Parisian. Samuel Foote's comedy *The Englishman in Paris* (1753) and its sequel, *The Englishman Return'd from Paris* (1756), lampooned his fellow countrymen for their poor command of French, love of money and cack-handed attempts to emulate French taste.

Indeed, the Londoner-in-Paris and the Parisian-in-London had become such stock figures that characters in plays such as Foote's *Englishman Return'd from Paris* could themselves comment on having seen Londoner-in-Paris characters on the Paris stage, alongside Parisian-in-London comedies by de Boissy.[8] Not that Foote wasn't above the odd piece of tub-thumping rhetoric, bemoaning the English love affair with Paris and in particular its luxuries, which were supposedly turning patriotic, stolid hearts of oak into mincing *petits maîtres*. In one speech a character named 'Classic' notes that, whereas in the old days Englishmen went to Paris as a contingent in conquering armies,

> Far other views attract our modern race,
> Trulls, toupees, trinckets, bags, brocades and lace;
> A Flaunting form, and a fictitious face.
> Rouse! Re-assume! Refuse a *Gallic* Reign,
> Nor let their Arts win that their Arms could never gain.[9]

But even as the audience cheered, Foote knew it wasn't quite that straightforward. Though they wrung their hands and clucked over the luxury, pride and vanity fostered by such useless baubles, Londoners loved their Parisian toys. Indeed, it was precisely this appetite among

FIG. 2: James Caldwell after John Collet, *The Englishman in Paris*, 1770.

the middle class that kick-started a process that we now call the Industrial Revolution, when Matthew Boulton's famed Soho Works in Birmingham began to churn out cheap gilt knock-offs of French shoebuckles and snuffboxes.[10] When writing his sequel, Foote included a prologue (addressed to the audience), which noted that Francophilia was *so* entrenched that, before his play began, the playwright 'dares demand Protection, Sirs, from you'.[11]

Fashion and taste were one axis on which the Paris–London relationship turned. Fashion dolls are recorded as passing from Paris to London as early as 1396.[12] Londoners recognized Paris as the capital of fashion and sought to keep up. Even if they sometimes saw these dolls as unmanning, demoralizing fripperies, or even as part of a deliberate conspiracy mounted against cherished English liberties, this exchange continued uninterrupted. An ongoing routine, it was remarked upon only when, as here, some mishap (such as a clumsy Huguenot dropping his book, a war – mere nothings, really, in the grand scheme of fashion) caused a hiatus. This scene inside a cramped London-bound diligence speaks of two cities locked together by such routine exchanges.

The Devil in the Channel

The Channel, Maundy Thursday 1780

The playwright Louis-Sébastien Mercier stood at the rail of the Dover packet as it sailed out of Calais harbour at six in the morning, thinking that there was something odd about the two men on deck. One tall, one short. The clothes they wore were that of a middle-class Englishman: decent, if a little simple, yet they did not seem to fit very well. The pair seemed nervous, keeping close together and not socializing with the other passengers, even though the crossing would take around four hours. They stayed on deck, rather than venturing below to the cabin, with its twelve little beds, each in its curtained niche.

Curious, Mercier resolved to observe them further. Like our first traveller, this Parisian was on his way to London to learn more about the English and their customs. Visiting London had become something of an enlightened fad after the publication of the great *philosophe* Voltaire's *Letters on the English Nation*. Born in 1740 on the Quai de l'École, between the Pont Neuf and the Louvre, Louis-Sébastien Mercier, the son of a sword-cutler, grew up in the heart of Paris. The family's wealth and income positioned them neatly between the middle class and the lower ranks. It was an ideal place from which to observe the manners of the city that Mercier would immortalize in his wide-ranging survey, the *Tableau de Paris* (1781–9).[13]

The *Tableau* consists of a series of short pen-portraits of Parisian social types, observations of street life and discussion of housing, religious institutions and civil administration, all larded with proposals for reforms intended to make Paris a more ordered and pleasant city in which to live. Whether it was protecting pedestrians from being run over by carriages, clearing overcrowded cemeteries or addressing the Parisians' fondness for small dogs, Mercier's urban commentary was a very enlightened mix of anticlericalism, utility and wit. The *Tableau de Paris* is justly celebrated as not only one of the finest portraits of Paris, but also of the modern city in general. [14]

Before he published his portrait of Paris, however, Mercier recognized that there was one thing he had to do: visit London, the largest city in Europe. It was impossible, Mercier believed, to pretend to know Paris without knowing something of London, too: 'Neighbour and rival, it is inevitable that in talking of Paris one comes to consider London. The parallel suggests itself. These cities are so similar and so different, yet bear such a strong resemblance to one another that, to paint the portrait of one, it is not, I think, out of place to take a look at some of the other's traits.'[15]

*

England was the only nation that could stand up to French power and influence. 'Paris holds sway in Switzerland, in Italy, in Germany and in Holland,' Mercier noted, but Paris did not hold sway in England; indeed, the relationship between Paris and London was that of rivals, rather than that of ruler and subject, a relationship characterized by mutual fascination, not by one-sided obedience.

And so Mercier found himself on the packet that Maundy Thursday in 1780. Eager to begin collecting information on the English, he decided to approach the mysterious couple, addressing them in their own language: English. Mercier knew it well, having learned it, like so many Frenchmen of his time, in order to read Shakespeare and Pope in the original. Upon speaking to them, however, he discovered that his fellow travellers were not English, but French. Furthermore, they were stars from the Paris stage, a world Mercier knew inside out. They were none other than the slack-rope artists Alexandre-Placide Bussart and Paolo Rédigé, known on the boulevard theatres of Paris simply as 'Placide' and 'The Little Devil'.

The two had adopted protective camouflage, they explained, trying to out-English the English in their dress, for fear they might be recognized as Frenchmen and attacked or insulted. And they were far from alone in their fear. It was widely believed in Paris that Londoners would rough up any Parisian foolish enough to appear in their streets. Addicted to cruel sports, the Londoner stalked his warren of streets with nary a Swiss guard or a policeman to keep his riotous tendencies in check. Visitors took their lives in their hands.[16] Another French traveller to London was warned by a friend that in London children stood at every upper window, ready to spit on any Frenchman who passed below.[17] Though Parisian fashion was admired, Parisians who appeared in fashionable dress in London streets during the 1780s were liable to meet with a frosty reception, and not just because France had fought on the side of the rebel colonists in what was called the United States. This made many Parisians fearful of travelling to London. In Paris, Mercier noted, 'they think that a Frenchman can't cross a London street without being insulted; that every Englishman is ferocious and eats raw meat.'[18]

Londoners themselves encouraged this stereotype, publishing prints like *The Frenchman in London* (1770) [Fig. 3]. Here a well-dressed Parisian has been trying to walk unmolested down a London street, only to find himself caught in a pincer movement: in front, a butcher (plenty of raw meat there) playfully holds up his fists, while behind him two women grab the tail (*queue*) of his fashionable wig, presumably making some unflattering allusion to monkeys, or to a particular part of this Frenchman's anatomy. The fact that this is a London print demonstrates Londoners' appreciation of this kind of behaviour. Though greasy and impolite, the butcher is more of a man than the cowardly, spindle-shanked Frenchman with his sword, ruffles and fine silk jacket, edged with gold lace.

Mercier was well aware of the comic potential of such clichés, and laughed much at the credulity of 'Placide' and 'The Little Devil'. They had nothing to worry about, he assured them. Although the French foreign minister Vergennes's strategy of aiding the rebel colonists in America had provoked some Londoners into excoriating French foreign policy, popular Francophobia had abated. The pair were visibly relieved at this. Seeing that there was nothing to fear and rejoicing to see the ship under sail, they began singing songs from comic opera. Comic songs, on Maundy Thursday, a day held in reverence by the English! From being too stiff and reserved, they had now gone to the opposite extreme of too much levity. Mercier quickly intervened, telling them to stop before they drew too much attention to themselves.

The journey from Paris to London was an all-in package costing 120 *livres tournois* (or francs). This included the diligence from Paris to Boulogne or Calais, the crossing to Dover and the journey from Dover to London, which was, mercifully enough, made by coach rather than

FIG. 3: Charles White after John Collet, *The Frenchman in London, 1770.*

diligence. It also included all meals and accommodation in hotels at Abbeville, Boulogne or Calais and Dover. But it did not include tips to the driver or to inn servants, custom fees and the cost of a visa at Boulogne, all of which added another eighteen *livres*. Passengers always stayed the night in Dover, regardless of how long the crossing took, at another hotel owned by the diligence company. The next day the coach left early, taking between four and five hours to reach Canterbury, where dinner would be eaten (the main meal of the day, eaten around midday). The horses and carriage were then changed. Passengers continued via Chatham, taking their evening meal at Rochester. Here they would be offered a choice between staying the night and pressing on to London.

Travellers approached London from the south, via St George's Fields, passing the obelisk at St George's Circus and crossing Westminster Bridge. The coach then rolled up Whitehall, past Charing Cross and up Haymarket, dropping off passengers at the eastern end of Piccadilly. Here a French-speaking manager could help them find their feet; it was best to spend the night at an inn next door for a shilling (twenty-four *sols*, with an extra half-shilling to the maid), looking for longer-term accommodation the next day. And Mercier would have needed such accommodation. He seems to have spent several months in London, observing the Gordon Riots at first hand. He could have hired a room in Jermyn Street for eight or nine shillings (ten or twelve *livres*) a week. There was a French *pension* in Leicester Square run by a Madame Artaud. An interpreter (if Mercier needed one) was one guinea (twenty-one shillings) a week.[19]

On his return to Paris, Mercier wrote a *Parallèle de Paris et de Londres*, a 152-page manuscript preserved in the Arsenal Library in Paris. In it he compared all aspects of life in the two capitals: bridges, prisons, food and drink, pets – even the different types of cold one was liable to catch. Mercier's *Parallèle* provides the ideal starting point for our journey, for it imagined the London–Paris relationship as a conversation about how to create the ideal city or utopia, or what the French philosophers of the eighteenth century called *la ville policée* ('the policed city', though 'police', as we shall see, meant something different then than it does today).[20]

La ville policée was ordered and well regulated, without being regimented. It was a city of plenty, luxury even, yet one free from the demoralizing effects of that luxury. Just as this book is about more than Paris and London, so Mercier addressed his readers, not as proud Parisians and Londoners, but as fellow members of the human race. 'Oh, poor humans,' he wrote, 'French or English! Your governments whip you up to set you on each other like dogs.' Instead, he insisted, they should compete in mutual emulation to see who could be more attentive to 'the duties of humanity'.[21]

In France, where the term 'police' originated, the concept derived from the idea of *policer ses moeurs*, 'policing manners'. In 1667, King Louis XIV established the *lieutenance générale de police*, which reformed the magistrature and took over a host of functions and responsibilities: for religion, public health, roads, paving, poor relief and security.[22] British writers found this concept useful, even if they struggled to translate the word into English. 'We are accused by the French, and perhaps but too justly, of having no word in our language, which answers to the word police,' wrote the collector and wit Horace Walpole, 'which therefore we have been obliged to adopt, not having, as they say, the thing.'[23] In the works of the moral philosopher Adam Smith and his fellow Scot Patrick Colquhoun, the remit of the 'police' embraced sanitation, paving and lighting, as well as the regulation of markets for provisions and the policing (in the more familiar, modern sense) of minor infractions of public order.[24]

The police of Paris were ever-present in the eighteenth-century capital, even if the popular image of the police spy or *mouchard* massively inflated their numbers. In London, the term 'police' had yet to denote a city-wide force of uniformed peace officers under a central command structure. Colquhoun's *Treatise on the Police of the Metropolis* (1796, first drafted 1792) did admittedly inspire the creation of the Thames River Police, the first force in Britain to carry that name. The Metropolitan Police Act (1829) that spawned the London 'bobby' was still several decades away, however. London would have to wait even longer, until the establishment in 1855 of the Metropolitan Board of Works (MBW), for there to be a single, city-wide authority able to coordinate slum clearance, sewer construction and other concerns understood as 'police' matters. In Mercier's day, therefore, municipal government in London was anything but an exercise in enlightened administration, being a patchwork of vestry committees and bodies regulating parish paving, lighting and night watches, which levied local rates and were staffed by individuals with little if any specialized knowledge or training. Nevertheless, these limitations did not stop Mercier and other Parisian observers from seeing London as a paragon of municipal policing.

In *la ville policée* cleanliness is paramount. Clean bodies and clean streets are healthy ones, and cleanliness requires circulation.[25] Mercier was obsessed with the circulation of air, water, effluent, bodies (both living and dead) and vehicles. He spent whole chapters of the *Parallèle* listing the Parisian buildings that he insisted must be torn down to improve circulation. Parisian bridges were to be widened: on top, by removing the houses that bordered either side of the roadway, as well as beneath, by removing the mill wheels that harnessed the river's flow even as they obstructed river traffic. London's Westminster Bridge (1750), its pavements and its street lighting made it a model of pedestrian-friendly circulation – in Mercier's eyes at least.

It was common to describe the city as a body, and so to equate any such blockage of circulation with a seizure or heart attack. This analogy was founded on William Harvey's discovery of the circulation of the blood early in the previous century, and was first made explicit by the diarist John Evelyn in his *Fumifugium: or the inconveniencie of the aer and smoke of London dissipated* (1661).[26] The concept in turn informed the straight avenues and wide market places that feature in plans for the reconstruction of London after the Great Fire of 1666; plans prepared by Christopher Wren and Robert Hooke, as well as by Evelyn himself. Though only a very small fraction of such utopian schemes were realized, post-fire regulations on the height of buildings and street widths did reflect a concern for circulation. So did the decision to relocate the general market from Cheapside to Honey Lane and to establish new markets to the west.[27]

But who is behind this 'police'? As Mercier put it: 'Once a problem is recognized and publicized, whose job is it to solve it?'[28] Does the city need an enlightened despot, assuming a person is to be found who can be trusted with such power? Can residents be trusted to each do their bit, in the expectation that, like Adam Smith's famous 'invisible hand', an intelligent system will emerge from the sum of their individual actions? The contrast between the highly centralized administration of Paris (which France's rulers have never lost sight of) and the patchwork of London, mentioned above, afforded Mercier and later writers the perfect opportunity to wrestle with such questions.

Mercier failed to find an answer to them. At times in the *Parallèle* he struck the pose of the obedient subject of the good King Louis XVI. If the king only knew about this or that abuse, Mercier insisted, everything would be made right. This convenient fiction – that the king could do no wrong and could be 'surprised' into a faux pas only by this or that wicked minister – helped many a would-be reformer protect himself from charges of sedition in late eighteenth-century London and Paris.[29] Yet Louis XVI is also presented as a remote authority, a monarch who sweeps past in his cavalcade, unaware of the suffering of his city's people.[30] Mercier was writing at a time when royal authority was contested, and not only by the *parlements* (courts charged with registering royal edicts).

In the end his position seems to be that of an enlightened absolutist. Mercier wanted to reform abuses of royal authority, rather than replace that authority. There is little sense of him appealing to a self-conscious 'public opinion'. He hailed the activities of voluntary associations on both sides of the Channel, such as the Société de Médecine and the Society for the Encouragement of Arts, Manufactures and Commerce. But Mercier did not see such activity as a reproach to the crown or to the state as institutions, nor as a case of outsiders (a rising middle class or bourgeoisie) using such 'public-spirited' activities to stake a claim to a role in government.[31]

This makes Mercier's vision of London as a *ville policée* rather strange. It is a place where disinterested, patriotic citizens take it upon themselves to act independently of the monarch. Compared to Louis XVI, the English sovereign is a much reduced figure. As Mercier noted, George III was regularly insulted in the public prints to be found in the windows of London's printshops. In contrast to Louis XVI's entourage, the English king travelled around town in a humble sedan chair, with no more by way of a retinue than three men armed with old pikes.[32] Even if much of it remained little more than a façade in Mercier's day, the royal palace of the Louvre was an astonishing architectural wonder compared to a ramshackle firetrap like St James's Palace. That George III moved into an aristocrat's house (Buckingham House) in 1761 rather than build his own palace speaks volumes about the relative poverty of the British court compared to the French. Yet rather than seeking to mimic this decentralized, consensual model, Mercier's plan to make Paris more like his ideal London was an absolutist, top-down master plan. His instructions were to be followed 'whatever the cost', 'by force' if necessary.[33]

There are moments where Mercier seemed to acknowledge the paradoxical nature of his position. Since the Parisian masses have been oppressed for centuries, it was, he conceded, unreasonable to expect them not to abuse whatever freedom they might be given by the French government. The latter, as 'the sole arbiter', held entirely in its hands their happiness as well as their unhappiness, and decided, apparently willy-nilly, which of them the *peuple* (that is, the common people) were going to get.[34] On the other hand Mercier had to concede that the strength of civil society in London partly depended on a toleration of disorder. Were the riotous masses (*la populace*) of London to be managed by a 'firm police', they would, he said, lose their courage and end up subject to a despot or a foreign power.[35] It is possible, therefore, to have both too much and too little *police*. In his struggle to reconcile the warring claims of authority, freedom and police, Mercier is very much of his own time, and of ours.

His project was to reimagine the metropolis as a polite, ordered, yet diverse and exciting place in which to live. Paris and London were the greatest cities in the world, he believed, and therefore had much to learn from one another. Much would get lost in translation, because of national prejudices or in armed conflicts fomented by regimes on either side of the Channel to keep their people at loggerheads. 'The French government fears nothing more than that the spirit of the English nation might arise in France,' Mercier noted, 'while the English nation fears nothing more than French tastes, fashions, manners and habits – and that the spirit of the French government might arise in England. This is what keeps the two nations apart.'[36] He urged Londoners and Parisians to stop playing the regime's game and discover the truth for themselves. This was very much an enlightened process, in the spirit of the Prussian philosopher Immanuel Kant's essay of 1784, *What is Enlightenment?* Londoners and Parisians needed to free themselves from jingoism and learn what they could from each other. As this volume demonstrates, they learned a lot, even if they clung to some prejudices and even fashioned new ones along the way.

This book is divided into six chapters, each devoted to one aspect of city life that emerged from, or was heavily influenced by, traffic between Paris and London. It argues that this dialogue formed part of a larger process by which the city-as-problem was tamed over the course of the eighteenth and nineteenth centuries, and metropolitan living moved from being the questionable exception to the fashionable rule. In the later middle ages and the early modern period it was commonplace to describe cities as monstrous growths, parasites that would, if left unchecked, sap the nation's body of its physical and moral strength. At a time when sanitation and medical facilities were poor, urban growth did indeed rely on constant replenishment from the country, rather than being self-generated.[37]

Thanks to this shift in both the lived reality and the perception of urban living, the monster was tamed, creating the modern European city, in which the mingling of different ranks is celebrated as exciting and fun, rather than resisted as frightening and politically dangerous. Here the dead are relocated to their own suburbs, rather than allowed to poison the living. Walking around is a delight, rather than a perilous chore. It is a place where people live piled up in layers, but they call their apartment a 'home'. This city has its own mythologies, which make even its most sinister corners and most disreputable activities an inexhaustible source, not of moral panic or fear, but of pleasurable suspense and thrill.

We start in the home, looking at the development of the apartment block in Paris and attempts to introduce this horizontal way of life to London. This might seem an odd place to begin, given the contrast between the Londoner's love affair with the terraced house and the Parisian penchant for living stacked up on top of each other. Where London sprawled, blurring any vestige of a city wall, Paris sprouted, hemmed in by its fortifications and other barriers. London's gates were left open from 1660; the gatehouses were removed for road widening in the course of the following century. Although Paris remodelled its walls as public promenades in the late seventeenth century, the tax wall (also called the Wall of the Farmers General, 1785) and later the Thiers Wall (1841–4) continued to restrict its expansion outwards, with entry possible only through gates.

London nonetheless experimented with what some architects called 'French flats', both as a replacement for the working-class slum and as 'mansion blocks' intended to provide the elite with a pied-à-terre.

Londoners knew all about what went on in Parisian apartment buildings (or, at least, they thought they did) from reading 'wicked' French novels by Zola. At the same time they recognized the advantages of horizontal living, both in terms of personal convenience and as a more sustainable model of urban development. Though Londoners continued to suffer from the English obsession with home ownership, these experiments did introduce a rival model that many twentieth- and twenty-first-century Londoners found appealing.

We then consider how Londoners and Parisians learned to walk. In the medieval and early modern city, nobody walked – at least, nobody who was anybody. Those who did travel through the city on foot scurried as their work and relative poverty dictated. They did not walk, they dodged – carts, carriages, their masters. In our own period the city became a place to walk, saunter, strut, parade and shop. For walking to become an activity in itself, and a polite one at that, street architecture needed to change. The public thoroughfare needed lights, benches, bollards, gutters and, above all, pavements. Perceptions of the city itself needed to change, too. The conurbation had to become a spectacle to be enjoyed, both day and night. The solitary, male urban walker or *flâneur* is held to be the quintessential representative of urban modernity, and no book on the modern city would be complete without him. He is traditionally seen as a nineteenth-century figure; here we explore his eighteenth-century origins.

Chapter 3 considers another Parisian import to London: the restaurant. Starting life in Mercier's time as an enlightened and surprisingly ascetic exercise in purging, the restaurant quickly broadened the range of its offerings. As we shall see, however, Londoners and Parisians viewed this institution differently: where the former saw a public stage, the latter perceived a retreat into anonymity. We then hit the town in Chapter 4, looking at resorts for dancing and singing in the late eighteenth and nineteenth centuries, in particular the music hall. From Champagne Charlie's heavy swell to the high-kicking *chahut*, the city's fizzing nightlife and even our notion of 'Gay Paree' were all shaped by cross-Channel dialogue.

The modern metropolis is at once a built environment and a text. It is composed of bricks and mortar, overlaid with that imagined entity that we all carry around with us in our imaginations. This city of the imagination weaves its web of metaphors, associations and fantasies around the actual buildings, streets and spaces. Meanwhile the buildings' design shifts to reflect those fantasies, in turn spawning new ones.[38] Chapter 5 considers one such imaginary city of the *fin de siècle*: the nocturnal criminal underworld, which provides the missing links that connect the most mundane, routine details of our lives with the remarkable, unspeakable exceptions. Here the *flâneur* becomes the detective.

Finally we arrive at the necropolis, the 'city of the dead' or cemetery, which emerged first in Napoleonic Paris, with the creation of Père Lachaise. Moving the dead from overcrowded, inner-city, parish burial grounds to new 'garden cemeteries' addressed a long-standing public health concern. The style and layout of Parisian cemeteries was closely followed at London's Kensal Green (1832) and at other privately operated cemeteries that opened over the following decade. This style itself reflected earlier English influences, as for example when an Anglomania prior to 1789 prompted French aristocrats to absorb English poetry and landscape architecture. Out of this hybridization emerged a new way of accommodating the dead. Sanitized of working-class 'scrubs', here the middle class created their ideal city, a model for the 'garden suburbs' in which the living would, eventually, find their own resting place.

The case studies presented here build on the study of architectural plans, paintings, drawings, prints and photographs, as well as newspapers and magazines. With a few exceptions, travelogues have not been used, representing as they do a discrete genre with its own set of conventions and concerns, very different from the concerns of those permanently resident in the city.[39] Fictional works are included, not only because they,

21

too, are based on close observation of actual buildings and behaviour (as Zola's realist novels certainly were), but because of the part they played in shaping how contemporaries experienced the capital in which they lived. For example, though voiced by a fictional character in a work of crime fiction, Holmes's injuction, 'Always carry a firearm east of Aldgate,' shaped how Arthur Conan Doyle's readers viewed the East End. If the specific writers considered here are less 'literary' than those normally cited in studies of Paris and London, they were certainly widely read at the time. They also range beyond the familiar, well-worked canon of writings on the city by Balzac, Baudelaire and Dickens.

It may seem odd that I have selected these two cities as my subject because for so long we have been used to seeing them as opposites: the ill-planned, hard-working 'Great Wen' that we associate with William Hogarth and Charles Dickens versus the Capital of Pleasure, 'Gay Paree', its boulevards thronged by Baudelairean *flâneurs* and other pleasure seekers. Britons in the eighteenth century, we are regularly told, defined themselves against a French 'other'. The British and the French were 'natural and necessary enemies'; they kept each other faithful to their assigned, but genuine characters.[40] Within an urban context, this made it possible for Londoners to view in a positive light their relative lack of fine churches and palaces. This absence was testament to the presence of liberty, as opposed to Roman Catholic 'superstition' and despotism, which Georgians summed up as 'wooden shoes': a reference to the clogs worn by penurious French peasants, in contrast to the leather shoes of their English equivalents. Parisians for their part could leave grubby industry and penny-pinching commerce to 'splenetic', 'melancholic' Londoners, who were congenitally unsuited to the real charms of life in the French capital.

Many books and exhibitions have documented the relationship between Berlin and St Petersburg, Paris and Rome, as well as several other pairings, even that of Paris and Edo, but none has addressed that of Paris and

London. While there is a truly enormous literature on London and Paris in isolation, no one has yet attempted to explore the relationship between these two cities across the centuries.[41] That is what this book attempts to do. It is not intended as a comparative history, however, nor even as a history of intercity transfer. For such a discussion to be possible, we would need to situate the reader in a separate, third place, equidistant from our two poles, in order to be in a position to assess similarities and differences. We would need to freeze time, acknowledging that all comparisons are taken from snapshots. We would have to presume a stable group of terms to denote what was being compared, ranging from, say, 'cemetery' right up to 'city'. We would need to identify such things as points of departure and arrival, directions of influence, etc. Even if we pinned down evidence that this or that London institution was in fact Parisian, discovery would come at a cost: in which case, we would have to accept that there is in fact some fixed notion of what was or was not 'Parisian', 'urban' and so on.

In the spirit of *histoire croisée*, this book concentrates on the process of crossing and exchange, on the city as a series of intersections. It recognizes that many of the terms we use are themselves artefacts of the process we are endeavouring to describe. This discussion is not interested in point scoring, in identifying this or that trait as constitutive of Paris or London in isolation. It might be possible to distil the story of the development of the two capitals as modern cities between around 1700 and 1900 into a game of cross-Channel tennis, of influence on one side, followed by reception on the other. As with a tennis serve, influences might be resisted, assimilated, modified or diluted. Yet the interaction described here is too complicated and too reflexive for this concept to be helpful. The crossings were more than exchanges. Paris and London did not become more or less Parisian or urban as a result of these crossings; they made them the great cosmopolitan centres they are today. New ideas, new activities and new understandings of the city developed in the crossing itself.[42]

A Boulevard in Marylebone

A summer evening in Marylebone Pleasure Gardens, 1776

There were less troublesome ways for travellers to make the journey between London and Paris than permitting themselves to be jolted to pieces inside a diligence or tossed about in the Channel. In the summer of 1776 the managers of Marylebone Pleasure Gardens [Fig. 4] printed and posted announcements informing the public that 'the Boulevards of Paris' could be enjoyed at their establishment for mere pence. Publican Daniel Gough had relaunched his pub and associated bowling green as a pleasure garden in 1738, charging one shilling admission and offering food, wines and a band performing 'concertos, overtures, and airs'. This venture was located on Marylebone High Street, on an eight-acre site covered today by Devonshire and Weymouth Streets. Though not quite as large and nowhere near as fashionable as its great south London rival, Vauxhall, Marylebone's pleasure garden had its tree-lined *allées* as well as a large assembly room and a temple or 'Great Room'. Like Vauxhall, it was on the edge of town, although the laying out of a major new thoroughfare to the north (Marylebone Road) in 1757 effectively cut it off from the fields that had previously been its backdrop.

'The Boulevards of Paris' consisted of a series of stalls set up in imitation of a Parisian shopping street, and may have built on the area's association with the French Huguenot community in London, whose church (St Marylebone) stood next to the Gardens. According to one newspaper's account, this theme-park-like extravaganza was pretty successful. 'As an attempt only to represent that busy chearful Spot, it is undoubtedly entitled to the Applause it met with.' The outside wall of the assembly room was originally fitted with a row of open wooden boxes in which parties could sit at small tables and order food and drink, watching the world go by. These had been converted into shops of the kind supposedly

FIG. 4: John Donowell, *A view of Marylebone Gardens*, 1761.

found on the boulevards of Paris, staffed by actors playing the parts of the shopkeepers, each with their name marked on a backlit transparency. There was Crotchet, a music shop; La Blonde, a milliner; Trinket, a 'Top Shop' (that is, a toy shop); Tête, a hairdresser; and so on. The actors initially failed to put their hearts into it, 'till the Humour of the Company had raised their Spirits by purchasing'.

As well as their names containing French puns (the hairdresser being named 'Tête', or 'Head'), the types of shop clearly referred to Paris's fame as Europe's toy town, in the Georgian sense of the word 'toy': a bauble or knick-knack whose only value lay in display. The placement of two kites in one otherwise empty stall was probably a visual joke, kites being associated with over-fanciful and foolish notions. Paris seemed to invent such toys faster than names could be found for them, as the catch-all English term 'kickshaw' (meaning toy or frivolous trinket) indicated, being Franglais for *quelque chose* ('something'). The nineteenth-century French word *nouveauté* did a rather better job of capturing this sense of a bibelot desired for its novelty rather than its utility.

The assembly room's interior was illuminated with coloured lamps and furnished at one end to look like the English Coffee House in Paris. The 'mistress' of this establishment again proved a disappointment, not being considered vivacious enough. As the newspaper observed, 'Even a Quaker might have taken his Oath that she had never been within Sight of Calais.'[43] Over the following weeks, the display was repeated and new features added, creating an even more elaborate effect. This was the new Paris of the Boulevard du Temple, the increasingly fashionable Rue Saint Honoré and the Champs Elysées: with straight lines, wide carriageways, new shops and new leisure resorts. A French gentleman visitor conceded that it did work, in a way. 'Ma foi!' he is said to have cried on entering the pleasure garden. 'It is a passing resemblance – but it is not quite right.'[44]

For Mercier, Rutlidge and other enlightened men of letters in the years around 1780, the ideal city was located somewhere between Paris and London, or perhaps in some hypothetical metropolis that was both at the same time. As travellers crossed from one to the other, going to and fro, in person, in print and in their imaginations, two cities that had initially seemed jealous rivals started to merge into one. At various points in his *Parallèle*, Mercier writes about Paris and London in ways that play fast and loose with their names, in a fashion that invites us to question just what 'a London' and 'a Paris' are. Is a city a location on a map? A collection of buildings? Or an assembly of people with a shared history?

Mercier writes at one point, referring to London, that '90 leagues from Paris is another sort of Paris.'[45] In another passage he states that many Londoners are in fact Parisians: French Protestants, the Huguenots, who fled the French capital after the Revocation of the Edict of Nantes in 1685. As Londoners, these former Parisians served in William of Orange's forces in Ireland. By their courage at arms and by their skill in manufacturing, they had, Mercier noted, 'done London much good'. 'And so, by this account, is it London which is in fact Paris?'[46] The search for *la ville policée* ends, not in London, nor in Paris, but in some invisible entity that is both.

How could one describe this city, this 'other Paris', this place that is at the same time both London and Paris, fantasy and reality? It was policed. It was chaotic. Its people were the most civilized in all Europe. Its inhabitants were riotous. It was an emporium of elegance, a metropolis of mud. It is this city that forms the subject of this book.

FIG. 5: Katherine Buildings, Cartwright Street.

CHAPTER ONE

The Restless House

I n 1789, on the eve of the French Revolution, Henri Decremps published his two-volume work, *Un Parisien à Londres*, intended to provide advice for Parisians travelling to England as well as to serve as a parallel of the two greatest cities in Europe. Then as now, the most important contrast was between London's sprawl and the high-rise, high-density dwellings found in Paris. As Decremps noted, whereas Parisian houses were at least four or five storeys, often reaching six or seven, the average London terraced house was just three or four storeys. 'People are more piled up on top of each other in our city,' he noted, 'where there may be fifteen or eighteen households in a single house, whereas in London there are only one or two.'[1]

This contrast in dwellings had wide repercussions. The Londoner's desire to have a house of his own supposedly reflected cherished notions of home. People tried to forget the existence of their neighbours on either side. A gentleman's home was his castle, a private space, even if it had to be shared with lodgers and a number of live-in servants, who slaved away in the basement and slept in the attics. A gentleman dined at home, even if it took him ages to get there, thanks to 'ribbon development': the tendency for developers to string out their terraces along the main roads leading out of the city centre. The expanding distance between the neighbourhoods where people worked and shopped marooned the genteel lady of the house within her own four walls.

Constrained by the city's walls, Parisians had no choice but to build upwards rather than outwards. Though they acknowledged its trials, apartment living was fully integrated into Paris's other institutions; for example, the invention of the restaurant, considered in Chapter 3, went hand in hand with the small kitchens that were common in apartments. Though Londoners could be scandalized at the thought of a family having dinner in 'public', Parisians did not sense this exposure. They found the terraces of London morbidly dull, while even Londoners were coming to recognize by the middle of the nineteenth century that the terraced house was unsustainable. This chapter begins by considering the terrace and the apartment block or *immeuble* as they came into existence in the seventeenth and eighteenth centuries. It then considers how the latter model was adapted, tentatively at first, in London.

Springing from the first social housing experiments of the 1840s and 1850s, apartment buildings were adopted by some of London's better-off in the 1860s. The development of the 'mansion flat' in the 1880s and 1890s involved taming the louche associations that 'French flats' had earned, thanks in particular to the novels of Émile Zola. His study of apartment living, *Pot-Bouille*, proved too hot to handle for would-be translators, as we shall see. Yet the course was set that would lead to our modern apartment block. From having been considered unthinkable, outrageous and Parisian, such blocks became humdrum, routine and international. A style of living apparently fit only to serve as the setting for scandalous French novels had been naturalized.

This process of domesticating the apartment raised disturbing questions. In settlements where people lived in such close proximity, where and how was a line to be drawn between private and public space? How could a very modern desire for privacy be balanced against the needs of the community? Familiar stereotypes held that the Englishman valued the privacy of his 'castle' more than did the Frenchman, and could never be persuaded to give up dreams of his own house and garden in the suburbs. As the distance separating their workplace from this 'castle' grew ever larger, however, Londoners began to reassess their expectations of what made a home. What use was a physical separation from their neighbours, if smells and sounds carried from house to house? Were servants a necessary part of a household, or just so many interlopers? In debating the merits of apartment living, Londoners and Parisians faced challenges familiar to the dwellers in all modern cities.

The Invention of the *Immeuble*

The six- or seven-storey, stone-faced apartment block, with its decorative balconies, arched entryway, communal staircase, bohemian garrets and internal courtyard, plays such an important part in our image of Haussmann's nineteenth-century Paris that it comes as something of a shock to discover that it emerged in the late seventeenth century and reached its mature form in the 1770s. Like all European cities, Parisian town houses were originally oriented towards the thoroughfare and constructed on narrow plots, with the ridgeline of the steeply pitched roof running at ninety degrees to the line of the street. The gable end was richly decorated, sometimes with dizzyingly high, crow-stepped gables that made the structure look taller and more opulent than it really was. Although families often took in lodgers, the norm was one household per house. There was no attempt to create an ensemble or a streetscape. Each house was a bald statement of the family's pretensions. Like so many racegoers struggling at the rail to show off their own hat to the best advantage, the effect made by a line of town houses in a medium-sized or large north European city around

1600 was anything but monotonous. In the case of both Paris and London, new building regulations adopted in response to the Great Fire of London would mark a watershed in their design.

In 1667 the French Bureau des Finances imposed height restrictions and banned gables, the latter being replaced with mansard roofs containing dormer windows. For the purposes of the regulations, a building's height was measured only up to the roof parapet, not up to the ridge of the roof. Squeezing one or two extra storeys into the roof space allowed owners to get the most out of their plot, especially if they replaced steeply pitched roofs with mansards. The 'Parisian' roof line was born. Even more importantly, the ridge of the roof now ran parallel to the street, presenting a broad, plain flank to the passer-by, rather than a narrow, made-up face.

Until the arrival of large property investment syndicates in the 1770s and 1780s, the main developers of apartment blocks were monastic communities. In 1669 the chapter of St Germain l'Auxerrois constructed a range of buildings on the Rue de la Ferronnerie, backing onto Les Innocents, the city's most crowded and noisome graveyard. These featured four levels of apartments stacked on top of an arcade of shops.[2] In 1715 the architect Dailly designed several ranges for the Abbey of St-Germain-des-Près. Each consisted of two shops either side of an arched entryway with a communal staircase leading off it. In the plans five rooms are indicated on each storey, without, however, any indication as to their purpose (whether *salon*, *chambre*, etc.). There are doors everywhere, allowing tenants a considerable degree of flexibility, as befitted spaces that were used as retail spaces, workshops, residences or some combination of all three.

While the plethora of doors and the apparent lack of kitchen arrangements would have seemed odd to nineteenth-century Parisians such as Zola, the design includes other features that hardly changed in the following century and a half: the mezzanine floor squeezed between the ground floor and the first floor, something that is also found in the earlier buildings on the Rue de la Ferronnerie, mentioned above. Intended originally to serve as storage for the shops below, in practice these spaces were often arranged as apartments distinct from the shop, suitable for the shabby-genteel, whose *amour propre* preferred these low-ceilinged rooms to the indignity of a more commodious suite at the top (and socially less desirable) part of the house.[3]

The architect Ramée's design for the house at 12, Rue du Mail showed how layouts had developed by 1789. A round communal staircase serves landings with one apartment on each storey, each with two adult bedrooms: one with windows onto the street for 'Madame' (a *boudoir*, to use the nineteenth-century term) and one facing onto the courtyard at the back for 'Monsieur', helpfully provided with access to a discreet back staircase. The kitchen was located on the opposite side of the courtyard to this second master bedroom, in a sort of miniature service wing.[4] The Maisons Armand on Rue Montorgeuil (1790) have three apartments on each floor, three internal staircases and several windows that are oddly placed (for the residents, at least).[5] Internal convenience was regularly sacrificed to the external appearance of regularity. Architects preferred to insert a blank window or have a window coincide with an internal wall rather than break the grid.

With this emphasis on serried ranks of windows it is unsurprising that critics soon complained that these *immeubles* were monotonous and overly regimented. In his *Essay on Architecture* (1755), Laugier complained of 'harmful uniformity'.[6] Royal decrees of April 1783 and August 1784 imposed maximum heights of 19.5 metres in streets of less than 10 metres diameter, and of 12 metres in those less than 8 metres wide, but developers continued to make good use of the attic area to add rentable space. They did little, however, to distinguish between floors, often overlooking the traditional emphasis of the first floor or *piano nobile*.

Such development seized up during the Revolution, only to reach unprecedented heights of activity in the thirty years after the Restoration of the monarchy in 1815, but declining thereafter. To take the Porcherons district (the 9th arrondissement) as an example, there were twenty such projects between 1769 and 1786, forty-five between 1818 and 1847, and twenty-six between 1853 and 1912.[7] Writing in 1778, Rutlidge's *Le Babillard* offers an early expression of bemused exasperation at the trials and tribulations of living in such an *immeuble*. In Paris, he observed, the rich enjoyed the peaceful isolation of their own mansion or *hôtel particulier*, while the humble citizen had to put up with his pokey bolt-hole in an apartment block, 'where the ensemble mirrors in a tumultuous and bizarre fashion that motley crew to be seen outside in the streets and in public places'. Although he deliberately chooses an unfashionable neighbourhood, the *Babillard* fails to find congenial company. During the day his nerves are frayed by the constant ringing of the bell of his neighbour, a businessman. At night this man's apartment falls quiet, just as the *Babillard's* other neighbours are getting started: a gambler to one side, a courtesan directly above.[8]

In London, the construction of houses was regulated by Building Acts following the Great Fire. The first of these came in 1667, the same year Paris laid down its own rules governing the relationship between street width and building height. The Building Acts of 1667, 1707 and 1709 laid down rules on the thickness of brick party walls and heavily restricted the use of wood. Wooden eave cornices were banned and the wooden boxes containing the sash window's counterweights henceforth had to be encased in brick. An omnibus Act in 1774 consolidated all this legislation and laid out four rates of building, each with its own set of rules.[9]

Fournier Street in Spitalfields is the best-preserved example of an early Georgian brick terrace, built between 1725 and 1731. As with most terraces it was the result of several different speculators working together. A builder could become a speculator in such projects without having to raise any capital. All he needed to do was acquire from the landowner the option on a building lease, paying a nominal rent for three to five years. In that time the builder would raise capital against the lease, quickly run up a house and hope to sell it before the grace period on the lease expired. In Fournier Street the builders seem to have raised pairs of houses, selling them on as shells to different classes of client. Hence some boast ornate interior panelling and chimneypieces, reflecting the wealth of their first inhabitants, while others are more modest. Cost-cutting extended to the incorporation of wooden beams in brick walls, whose face bricks were often poorly bonded into the place bricks behind.

Although the landowner needed to ensure that standards did not slip too much, his interests were otherwise well served; the system incentivized builders to put up houses fast. Despite this emphasis on speed, a surprising uniformity of exterior proportion was nonetheless achieved. In part this was dictated by the materials. The average softwood tree trunk produced beams of twenty to twenty-five feet, setting the width. To build higher than three or four storeys in brick would have required deeper, stronger and hence more expensive foundations. The widespread use of pattern-books such as Isaac Ware's *A Complete Body of Architecture* (1756) also helped.

In the West End the distribution of landownership was different from that of Soho and Spitalfields, being focussed around large estates owned by the dukes of Westminster, Bedford and the like. This enabled the construction of more ambitious squares, whose terraces were designed to appear as if they were four distinct palaces, with more expensive carved stone ornamentation taking as its focal point a fine central pediment. The 1776 contract for Bedford Square shows two builders, William Scott and Robert Grews, agreeing to follow a plan held by the Steward of the Bedford Estate and stick to stipulated floor-to-ceiling heights. Scott and Grews sold sub-leases to other builders. One of these, the architect Thomas Leverton, built the extra-large, five-bay house in the centre of the east side.[10] On the north side the central six bays were divided between two houses of three bays – the width of a typical terraced house. This required the placing of a five- rather than a four-pilaster pediment over the two houses, which had the unfortunate effect of there being a pilaster in the middle: a howler of a mistake in a classical building.

The eighteenth-century terraced house commonly had a basement half or completely sunk below street level, in which the kitchens, larder, scullery and other 'offices' were located. The façade was set slightly back from the street, creating an open area that allowed light and air to reach this basement. A bridge of steps led across this to the front door, while a small exterior staircase gave direct access to the kitchens. Coal could be delivered by simply pouring it through a coal hole in the pavement outside, which communicated directly with a coal cellar under the street. Whereas in the *immeuble* one house contained several small kitchens leading off the main stairs, tucked into odd corners of the building, in London there was one commodious kitchen in the basement that could be reached by servants and delivery boys without getting in the residents' way. Parisian observers struggled to explain this arrangement, referring to the area as a courtyard or even a moat, but they admired its practicality.[11]

Although this layout was not uniformly followed, generally speaking the front room on the ground floor was used as a dining room, with a parlour or breakfast room behind, in which the family spent most of its time. The more formal drawing room was above the dining room, with a dressing room or perhaps a bedroom behind. The upper floors were all bedrooms, two or three to a floor, with the servants in the roof area, under the leads. 'Closets' and small secondary staircases could be tucked into corners, the former varying in size and use from small storage spaces to rooms that could be used for writing, dressing, or for a servant to sleep in. The average terraced house in late seventeenth- and eighteenth-century London would house eight people: the master and mistress, their three children and three servants. In the larger houses on the finer estates this number might rise to fourteen, including a nursery maid, a groom, a coachman, a butler, footmen, a cook, housemaids, a governess and a housekeeper. Even then, the footmen, groom and coachman would have slept over the coachhouse, reached off a back-alley or mews that ran behind the row of houses.

Slums in the Sky

Of course, poorer Londoners could not afford to have a whole terraced house to themselves. They had three options: to go into service, in which case they would be allocated living quarters in their employer's attic; to share a house with several other households; or to sleep rough. The five-storey houses on Bentinck Street, Soho, finished in 1737, contained by 1801 four, five or six families each.[12] Behind and between the new squares and the serried ranks of terraces lay much pre-Georgian housing stock, above all in areas untouched by the Great Fire, such as Southwark. One or two such wooden-frame buildings survive, for example in the narrow alleys leading off Borough High Street. These premises, grandly known as 'courts', stretched back from the main street, culminating in a shared well and darkened by the upper storeys cantilevered out over the alley on either side. Hundreds of people lived in these wooden firetraps, such as in the warren of dwellings in the Mint, a debtors' sanctuary a few hundred metres to the west.

Those fortunate enough to lease land within the limits or 'rules' of the Mint had no need to tempt tenants with an elegant façade or even the most basic conveniences. Eager would-be tenants facing imprisonment for debt would present themselves anyway, only too grateful to find refuge in a special jurisdiction beyond the reach of the law. Thanks to the site's former use as a royal mint, the neighbourhood's residents purportedly enjoyed a form of immunity. Though Southwark Mint was suppressed in 1724, the buildings remained a slum until the 1880s, when the Metropolitan Board of Works (MBW) razed the area, pushing through a new thoroughfare

(Marshalsea Road) and encouraging the construction of new working-class housing on the cleared land. Erected by the Peabody Trust and the MBW itself, these 'model dwellings' were surrounded by streets renamed after characters from Charles Dickens's *Little Dorrit*. Although the names of Mint and Sanctuary Streets are a nod to history, we have otherwise entered a curious realm in which poverty is retrospectively sanitized by associations with a work of fiction.

These 'model dwellings' took the form of seven-storey apartment blocks. They bear witness to the surprising fact that the first apartment blocks to be put up in London were intended, not for the middle class or the elite, but for the working class. These 'model dwellings' emerged in the wake of a parliamentary inquiry in 1842 into the sanitary conditions of the metropolis, driven by the indefatigable Edwin Chadwick, who carried out detailed investigations into poor relief, workhouses, graveyard overcrowding and other matters relating to what we today would call welfare. Known colloquially as 'the Prussian Minister' for his humourlessness and fondness for statistics, Chadwick could normally be counted on to advocate the establishment of a centrally funded inspectorate or other office to impose a more efficient and 'scientific' solution to social problems. However, such was his irritation with the government's dilatory response to his evidence linking unsanitary dwellings with drunkenness, cholera and family breakdown that he and his friends resolved to turn to the free market for a solution.

They developed an innovative funding model that became known as 'Five Per Cent Philanthropy'. Under this system, joint-stock Model Dwelling Companies (MDCs) took investors' capital and used it to build sanitary, high-density residential buildings for the working man. By this means the respectable poor would be rescued from the slums in return for a modest weekly rent of around two shillings and sixpence, while the investors would receive dividends of between 4 and 7 per cent. These dividends were modest enough by the standards of the time, but higher than the 2.79 per cent paid out by other secure long-term investments, such as government consols.[13]

Today such a scheme would be called an 'ethical investment'. Over time, MDCs such as the Metropolitan Association for Improving the Dwellings of the Industrious Classes (MAIDIC, est. 1846) and the Improved Industrial Dwellings Company would be 'crowded out' after 1890 by the flat-building efforts of the London County Council (LCC). Nevertheless, between 1856 and 1914, MDCs and charitable organizations such as the Peabody (est. 1862) and Guinness Trusts provided between 11 and 15 per cent of new working-class housing in London.[14] This was a remarkable achievement, considering the difficulty of finding sufficiently large plots of land in central London, compounded by popular widespread prejudice against having an apartment block built on a householder's doorstep.

It also meant that multi-storey life in London was first experienced by the working class, in contrast to the usual pattern in which they would get the leftovers of the London lettings market. Eighteenth-century housing stock in formerly genteel neighbourhoods was bought up by speculators, who divided what had once been one-family homes into multiple one-room dwellings, each intended for whole families. Partitions would be inserted where necessary to increase the rentable value, without improving or even maintaining the already outdated sanitary and cooking facilities. With the introduction of apartments, the working man and his family were pioneers – or guinea pigs. The results changed the look of neighbourhoods like Whitechapel, Shoreditch and even parts of Chelsea, as we can still appreciate today.

MAIDIC put up London's first apartment block in 1847, and by 1854 was trumpeting its success in *Healthy Homes*, a report discussing ways in which its model could be expanded more widely. In an example of local ethical investment, in 1853 a group of subscribers from the local parish erected a four-storey block of flats in Grosvenor Mews, Berkeley Square, including 'eight sets of two rooms, with two [water-]closets, sink, and dust-shaft ... These rooms are approached from open external galleries, to which a central staircase (of slate and iron) conducts.' Though they hadn't a word for this 'building to accommodate thirty-two families', the parishioners were clear that it afforded 'a boon to the industrious classes' *and* 'a fair rate of return'.[15]

In the 1850s, however, these blocks were still oddities. The Improved Industrial Dwellings Company (IIDC), the Peabody Trust and the Artisan and Labourers' General Dwellings Company were founded in 1861, 1862 and 1867 respectively. Acts of Parliament passed in 1866 and 1867 made it easier for such entities to borrow over long periods at low interest. Early 'model dwellings' were small blocks, like the IIDC's Cromwell Buildings near Borough Market, which still survives. It has five storeys served by an open central staircase, with four two-room apartments on each floor. Larger developments required the kind of plot that became available only when the Metropolitan Board of Works cleared away slums, using powers granted to it under the so-called Cross Acts of 1875 and 1879, named after Disraeli's Home Secretary, Richard Cross. To an extent, therefore, the MDCs and the Peabody Trust benefited from government assistance, being allowed to purchase such plots at very favourable prices.[16]

When sufficient space could be found, these large-scale developments certainly attracted attention. MAIDIC's Farringdon Road buildings had a frontage of 300 feet, with five blocks seven storeys high, set at ninety degrees to the street. The premises were opened in November 1875 by Richard Cross. Here the ground floor was given over to shops, while the space between the blocks was intended to give tenants' children a safe place to play. Like most 'model dwellings', Farringdon Road was made of stock brick (yellow, but with the odd band of red), with artificial stone (in this case, a mixture of Portland cement and coke residuum) used to decorate the windows, doorways and parapet. Its roof was flat, covered in asphalt, and easily accessible to tenants as 'drying grounds' or for recreation. Like the communal laundry, use of these grounds was regulated by a rota.

On each floor the four apartments were divided into pairs, with one balcony for each pair, separated from the main stone staircase by a lockable metal grille. Open staircases and semi-private balconies were a feature of many 'model dwellings' (including Cromwell Buildings) and were felt to lessen some of the risks associated with shared 'public' staircases. These open stairs were draughty and unheated, definitely not places to pause for a chat. Grilles and balconies ensured that those using the stairs did not see the doors of any residence other than the one they inhabited. The fact that 'no doorway opens on to a public passageway' was clearly felt to be very important,in that it supposedly limited potentially harmful interaction between residents.[17]

The original plan for an external gallery was probably dropped on similar grounds. As is clear from the notes jotted down by one middle-class observer, Charles Booth, on his forays compiling data for his famous poverty map of London, any street in which residents leaned out of windows, left doors open or sat on stairs was clearly inhabited by the semi-criminal classes. There were even those who objected to a balcony being shared by two flats. In a letter to *The Builder*, Francis Butler insisted that tenements had to be planned as a series of entirely self-contained units, so that the working man 'might still feel [his flat] to be his castle, so to speak, and that he dwelt there without any loss of those home associations so dear to English people'.[18]

At Farringdon Road each block had fifty-two 'tenements', meaning that the entire project housed more than 1,000 people, at a cost of less than £40,000. Entities like the MBW are sometimes accused of 'clearing' slums only to leave former residents homeless, with no option but to move to new slums further afield, in the same way that the new boulevards of Haussmann's Paris pushed thousands out of the city, or into already crowded corners of their own neighbourhoods.[19] Where MDCs and the MBW collaborated, however, genuine slum clearance, rather than slum relocation, could and did occur. Demand clearly outstripped supply, causing a certain amount of resentment. When slum dwellers were asked by middle-class notables such as the Revd Wyatt Edgell why they did not move to 'model lodging houses, instead of paying such a high rent as 4s. 6d. for a single room . . . in the worst part of London', they claimed that, when they tried, they found blocks already filled to capacity with 'clerks', white-collar workers supposedly favoured as tenants by MDCs over artisans and labourers.

In fact, the occupational make-up of such blocks closely matched that of working-class Londoners as a whole, though MDC blocks were statistically overstocked with children relative to the general London population.[20] Perhaps oddly, given the choice between letting a two-room apartment to a married couple without children or to one with two children, companies like MAIDIC often stated a preference for the latter.[21] Both slum-dwelling Londoners and apartment-dwelling Parisians were supposedly wont to change their lodgings regularly. However, census returns for 'model dwellings' indicate that their inhabitants tended to stay put. These apartment blocks may have been noisy at times, but only because so many children lived in them, not because their adult tenants were shifty. Far from housing the 'criminal classes', these dwellings were hailed on account of 'the facilities they afford for the detection and suppression of crime'; this was not bad going, considering that they did not have concierges, only a resident superintendent and a handyman.[22]

One anonymous account of life in an east London model dwelling appeared in the first volume of *Labour and Life of the People in London*, published in 1889 by Charles Booth. The 'Sketch of Life in Buildings' may have been written by Margaret Harkness, a clergyman's daughter who had come to London in 1877 after refusing to get married. Having initially trained as a nurse, in the early 1880s she set out on a career as a journalist and novelist, much like Annie Besant, Eleanor Marx and other socialist writers who combined social work with women's advocacy. Model dwellings afforded such ladies an opportunity to enter what had previously seemed no-go slum areas, dispensing Christian charity as Victorian 'Lady Bountifuls' or collecting evidence of capitalism's failure to provide the poorest Londoners with a means of supporting themselves. Other women were drawn into such work simply by a desire to escape the grinding monotony of genteel life and to experiment with an activity that might turn into a career – one of the few open to educated 'New Women' in the 1880s and 1890s. Heady accounts that compared London's slums to 'darkest Africa' made such work exciting: a chance for female explorers to have their go at being Henry Morton Stanley in another 'dark continent'.[23]

Cut off from her family and living off her pen, Harkness wrote an account (if it is hers) that may draw on her experience of living in Katharine Buildings, East Smithfield, a complex of one-room flats erected by the East End Dwellings Company and managed for a time by Beatrice Webb, a socialist who went on to found the London School of Economics and the *New Statesman*. Though other patrician women may have spent time visiting such places, it must have been a daring step for someone of Harkness's background to go and live in one. The 'Sketch' describes a typical twenty-four hours in an unnamed model dwelling, beginning at 5 a.m., when the writer hears the man upstairs getting ready to start work at a railway goods depot, his wife having been at work on her sewing machine the previous evening until one in the morning. At eight o' clock the widow next door is heard scraping out her stove and gossiping. A lull sets in after the children of the building go to school, returning at noon. The afternoon is also quiet; the children play cricket in the courtyard and the women visit one another. After 6 p.m. the stairs fill with the sounds and smells of cooking as the main meal of the day is prepared. In the evening some men go out to the pub to sing and talk politics, but most stay at home with their wife and children. This being a set of dwellings with a good reputation, all is quiet by 10 p.m.

The overall conclusion reached by the author of the 'Sketch' is that the advantages of such places far outweighed the disadvantages:

Cheapness, a higher standard of cleanliness, healthy sanitary arrangements, neighbourly intercourse both between children and between the grownup people, and, perhaps above all, the impossibility of being overlooked altogether, or flagrantly neglected by relatives in illness or old age, seem to be the great gains; and the chief disadvantage, the absence of privacy and the increased facility for gossip and quarrelling, though it may sometimes be disagreeably felt, introduces a constant variety of petty interest and personal feeling into the monotony of daily life.[24]

Inevitably, perhaps, most of the accounts we have of model dwellings in this period are written by the men who designed them, or who wrote about them for architectural reviews after a hasty inspection of ground plans or perhaps a quick walk around a newly finished (and therefore empty) block. Though invaluable as a reflection of how the middle classes viewed these buildings and their residents, they convey little sense of what it might be like to live in one. While the author of the 'Sketch' was certainly far better educated than her neighbours, her account suggests that the architects were unsuccessful in their struggle to prevent 'consorting' among residents, but that this did not in itself represent a failure.

Was it the way of the future, though? One architectural critic, James Hole, who delivered a paper to the 1884 International Health Exhibition, was clear on this point. 'I do not think a city of tall blocks fitted with one- or two-roomed dwellings is a satisfactory ideal for the next generation,' he opined, 'or that the kind of existence which it represents should be the horizon of our hopes and aspirations.'[25] There were housing reformers, most notably Octavia Hill, who rejected the block model in favour of one in which small terraces of two-storey, cottage-style buildings were gradually erected as pocket-sized sites became available. Three of her projects from the 1880s survive in Southwark, tucked away on side streets. Gable Cottages on Sudrey Street is a charming oasis, but simply unviable as a template.

Yet model dwellings had proved beyond a doubt that high-density housing did not have to mean high-mortality housing. After a burst of enthusiasm following the creation of the LCC in 1889, its own housing activities began tentatively in the 1890s, opening its first apartment block in Boundary Street in 1893. Its model borrowed heavily from that of the MDCs, right down to the insistence on a net return of 3 per cent.[26] A similar body established in Paris in 1849, the Société de cités ouvriers de Paris, was far less successful. There were plans to build copies of its first project, a group of four three- or four-storey blocks on the Rue Rochechouart, named the Cité Napoléon. These were shelved, however, as workers resented the hundred by-laws regulating life inside the 'barrack' (as they dubbed it), while the authorities feared the political repercussions of housing large numbers of working-class Parisians in close proximity to one another. Communal living might encourage 'socialist follies', as well as sexual promiscuity and intemperance.[27]

Piping Hot!

Percy Pinkerton must have been delighted and somewhat relieved to see his English translation of Émile Zola's novel *Pot-Bouille* appear in 1895, under the title *Restless House*. A polyglot man of letters, Pinkerton had years of experience translating opera libretti (including *La Bohème*), memoirs and other works into English from German, Italian and Russian as well as French. Zola was enjoying something of a boom in England. In 1891 a version of *Thérèse Raquin* was staged at the Royalty Theatre. Among the other Zola translations to appear in 1895 were those issued by the publisher and translator Henry Vizetelly, which included translations of *Les Mystères de Marseilles*, *Une Page d'Amour*, *Au Bonheur des Dames* and *Contes à Ninon*. Like *Pot-Bouille*, *Au Bonheur des Dames* and *Une Page d'Amour* were part of Zola's famed Rougon-Macquart: a twenty-novel panoramic survey of Second Empire France that exposed every corner of political, religious, artistic, economic and social life with unprecedented realism. *Pot-Bouille* was devoted to the corrupt goings-on inside a fictional Parisian apartment block on the Rue Choiseul.

Pinkerton would not have been scanning the pages of London's literary journals for reviews, however. *Restless House* was not reviewed. It was not even for sale. Distribution was limited and potentially dangerous. When Henry Vizetelly had published his translation of *Pot-Bouille* back in 1886, he had been hauled before the court and charged with obscenity. He had expurgated and bowdlerized *Pot-Bouille* to such an extent that *Piping Hot!* was not only lukewarm, it was short measure: two-thirds the length of the original, in fact.[28] Nevertheless, it was still too hot for the National Vigilance Association (NVA). After a two-year court battle, *Piping Hot!* and other Zola translations were banned and Vizetelly was fined £100. The Liberal MP and NVA activist Samuel Smith claimed that Vizetelly and other booksellers were in cahoots with brothels, supplying them with young girls whose minds had first been 'polluted and depraved' by reading such works.[29] Zola was not for the uninitiated. When Arthur Conan Doyle went to see *Thérèse Raquin* on stage, he left his wife safely at home.[30]

Restless House had been privately printed for a recently established group of subscribers, the Lutetian Society, named after the Roman name for Paris, Lutetia. Members acquired it as one of a set of six translations of Zola novels published in 1894–5, for which they paid the princely sum of twelve guineas. The set also included Havelock Ellis's translation of *Germinal* and Arthur Symons's of *L'Assommoir*. As their flyleaves proclaimed, these volumes were a numbered edition of 300, 'Printed by the Lutetian Society for Private Distribution among its Members', on handmade paper. They appeared 'by the special permission and under the direct auspices of M. Zola', who had met the Lutetian Society's founder in London in October 1893. If this was an attempt to cock a snook at Victorian respectability, however, it was rather tokenistic. After all, almost every single one of the Society's members could speak French and could have read the originals. Even with a small print run, the series failed to make a profit and plans to translate other novels were shelved.[31]

Although Émile Zola had been born in Paris in 1840, his family had relocated to Aix when he was three. When he moved back to Paris in 1858, therefore, Zola was – like the hero of *Pot-Bouille*, Octave Mouret – a young man new to the city. The apartment block's repertory of stock characters and hackneyed episodes was by then well established, from the wizened, witch-like and omniscient concierge who observed every coming-out and going-in from her *loge* just inside the main entrance, to the penniless painter and pathetic maker of artificial flowers who froze or baked (depending on the season) under the leads. Honoré Daumier's *Locataires et Propriétaires* (*Tenants and Landlords*, 1847) made light of the minor trials of apartment life, such as the concierge's feeling miffed at not having received enough by way of a New Year's gift from an impecunious tenant.

Paul de Kock was the first novelist to exploit the apartment block's potential for voyeuristic tales of sexual shenanigans, above stairs, below stairs and in their general vicinity. *La Demoiselle au Cinquième* (*Her on the Fifth*, 1856) and *Mon Voisin Raymond* (*My Neighbour Raymond*, 1842) are lightweight affairs, with all the character depth of poor American sitcom. The latter describes the petty travails of Eugène Dorsan, a young man of private means who haunts the boulevards and *bals publics* such as the Tivoli, spending whole days away from his Montmartre apartment in an effort to avoid his suspicious concierge (Mme Bertin), his pesky neighbour (the avant-garde painter Raymond) and his jealous mistress (Agatha, a milliner). English translations of such works ensured that 'French flats' had a dubious reputation, even before Zola wrote his masterpiece.

Published in 1882, Zola's *Pot-Bouille* is set twenty years earlier, in a fictional apartment building on the Rue Choiseul that Mouret's cousin, the architect Campardon, claims is twelve years old. It thus dates from around 1850, near the end of the busiest era of apartment building. As we have seen, by then the basic layout and design of the *immeuble* had been long established. Architectural treatises such as Louis Le Normand's *Paris Moderne* (1837) rehearsed minor variations on this tried and tested model. Zola's four-storey building is unusual only in the quality of the balcony ironwork and the appointments of the heated main staircase, with its mahogany handrail, thick red carpet and scagliola panelling.

Met by his cousin, the architect Achille Campardon, Octave is introduced to the concierge Monsieur Gourd, who lives with his largely immobile wife on the ground floor, to the left of the *porte cochère* that leads from the Rue Choiseul into the paved courtyard, with its stables at the back. On the right side of the passageway is the silk shop operated by the landlord's son, Auguste Vabre, who also leases the mezzanine floor, where he himself lives with his wife Berthe. At first the layout seems simple: two apartments on each floor, the larger and grander facing the street, the other facing the courtyard, their mahogany doors facing each other across a landing.

As they climb to Campardon's apartment on the third floor, the architect reels off the names of his fellow tenants. The landlord, Monsieur Vabre, a retired Versailles notary, occupies the finest suite on the first floor, together with his daughter Clotilde, her husband Duveyrier, aged forty-five, a judge, and their son, Gustave. Vabre's other, less commercially minded son Théophile lives at the back with his fascinating wife Valérie. On the second floor the front apartment is occupied by a nameless writer, his wife and their two children, who are described as wealthy (they keep a carriage in the stables, something not all residents can afford). Gourd is dismissive of them, partly because this scribbler once threatened the block's reputation for respectability by getting into trouble with the police – for, of all things, writing a book about the scandalous goings-on in an apartment building.

Zola thus inserts himself and his family into the heart of the building, even if they keep a low profile.

Before showing Mouret into his own apartment on the third floor, Campardon takes him up to the fourth. A line has clearly been crossed, as Mouret notes to his chagrin that the fine red carpet stops on this floor, giving way to a plain grey covering. On the exterior, this is where the façade breaks, creating a terrace. At the front live the Josserands, an apparently respectable household dominated by the formidable Mme Josserand, who is determined to marry off her daughters Berthe and Hortense before anyone realizes that their carefully maintained veneer of wealth is a lie, her husband being a mere cashier at a glassworks. Their son, Saturnin, is mentally unstable, though this handicap seems to give him a preternaturally acute sense of the corruption at the house's core. At the back of the fourth floor lives a clerk in the civil service, Jules Pichon, together with his wife Marie and their baby girl, Lilitte. The rest of the block's families are on good terms, inviting each other to their black-tie musical soirées. But the Pichons are clearly a class below, and are invited nowhere. Mouret's apartment consists of one room at the end of a long passageway on the courtyard side. He must pass by the Pichons' on his way in and out, while Marie Pichon must cross the passageway to reach her kitchen.

At the very top of the house are two corridors, one running along the roofline on each side of the top-lit central staircase. Here are the bedrooms for the servants. All the residents except the Pichons have domestic help of some kind. The Josserands get by with a Breton cook. The Compardons have a maid and a cook, while the Duveyriers have both plus a coachman. Although their masters seem to Mouret's innocent imagination to be sealed off from one another, barricaded behind the impossibly sober mahogany doors of their respective apartments, in the attic the servants of different households are jumbled up, separated from each other only by flimsy matchboard partitions. There is little privacy up here. Many servants opt to leave their doors open, especially during the summer, when the attic is unbearably hot. One of the attic rooms is let out, initially to a carpenter, then to a boot-stitcher. Gourd fights a running battle with these hard-working artisans, considering them to be disreputable interlopers carrying in all kinds of bad influences from outside. As it turns out, in evicting them Gourd is chasing out the only honest inhabitants. Working-class artisans were indeed being driven out of such garrets after mid-century, and the public works pursued under the Second Empire further encouraged migration to the untaxed wasteland of wooden hovels between the city's tax wall and its fortifications.[32]

A second, servants' staircase rises from the courtyard right up to the attic, with three doors on each landing, one leading to the kitchen of the main apartment at the front, one leading into the kitchen of the second apartment and a third leading onto the rear passageway. Mouret's bedroom is thus directly opposite one of these doors. This staircase is Berthe Vabre's salvation when she and Mouret oversleep after a night of adulterous passion in Mouret's room: she can slip down two flights using the back stairs and enter her own apartment via the kitchen door. Unfortunately her maid is waiting in her boudoir, staring at her mistress's bed, which is still made up. Unlike Campardon, Berthe has not realized the importance of unmaking her own bed 'for the sake of the servants' before climbing into someone else's. A bribe silences the servant, temporarily.

The next time Berthe visits Mouret the lovers are interrupted by her husband Auguste, who breaks down the door and confronts Mouret. Once again Berthe flees down the back stairs, only to find her kitchen door locked. She runs back up two flights, along the passage and down two flights again, this time using the main stairs. But when she reaches the front entrance to her apartment she finds another locked door. Refusing to contemplate returning to her parents, she frantically rings the Compardons' bell, throwing herself on their mercy. Irritable at having been roused from his adulterous slumbers with his cousin Gasparine, Campardon insists that Berthe leave his 'respectable' home. Once again, Berthe finds herself on the stairs. 'Never had the house appeared to her so saturated with purity and virtue.' She shivers, 'terrified that she might see the spectre of Monsieur Gourd emerge in velvet cap and slippers'.[33] Though the whole house is awake by this point, only poor Marie Pichon is willing to take in this stray, who is still in her peignoir, and provide her with a sofa to sleep on.

The servants' staircase is lit by a light well, a small open courtyard inside the block that also provides the kitchens with ventilation. There are two kitchens on each floor, one for the street-side apartment and one on the other side, which belongs to the larger of the two rear apartments (Mouret does not have the use of a kitchen). The kitchens' windows face each other across the internal courtyard, allowing the servants to gossip with those working in other kitchens. 'This was the sewer of the house, draining off the house's shames,' Zola's narrator notes, 'while the masters lounged about in their slippers and the front staircase displayed all its solemn majesty amid the stuffy silence of the hot-air stove.'[34] This sewer corrupts innocents like Campardon's fourteen-year-old daughter, Angèle, coached in hypocrisy by her family's maid, Lisa, who has the girl mime the unspeakable acts committed by the adults.

As Mouret combs the block for 'safe corners' in which to bed its female residents, he keeps coming across the concierge, Gourd, 'prowling about, looking mysteriously ill at ease'. One night Mouret finds the concierge keeping watch in the dark at the end of Mouret's corridor, leaning against the door opening onto the back stairs. 'I want to find out something, Monsieur Mouret,' explains Gourd, before padding off to bed.[35] In Zola's restless house the concierge, a figure normally depicted as a fierce, omniscient tyrant, becomes a pitifully powerless revenant.

With one or two exceptions, Gourd's attentions seem to be devoted to the building, to its façade, its internal walls, carpet and fittings, rather than to its foul-mouthed and licentious inmates. Alone in the dark on the fourth-floor back passage, he might seem to be blocking Mouret's access to the back stairs. It is perhaps more helpful to describe him as listening to the building itself, trying to detect a false note in its audible silence. Elsewhere Zola's narrator describes Gourd as inspecting the fabric of his apartment block so sternly that the 'walls blushed'. But was it in fact the walls – the apartment block and its layout – or the residents who were at fault and should blush with shame? Would the Compardons, Josserands and Vabres have behaved better had they been transplanted to a genteel London house of a similar vintage, to a Gothic Revival terraced house in Clapham, perhaps, or to a detached villa in a north London development like Tufnell Park? In short, did the house make the household, or the household the house?

Commenting on 'French Flats' in 1857, the journal *Building News* was clear on one point: good, decent English people would never condescend to live stacked up and squeezed in like their neighbours across the Channel. 'Although the French have introduced our English word "*comfort*" into their language, they certainly have not introduced the thing itself into their houses,' it opined. French families might not be concerned with privacy; they might well see nothing wrong in having a bedroom leading directly off a sitting room, an arrangement no respectable English family would tolerate. The French might be highly talented in fitting up a boudoir, but in a well-regulated family, 'a boudoir, be it fitted up and finished up ever so tastefully, is not everything'.

Building News conceded that it was of course necessary to have a kitchen in a dwelling, but that was no excuse for the unforgivable French habit of siting their kitchens next to their dining rooms, separated by only a single door, so that sounds and smells could intrude. And compared to the London terrace's kitchen, with its scullery, pantry, larder and store-cupboard, Parisian ones were tiny, little more than a closet. This reflected the Parisian's neglect of 'comfort at home' in favour of 'amusement abroad', out in the city. It was painful to relate, if nonetheless true, the anonymous correspondent continued, that the Parisian was happy to dine out, at a restaurant, and even take his wife or family with him. The Frenchman wasn't in the market for a real home, and wouldn't know one if he saw it. 'His idea of a house scarcely extends beyond a *salon* and a *salle à manger*, and, provided they be showily fitted up, he himself puts up with much that to an Englishman would be intolerably annoying.' Among these annoyances was a shared staircase, it being insupportable for an Englishman to pass members of another family or their tradesmen on the way to his own front door.[36]

Two decades later, little seems to have changed, except that the criticisms could now be found outside the specialist building press. In a piece entitled 'Living on Flats', the *Saturday Review* added fraternization among servants to the concerns raised earlier by the *Building News*. It also pointed darkly to the concierge, claiming that Parisians were powerless in the face of this 'spy', 'tyrant' and 'cheat'.[37] Yet the author of 'Living on Flats' has to concede that numbers of apartment blocks were rising in London, and had been for some time. As *The Builder* noted a few months later, it was all very well to repeat what it called 'the old theory' about 'the Englishman's home being his castle'; however, it remained a 'fact that the system of "flats" is being talked of, and when a thing gets talked of in England that is the most decisive step towards the adoption of it as a fashion, or at least towards the removal of the prejudice against it as "unusual"'.[38]

Behind the familiar criticisms that a flat could not be a 'home', a quiet change in attitudes was afoot. By 1870 it was becoming clear that spinning out ever-longer lines of suburban terraces was unsustainable. A shoddily built terraced house (some collapsed before they were even finished) was not much by way of a 'castle'. Even if the man of the house had a cheery fireside of his own waiting, how much time to enjoy it was left to him after he had traversed the 'two miles of omnibus, five miles of railways, and a mile of walking' that might separate it from his place of work?[39] Bayle St John contrasted the affordable life of apartment passages and staircases with the expensive dullness of a London suburban street: 'a cheerless double row of houses, whose inhabitants seem to have just received news of the arrival of a pestilence or an invading army'.[40] To Parisian eyes, London terraces looked like prisons.[41]

As *Building News* had noted in 1868, there was something odd about developers building terraced houses in Foley Street (off Langham Place) following the traditional design (that is, designed around the needs of a single household), but fitting six bell-pulls next to the front door (indicating that the property was to be divided up). In this example the ground floor and main kitchen were to be let at a weekly rate of thirteen shillings, the first floor for twelve shillings, the second floor for eleven shillings and the third (top) floor for ten shillings. The small back kitchen would be shared by three households. No wonder young men were losing a taste for home life, *Building News* observed, when they were raised in houses where domestic privacy was impossible.[42] What with these new 'one-family' houses and the widespread tendency for those in older housing stock to take in lodgers, the London home was, it seemed, as riven by contradiction as any Parisian apartment block. From the lodger, who pretended he rented the whole house, to his landlady, who would rather die than have her name appear in the Postal Directory under 'Lodging-House Keepers', Londoners, like Parisians, were living a lie.

Mansions in the Sky

Although this trend was less noticed, the 1850s and 1860s had witnessed the construction of some apartment blocks for the wealthy: the antecedents of what we know today as 'mansion blocks'. The earliest of these was erected in 1853 by a private developer, Mr Mackenzie, on Victoria Street. Mackenzie's blocks had a street frontage of 117 feet and were 82 feet high. Although they had flat roofs, otherwise they were very Parisian. Each house had six shops on the ground floor. There was a resident porter, and a separate staircase for tradesmen, with a service lift. 'The advantage of such residences to parties who remain only a portion of the year in London is obvious,' it was noted, 'as the porter in their absence takes charge of the apartments.'[43] Mackenzie was clearly eagle-eyed at spotting an opportunity. The development of Victoria Street was still being pushed through Westminster in 1857, its otherwise straight course adjusted to allow the MBW to clear a notorious slum.

In the 1870s and 1880s, Victoria Street became London's answer to the Boulevard de l'Opéra, lined with the unprecedentedly massive Westminster Palace Hotel and fine apartment blocks such as Oxford and Cambridge Mansions (1882–3) and Prince's Mansions (1884). Unlike the one- to three-room flats of model dwellings for the industrious poor, model dwellings for the rich had eight to ten rooms, accommodating servants as well as their masters. As with Mackenzie's block, they were targeted at those whose main home was elsewhere and who visited London only for the season. They also proved popular with well-off professionals of both genders, MPs (who valued proximity to the Houses of Parliament) as well as music-hall artistes such as the skirt dancer Kate Vaughan, whom we shall meet in Chapter 4.

Whereas *The Builder* had dismissed 'French flats' in 1857, by 1868 *Building News* was anticipating their being embraced by the middle classes. '[French flats] having . . . been partially adopted by both extremes of English society', it hoped 'before long to see them adopted by the middle strata, and when they shall have had experience of their comforts, privacy, and convenience, they will wonder that they have themselves been such "flats" [i.e. fools] as for so many years to dwell in lodgings.'[44] Ten years later, *The Builder* had come round, presenting Paris as a model to be followed, rather than avoided.[45] Whether these new houses were to be called 'dwellings', 'mansions', 'buildings', 'residences' or simply 'flats' was secondary. The main question now was how to adapt Parisian designs and layouts for Londoners. This apparent conversion, however, did not mean that Londoners shed their preconceptions about the immoral goings-on inside Parisian apartment blocks.

The architects William H. White and Frederick Eales played a crucial role in fostering this debate, at the Institute of British Architects (IBA), the Architectural Association and the Royal Society of Arts. They encountered considerable opposition from their professional peers, especially those of the older generation such as Charles Barry, architect of the Palace of Westminster. 'Mr White is a revolutionist in every sense of the word,' Barry had thundered at the IBA in 1877; 'he not only wants to revolutionise the arrangements of our houses, but to entirely alter ourselves in all our wants, habits, and mode of life.'[46] Yet Eales and White had at heart the interests of the profession, for there were those who claimed that apartment blocks could be put up without the help of an architect. Matthew Allen, a contractor who built residences for the IIDC, insisted that architects knew nothing about how to put up this particular kind of dwelling. Such contractors sometimes went on to build their own apartment blocks as a private speculation, targeting a slightly better clientele. Whether they were building blocks for a Model Dwelling Company or for themselves, they saw architects as a needless and perhaps a harmful luxury.[47]

White and *The Builder* agreed: London architects had no idea how to design 'a block of flat houses'. Were they to inspect the blocks on the Boulevard Haussmann or Boulevard Malesherbes, they would, *The Builder* argued, be astonished to note that, rather than being uniform barracks, each was slightly different from its neighbour, and that they had been designed by well-respected architects.[48] If model dwellings in London were barrack-like, that was because they had not been designed by architects. Staircases provided plenty of opportunity to add 'architectural character' to an apartment block.[49] British architects simply needed to learn from French examples, as well as from their own failures, such as H. A. Hankey's Queen Anne's Mansions (1873) and Norman Shaw's Albert Hall Mansions (1878). Fourteen and nine storeys respectively, both having communal kitchens and dining rooms, these buildings had been criticized for being too tall.

Queen Anne's and Albert Hall Mansions were seen less as 'French flats' than as 'American buildings', their monotonous grids of windows representative of 'the American hotel system'.[50] Though American models were not cited anywhere near as frequently as French ones, there was a sense in which New York represented the opposite extreme to Paris in such discussions. If French apartment blocks were *Piping Hot!,* with too much fraternization to be decent homes, then American ones were too cold, symptomatic of a broader tendency by which 'individual character is more and more in danger of being merged and lost in the complicated social machinery of modern life'.[51] For architects like Eales and White, therefore, the aim was to find a compromise that was neither too hot nor too cold.

One major concern centred on the servants, on how to accommodate them and their activities within a single, self-contained unit. Everyone agreed with the *Saturday Review* that 'herding' servants together in the roof space as they did in Paris was 'barbarous'. Though it would have been impolite to go into details or even profess to have knowledge of exactly what went on, it was obvious that the results were, well, such as could not be described, except for those decadent members of the Lutetian Society, who liked reading about that sort of thing. Though the tone adopted by the *Saturday Review* in its 1875 piece on 'Living on Flats' was satirical, on approaching this sensitive area it suddenly became serious. 'The immorality among the servants is, we believe, scandalous. It could scarcely be otherwise, when we consider that they have a separate staircase, often into the street, and no supervision.'[52]

While *The Builder* took the author of 'Living on Flats' to task for what it considered ill-informed criticism of flats, it had to agree that the greatest problem associated with 'the Paris plan' was the way that servants of different households were lodged, promiscuously and without supervision, in the attic. But housing the servants in the same self-contained unit as their masters only created another problem: how to keep them conveniently close, yet out of sight. In a terraced house the servants and tradesmen never used the front door, but rather descended by an outer stair into the 'area' below, giving access to the kitchen. It was unacceptable for them to use the same staircase as their masters. Though it made planning complicated, *The Builder* insisted that a secondary servants' staircase was necessary, 'only it should be so placed as to be in the way of being a good deal overlooked by the residents, and not in a too removed and out-of-the-way corner, otherwise the facility for gossip, &c, would be almost as great as in the Parisian system'.[53]

This, however, was not a straightforward solution, which may have led promoters to claim that it took only one rather than the usual three servants to run a genteel middle-class household inside an apartment building. As respectable suburban terraces spread further and further out of the city centre, it had become harder and harder to find servants to service them. These terraces had been built on green-field sites where there was no resident working-class population to be employed, while many of those who fifty years earlier might have jumped at the chance to enter service had become less enthusiastic. For there were better paid alternatives now, as well as a growing stock of affordable working-class homes that were more comfortable than a pull-out bed in an employer's kitchen or a freezing room in his garret. Flats thus held out the prospect of solving 'the servant problem' by a process of elimination. With fewer servants a wife could be 'more like the mistress of her home than many a wife is at present', and supervise her children more effectively.[54] Technology could help, too. With the installation of goods lifts, servants would have less call to walk up and down these stairs, while tradesmen could be kept off them entirely.[55] The emergence of restaurants from the 1860s onwards, at which ladies could dine without compromising themselves, made it possible to eat well and entertain friends without necessarily having to hire and house a good cook.

The second major objection to flats was the concierge, who in Paris handled the inhabitants' mail (which in some cases included reading it) and collected rents as well as manning the main entrance. Charlet's depiction of a wizened harridan denigrating perfectly respectable tenants as *canaille* (low-lifes) simply because they keep to themselves [Fig. 6] is a typical representation of the concierge. As Blanchard Jerrold noted, the concierge was the *bête noire* of the Parisians.[56] At Jerrold's block in the Rue des Quatre Vents, the concierge used his control of the string (or *cordon*) that lifted the front door latch to inspect everything and everyone, on the way in and on the way out.

FIG. 6: Nicolas Toussaint Charlet, '*Ces petites gens du second ...*', 1826.

His nose was in every bag of roasted chestnuts that entered the house. In vain I cried, '*Cordon, s'il vous plaît,*' in a winning voice, as though I were calling a bird to its sugar: I must be surveyed before I could pass into the street. When I returned home and pulled the bell, a brown wrinkled face, with no more shape nor complexion than a dried Normandy pippin, crowned with a cotton night-cap, was thrust out of a little window by the door, and I underwent another searching examination before the string was pulled.[57]

As we have seen, with 'model dwellings' in mansion blocks there was no concierge, only a superintendent, who lived on site, but did not have much control over who came and went, or at what hours.[58]

A final concern was sound spillage. Though it was, as some were prepared to admit, a fine distinction, to the Englishman, hearing a neighbour's piano and domestic quarrels through the walls was preferable to hearing them above his head, through the floor. In Zola's *Pot-Bouille* the main staircase's silence is deepened rather than broken by the hiss of the central heating, and even the muffled sound of pianos being played on each floor only renders the house's sober atmosphere more stifling. The walls of the internal courtyard, meanwhile, are lined with white glazed brick that seems to amplify the coarse oaths and gossip of the servants. As noted before, Londoners preferred to endure cold food rather than put up with having to hear sounds from the kitchen, so viewed a kitchen opening into a dining room as something shocking.

When the manager of St Anne's Mansions asked Eales what could be done about sound spillage, the architect dodged the issue somewhat. Thinking perhaps of 'model dwellings' with their hordes of children, he observed that flats were unsuited for children, it being 'most disagreeable' to encounter them on the stairs.[59] Other people simply called for thicker, soundproof party walls and floors. One of the common criticisms made of Albert Hall Mansions even before it was built was that it did not have enough internal party walls, to keep sounds from travelling between separate dwellings. As the pianos in *Pot-Bouille* made clear, sounds could carry heavy moral baggage, or, as *The Builder* put it: 'A party-wall has a moral as well as a fire-resisting value.'[60]

Neither a set of 'model dwellings' for the 'industrious classes' nor a mansion block for the elite, Palatinate Buildings (1875) near Elephant and Castle is a good example of Victorian middle-class flats. The Buildings were put up by a private contractor, Messrs Sutton and Dudley, had a 200-foot frontage on the New Kent Road and covered nearly two acres. The ground floor was given over to large shops, with a spacious central entrance and staircase giving access to the flats above. Built of stock brick with windows and doorways trimmed in artificial stone, the main blocks had flat roofs for drying, as well as decorative iron balconies on the second and fifth floor: a cut above designs found in model dwellings for the poor. The site was large enough for the developers to include two new streets, lined by blocks with bay windows: a homely touch redolent of an old-fashioned terraced house.

These apartments were explicitly intended for large- and medium-sized families of the 'trading and middle classes'. When finished, Palatinate Dwellings contained more than 300 flats.[61] As we have seen, the challenge of domesticating 'French flats' lay in striking a balance. Too little ornament and the architect risked being accused of designing a 'barracks'. Too much, and the architect left himself open to the charge of designing a bordello. London flats would need to be controlled, but not regimented; they must be comfortable, but not flashy. Buildings like Palatinate Dwellings demonstrated that Londoners could pull it off, creating a model of horizontal urban living that has become normal for most Londoners, as well as most city-dwellers. Though their differences had seemed insurmountable, in less than fifty years Londoners and Parisians had achieved the impossible. Together they had made the Restless House a home.

FIG. 7: Unknown artist after Robert Dighton, *A pleasant way to lose an eye*, 1820–5.

CHAPTER TWO

The Street

In September 1889, the poet Arthur Symons paid his first visit to Paris, aged twenty-four. The son of a Wesleyan minister, he had been born in Milford Haven, and his formal education had ended at seventeen, when his family moved to Somerset. Arthur had just published his first collection of verse, *Days and Nights* (1889). A fervent admirer of Paul Verlaine and other Symbolists, Symons took as his travelling companion the sexologist Henry Havelock Ellis, then a medical student. For Symons the trip was a long-awaited opportunity to experience at first hand the city whose authors and poets he venerated. On his first Sunday there, he ambled up and down the Boulevard des Italiens 'from 9 to 12 taking what Baudelaire calls a "bath of multitude"'. The election results had just been posted up, so he 'had the delight of observing the humours of a French crowd'.[1] While in the French capital he also had the chance to meet the poets Stéphane Mallarmé and Paul Verlaine. Arthur wasn't in Yeovil any more.

Symons's career as a cultural ambassador, forging a link between Paris and London, had begun. He returned to Paris the following year, staying three months. Though he set up house in London's Fountain Court, just off the Strand, in 1891, he kept going back to Paris and considered relocating there permanently. In London he moved in the circle of George Moore, W. B. Yeats and Aubrey Beardsley. The author of thousands of reviews, Symons did more than anyone else to encourage Victorians to appreciate Symbolism and aestheticism as something more than a crude assault on middle-class morality or an outlet for the frivolity we still associate with the 'Naughty Nineties'. Though his career came to a stop in 1908 as the result of a nervous breakdown, we have already encountered Symons as a translator of Zola's wicked novels, and will meet him again as a champion of music hall. Here we are more concerned with establishing just what Symons thought he was doing on the Boulevard des Italiens on that morning in 1889.

The reference to Charles Baudelaire is the key. In 1863 the poet published an essay praising the artist Constantin Guys, entitled 'Le Peintre de la vie moderne' ('The Painter of Modern Life'). Baudelaire hailed a way of seeing the city in Guys' work that he identified as characteristically modern. Rather than seeking to regulate or restrict the ever-accelerating production of increasingly ephemeral goods, the apparently random circulation of crowds and the constant creative destruction of the city itself, Guys embraced all its facets. This way of seeing was embodied in the figure of a solitary male walker, who sauntered around the city streets without any goal or purpose in mind, intent only on collecting impressions: a line of buildings, the feel of a piece of fabric on a shop stall, a snatch of conversation, a glimpse of a woman's face in the crowd. Neither a *promeneur* (a promenader) nor a *batteur de pavé* (literally 'pavement pounder', a vagrant), this walker was something else, a *flâneur*.

Baudelaire's *flâneur* made his home in the crowd, relishing the anonymity it brought, an anonymity that (unlike that of the lowly 'pavement pounder') was both thrilling and ennobling.[2] As any reader of 'À une passante' and other verse published in his collection *Les Fleurs du Mal* (1857) can attest, Baudelaire's poetry closely followed this model, 'distilling the eternal from the transitory'.[3] The 'bath of multitude' (*bain de multitude*) comes from a later essay, 'Les Foules' ('Crowds'; 1869), part of Baudelaire's multi-volume *Le Spleen de Paris*. 'Taking a bath of multitude is not vouchsafed to everyone,' Baudelaire wrote, 'multitude, solitude are one and the same for the active, fecund poet,' whose wandering soul entered this or that passer-by at whim, in an 'ineffable orgy', a 'holy prostitution of the soul'.[4] As a pose, the *flâneur* is therefore at once self-effacing and outrageously arrogant. Though he may disdain wealth or love, his appropriation of the city as his demesne has a swagger to it that Symons and many others since have found attractive. This *suffisance* derives from a conviction that all other inhabitants of the city are in some way blind or deaf to it, that the city reveals its secrets to the *flâneur* alone.[5]

The *flâneur* has become something of a stereotype, an urban cliché. Though Guys (who lived in London between 1842 and 1848, and may have worked for *Punch*) is forgotten, the Impressionists are held to have adopted the *flâneur*'s vision in their depictions of the city and its outskirts.[6] This fawning attention to the *flâneur* is largely due to an early twentieth-century sociologist, Walter Benjamin, author of *Das Passagen-werk*, a project on nineteenth-century Paris. Benjamin's introductory essay to this incomplete work, entitled 'Paris, Haupstadt der 19. Jahrhundert' ('Paris, capital of the nineteenth century'), has been enormously influential on the way in which the city has been viewed since. Benjamin's conclusion – that Paris created the *flâneur* – is widely accepted.[7]

It also happens to be incorrect. The first *flâneur* was not Baudelaire's 'passionate spectator', but Joseph Addison's and Richard Steele's Mr Spectator, the eponymous editor of their periodical, *The Spectator*, published between 1711 and 1712.[8] That this type of urban walking appeared so much earlier in London reflected the improvements in urban design – pavements, gutters, street lamps – adopted after the Great Fire of 1666, particularly in the fashionable squares of the city's western fringes. These made it possible for this peripatetic philosopher to wander the streets without getting doused with mud, assaulted by thieves or run over

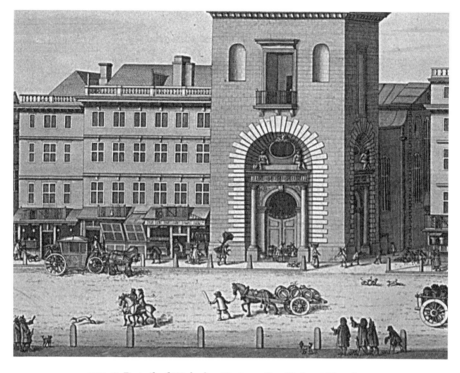

FIG. 8: Detail of Nicholas Yeates after Robert Thacker,
View of St Mary le Bow, c. 1680.

by a carriage. Such improvements came to Paris achingly slowly, much to
the frustration of would-be French Mr Spectators like Mercier and, seventy
years later, Théophile Gautier. But come at last they did.

The process by which Londoners and Parisians learned to walk at leisure
is more complicated than it might seem. At the start of our period the idea
that one might walk the streets for pleasure, the notion that the trivia of
paving stones, signs and advertisements might be a source of diversion or
even fascination, would have struck city-dwellers as deeply strange. Who
would choose to walk when he or she could take a carriage? Why would one
want to draw out the 'running' of errands into a relaxed saunter, let alone
make it an activity (that is, shopping) in its own right? What on earth was
there worth looking at? As we shall see, in learning to walk for the sake of it,
Londoners and Parisians also learned to see the city for the first time.

Mean Streets

The contrast between London, so friendly to pedestrians, and Paris, where the carriage was king, is clear in the work of late eighteenth-century Parisian commentators such as Louis-Sébastien Mercier, Rétif de la Bretonne and Henri Decremps. Decremps's *Un Parisien à Londres* included a section advising readers on how to walk on the pavements of London. 'Certain streets in this town are so wide and furnished with sidewalks so fine and clean,' he noted with wonder, 'that they can be used as promenades.'[9] This was thanks to the fact that main streets were divided into a central roadway flanked by sidewalks, with bollards to stop carts and carriages encroaching on them. A print of Cheapside in 1680 shows these arrangements already in place, whereas a print of the Rue Quincampoix in Paris from 1720 [Fig. 9] shows no such separation between pedestrians and traffic.

Though the streets of London were dirty enough by contemporary standards, there was no equivalent to the *décroteurs* of Paris: boys and men who gathered on bridges and major road junctions, offering to remove the filth from one's footwear. The mud of Paris was notorious in the

FIG. 9: Detail from Antoine Hublot, *Abbildung des auf der Straße Quincampoix in Paris entstandenen so berühmten Actien-Handels*, 1720.

seventeenth, eighteenth and early nineteenth centuries, and even today the *flâneur*'s enjoyment is limited by the necessity of constantly watching out for dog excrement. As Mercier noted, there was little need for *décroteurs* in London.[10] Early in the eighteenth century, developers of the great West End estates took steps to write into their leases stipulations regarding paving and pavement cleaning, practices regularized and extended under the Westminster Paving Act, the London Lighting Act (both 1761) and the Building Act of 1774.[11] In his *Parallèle*, Mercier demanded that London-style sidewalks (*trottoirs*) be introduced in Paris. Otherwise, he noted, London, where the pedestrian came first, would always shame Paris.[12]

Carriage and cart accidents involving pedestrians were so common in Paris that the police were forced to adopt a ready rule of thumb. If a pedestrian was run over by the vehicle's front wheel, the pedestrian was at fault, on the understanding that he or she should have got out of the way. If the pedestrian was run over by the back wheel, however, it was the driver's fault, on the understanding that if the driver had been paying sufficient attention, he could have stopped in time to prevent the back wheels rolling over the victim.[13]

The combination of sludge and fast-moving vehicles also meant that pedestrians were sprayed with mud flung up by the wheels. And not just any mud, but Paris mud, whose sticking power was proverbial (*il tient comme la boue de Paris*; 'it sticks like the mud of Paris'). Helped by the apparent indifference of householders and the lack of sewers, the mud consistently resisted the efforts of the *service de la voirie*, the city's sanitation service, which see-sawed back and forth between trying to get householders to perform their duty to sweep the area in front of their properties and contracting out street sweeping to entrepreneurs.[14] The necessity of dodging muddy puddles and delivery boys shouting 'Gare! Gare!' ('Coming through!') made the idea of being a *flâneur* in Paris ridiculous.

Nor could one dress so as to provide a spectacle for others: one's nice, expensive clothes would be covered in mud from the single gutter, which ran down the middle of the street, rather than, as in London, at the side, between the roadway and the pavement. The middle class of seventeenth- and early eighteenth-century Paris therefore sought to emulate the elite by avoiding the streets as much as possible. To walk on foot rather than ride in a carriage was tantamount to *encanaillement* (making oneself one of the *canaille,* or mob).[15] Of course, this only added to the risks run by pedestrians. Eighteenth-century Parisian *flâneurs* editorialized freely about how these carriages prevented the social mixing of the kind that might make people more patriotic. 'You mad dog, you!' cries Rétif de la Bretonne in one rant of 1788. 'Who gave you the right to cover us in mud?'[16]

There were, however, places in Paris where one could promenade in one's finery: the boulevards. These public promenades had been constructed from 1670 onwards along the line of the city's fortifications.[17] Between 1670 and 1676 the ramparts from the Porte Saint Antoine to the Porte Saint Martin became the first segment to be transformed. The boulevards eventually stretched to over 4.5 kilometres in length. These promenades were, along with the gardens of the Tuileries, the Luxembourg and the Arsenal, a distinct preserve, with a limited number of ways both in and out. The city authorities sought to prevent the boulevards from becoming part of the city's traffic system, restricting the number of roads leading from them back into the city as well as the kind of traffic that could use them.[18]

Therefore when Decremps said that the streets of London were like promenades, he meant that they could be enjoyed in the same way as could the boulevards and royal gardens of Paris: as an inviting place to go, to see and be seen. 'But one should not do so,' he added, 'without first taking certain precautions.' Here the stock image of 'the Parisian in London' reared its head yet again. The Parisian should not walk the streets dressed 'à la Française', Decremps insisted: that is, in silk garments, with a long tail-wig and a sword. While middle-class people would only laugh, the mob would jeer and maybe even throw mud.

Foreigners might well balk at this, Decremps conceded. Allowing such things to happen unchecked indicated a want of 'police' as well as exposing the gross manners of the common folk. But then, he asked, were a Londoner to come to Paris and seek to speak 'à l'Anglaise', discussing politics in a loud voice, wouldn't Parisians say that such behaviour was imprudent (given the presence of police spies, who supposedly listened to every conversation)? One city, in other words, had too little 'police', the other too much. One of the reasons for studying the Paris–London relationship was to find out where the balance lay.

When it came to native customs, Decremps observed, the common folk of London were their own masters, and their customs had to be respected. Pedestrians in eighteenth-century cities sought to avoid the mud by walking close to the wall of the houses on either side. Thus when two pedestrians walking in opposite directions approached each other, there were conventions as to who could move away from the wall and who could remain in position. As John Gay noted in his *Trivia; or the art of walking the London streets* (1716), one had to know when to hold the wall, and when to give way.[19] Most commentators felt that rank should trump all other considerations, even a respect for the weaker sex. In London, however, Decremps advised his genteel foreign visitor to give way, always, even to a humble porter or fruit-seller. 'Even the greatest *seigneurs* do the same, and this step, far from being humiliating, only serves to declare the politeness of a gentleman.'[20] The visitor should avoid other, more traditional means of announcing his rank. While it was merely foolish (*une fatuité*) for a Parisian dandy to display his two pocket watches in the streets of his home town, to do so in crime-filled London was lunacy (*une démence*).[21]

One of the native customs in which Londoners' rights were not to be challenged was the fist fight. Although he ridiculed the popular notion that in London 'they do nothing but beat each other up from morning to night', Decremps advised his readers that they should not be surprised if they came across impromptu boxing matches in the street. Once a fight was over everyone watching shouted 'Huzza!' three times. The combatants shook hands, then repaired to the nearest pub to have a drink together.[22] Far from a Parisian running the risk of a dust-up at every step, in reality a man had to indicate that he was ready for a fight by removing his jacket or placing a bet, before bystanders would stop to form a circle and direct the fight. Were anyone to punch someone who had *not* so indicated his readiness, then he would be severely punished, and more severely, Decremps claimed, than in any other country. 'In this regard the common English people are, it seems to me, the most civilised in Europe.'[23] Londoners were savages, but civilized ones.

Even on the Strand, the busiest and most congested thoroughfare in London, the mean streets had a gentler side, Decremps revealed. He described an experiment carried out the previous year (1788) by an Englishman, who carried a five-year-old boy to Charing Cross and then had him walk, alone, to his father's house at Temple Bar (near where the Royal Courts of Justice are located today). This experiment was apparently made to test the child. The result was surprising.

> Not only was he not attacked, more than two hundred
> individuals went out of their way to let him pass; wherever
> he might be expected to walk in the mud to cross from one
> sidewalk to another he found kindly women to carry him
> over, caressing him all the while. He arrived at his father's
> house, safe and sound, eating the sweets that had been
> given him on the way. An experiment intended to prove
> the boy's intelligence ended up proving the gentleness and
> politeness of English manners.[24]

Though intended to be reassuring, a corrective to the many accounts of wanton violence retailed in France, Decremps's account probably confused his readers more than it enlightened them.

Even at a time of Anglomania, French images of England were riven with paradoxes. The English constitution, such as it was (and it wasn't a written document, as was the American one), was much admired, but little understood.[25] English patriotism was credited with having led the nation's forces to victory in the Seven Years War. Yet such strength came at a cost: a level of political instability that seemed too high for many French observers.[26] The Wilkite disturbances of 1768 and 1771, the American Revolution of 1776 and the Gordon Riots of 1780 regularly confirmed the prejudices of those of the French elite who expected Britain to tear itself apart, a victim of its own contradictions. 'The English can never destroy each other as much as we would like,' wrote the French prime minister the Duc de Choiseul in May 1768, shortly after one bloody riot in St George's Fields.[27] A nest of republicans and regicides, periodically incinerated by revolutionary unrest, London was a city whose very walls reeked of blood – at least, according to one French pamphlet published after the Gordon Riots.[28] It was only a question of time before it all came crashing down, and the French secret service was doing its bit to help things along, either by covert arming of the American rebels or plots to support Wilkite agitation.[29]

Such contradictions were reflected in the way Parisians viewed London, a much bigger and more populous, yet much less policed city than their own. How could one make sense of a city where novel, broad sidewalks made for promenading served as stages for time-worn, violent rituals in which two individuals sought to beat each other to a pulp? A city whose residents were so solicitous of horses that anyone who ran his mount through in a moment of passion (as Parisians were known to do: at least, according to Mercier) risked being cut down on the spot?[30] Mercier had been an eyewitness of the Gordon Riots of 1780, a week-long orgy of mayhem and anti-Catholic mob violence sparked off by Lord George Gordon, leader of the Protestant Association. Though the rabble attacked the Bank of England, broke open prisons and committed many acts of arson before 11,000 troops were brought in and began shooting (killing several hundred), according to Mercier's account the mob's violence was precisely targeted.

So disciplined were the rioters, he wrote, that as they carefully smashed the windows and property of the ministers who had drawn their ire, those resident in the houses on either side were able to watch them at work, in total safety. Those debtors who found themselves at liberty went home, but only temporarily. 'Most of those imprisoned for debt subsequently returned of their own accord,' Mercier noted. 'Other debtors wrote immediately to tell their creditors where they were and not to worry.'[31] For Mercier it was the working-class Londoner's sense that he and his fellows were 'at all times their own master' that made him monitor and control his own behaviour. In contrast, were their Parisian equivalents to wake up one day and discover themselves to be free of the watch and the police, the result would be chaos.[32]

Window-Shoppers

The first sidewalks in Paris appeared in the 1780s, as part of the redevelopment of the Odéon quarter. New streets were created converging on the Place de l'Odéon, where the theatre of the same name stood. This was one of a series of large-scale developments of *immeubles,* funded by speculators, discussed in the previous chapter. There were, admittedly, raised flat terraces on either side of the Pont Neuf, built at the King's expense between 1578 and 1607. But these were intended to provide room for stalls selling goods, not for pedestrians to walk on.[33] The Pont Neuf was for centuries one of the main sights of Paris, admired as a wonder of engineering as well as for its unparalleled views of the city, views impossible from the other bridges, thanks to the houses built on them. In the late

1780s the houses on the Pont Notre Dame were finally cleared, a moment immortalized by the painter Hubert Robert.

With the exception of such new developments, however, pavements in Paris were rare. When the *voyageur* Babillard tried to stroll down the Rue de la Seine, the result was a disaster: he got lost, was stopped, then shoved around by porters, and finally almost drowned in overflowing gutters. Eventually he gave up attempting to be a *flâneur* and hailed a hackney carriage, rueing the fact that Paris lacked London's pavements.[34] The French capital's filthy streets continued to provide a good living for *décroteurs* well into the nineteenth century. In 1822 it could boast just 267 metres of sidewalk in the whole city.[35] Along with the royal gardens of the Tuileries and the Luxembourg, London-style 'Wauxhalls' or pleasure gardens provided the only places one could stroll and shop in *ancien régime* Paris. At the Colisée, which opened on the Champs Elysées in 1771, three distinct arcades ran off the main central ballroom, each with ten shops on each side, selling jewellery, fashion and lottery tickets. Unfortunately the Colisée proved too remote for most people and closed two years later, taking with it this early form of Parisian shopping mall.[36]

Dandies thus fled to the *passages* (covered shopping arcades) to be found in the area north-west of the Palais Royal. The Galerie de Bois, a range of wooden shops linking the two ends of the arcades of the Palais Royal, opened in 1786. The Passage Feydeau and the Passage du Caire opened in 1791 and 1799 respectively. However, the heyday of the *passages* came in the years between 1822 and 1837, the age of the Passage Colbert (1826). These provided *flâneurs* with an opportunity to stroll under glass at all times of the year, ogling passers-by as well as the luxury goods displayed in the boutiques on either side. Protected at night by a grille at both street entrances, these establishments could dispense with the massive shutters (*volets*) put up at the close of business by shops out on the street.

Shopfronts in seventeenth- and early eighteenth-century London usually had a narrow door flanked by two wider openings covered by shutters, which divided horizontally. The top half opened to form a canopy; the bottom had folding legs that enabled it to serve as a shopboard. Goods thus spilled out into the street. In Paris many shops had no fronts at all. In 1767, Gabriel de Saint-Aubin depicted the shop of Périer, a *quincaillier* or ironmonger, possibly for a trade card intended to advertise his premises, as being at the sign of the Moor's Head on the Quai de la Mégisserie.[37] This set-up seems to have been the case even for the emporium of picture dealer Edmé-François Gersaint on the Pont Notre Dame, depicted in Antoine Watteau's famous *L'Enseigne de Gersaint* (1720) [Fig. 10]. Gersaint's staff would have had to move all the paintings, chairs and crates, shown in the illustration, in and out of the back room, every day. The walls are bare stone, making the space look more suitable for stabling horses than selling luxury goods to well-dressed aristocrats.

Such a venue would have been unthinkable in early eighteenth-century London. It would have had a proper shopfront, with windows and a neatly plastered interior. Even before the Great Fire, Parisians like Samuel Sorbière found London shops striking for their ornament, 'delighting the gaze and

FIG. 10: Pierre Aveline after Antoine Watteau, *L'Enseigne de Gersaint*, 1732.

attracting the eye of passers-by'.[38] English observers, too, were taken by the speed with which open shops were being supplied with glazed shopfronts. 'Never was such painting and guilding, such sashings [i.e. installation of windows] and looking-glasses among the shopkeepers, as there is now,' Daniel Defoe complained in 1726. He compared London's gaudy stores somewhat unfairly with a foppishly dressed Frenchman.[39]

Though windows were taxed, the various English glassworks competed freely with one another, keeping prices low. Their French equivalents such as St Gobain (established by Colbert in 1665) enjoyed the protection of royal monopolies. London shopfronts continued to astonish Parisian visitors throughout the eighteenth century and well into the nineteenth, not only because they had windows but because those on major streets were illuminated at night, staying open until 8 or 9 p.m.[40] In 1831, Edward Planta was still remarking on how few Parisian shops had proper shop windows.[41]

The construction of Regent Street, designed by the royal architect John Nash and pushed through Marylebone between 1817 and 1832, may have opened a new traffic artery running north–south, but it was mainly hailed as the heart of a new shopping quarter.[42] With its arcades lined with shops having terraces above and ample sidewalks below, Regent Street was the envy of any Parisian *flâneur*, as well as being the haunt of dandies such as Tom, Jerry and Logic, the heroes of Pierce Egan's *Life in London* (1821). Nash's attempt at a *passage,* Royal Opera Arcade (1817), was, by contrast, a failure. Though Burlington Arcade (1818) was more successful, London did not really need *passages* when Oxford and Regent Street provided shoppers with the same experience, on a much larger scale. Only with the appearance of the great department stores such the Samaritaine (1869) did Paris supplant London as the home of window shopping, as the place where shopping became an art form in itself.[43] Today's Parisians are known for their fondness for 'window shopping' (or 'window licking', as they put it). Before the second half of the nineteenth century, there were few shop windows in Paris to lick apart from those of the arcades, and those few were little noticed.[44]

Shopping and haggling no longer went together, but parted ways as the purchasing of goods became more of a spectacle and less of a drama. Although haggling might have afforded a rich seam of material for *flâneurs*, they heartily welcomed the introduction of fixed prices, as did shoppers (the distinction is important: for the *flâneur* was not out to buy anything, but simply to gather sights, to window shop).[45] Fixed prices had become the norm in London shops by the time Mercier visited in 1780. By then only the most aristocratic clients could count on getting credit of the sort still common in Paris.[46] Everyone else paid cash. Mercier appreciated the resulting speed. 'Walk into a shop in Paris and you are invited to take a seat,' he noted; 'each party salutes the other, you talk of a thousand different things while you bargain, even about the shopkeeper's family life or public events, haggling, much haggling over the price.'

All too often this time-consuming exercise was in vain: buyer and seller would part, 'the one driven to distraction by all the merchant's babble, the merchant riled at having failed to sell anything, ready to lash out at the next person who comes in'. In London shopping was faster, almost curt in its rhythms. Buyers entered a shop without receiving any formal greeting, and without removing their hats. Once informed of what the buyer was looking for, the shopkeeper went and got it; there was no beating them down on the price. It was take it or leave it. 'You pay, job done. Merchant and customer alike have saved time.'[47] Mercier's businesslike transaction contrasts sharply with that described in Laurence Sterne's earlier *Sentimental Journey* (1768). Here the hero, Yorick, pauses in a glove shop to ask directions to the Opéra Comique and ends up engaged in a highly sensual, if not downright erotic, exchange of caresses with the shopkeeper's wife, Madame Grisset, while her husband watches.[48] In the 1670s this sort of flirtation had been a key part of seventeenth-century shopping in London's exchanges (covered arcades for luxury goods). By Yorick's day it was a distant memory.[49]

The contrast between sentimental tourist and splenetic *flâneur* is clear. Given a choice between pausing to interact with his surroundings or moving on to the next sight, the *flâneur* prefers the latter. That is part of what makes him modern. Whereas Yorick pays Madame Grisset compliments and holds her hand in an orgy of polite *galanterie,* Mercier just wants to get on with it. Whatever 'it' is, it certainly has nothing to do with physical contact. Behind the apparently aggressive ogling, the *flâneur* is an asexual, perhaps even ungendered, being.[50] Whether the 'goods' are gloves or the women who sell them, the *flâneur* never buys. He is always 'just looking'.

It may seem anachronistic to discuss Mercier, let alone Mr Spectator, in terms of the *flâneur*.[51] The first appearance of the word in print occurs in an anonymous review of the Paris Salon of 1809, entitled *Le Flâneur au Salon, ou Monsieur Bon-Homme.* This figure is described as having a private income of around 2,000 francs: a *rentier* therefore, who lives on the fourth floor of number 27, Rue de Fleury, near the Louvre. His day is described, hour by hour. He starts at nine with a round of watching construction and destruction work around the Louvre, where a new street is being pushed through to the Carrousel. He gazes at print-shop windows, has his morning cup of chocolate, looks at theatre posters and talks to actors he knows, indulging in yet more print-shop gazing before hitting the boulevards in the afternoon:

> At around two o'clock, he is on the boulevards, which
> he follows as far as the Passage des Panoramas. He has
> reviewed every shop, examined every new bonnet, new
> novel, new toy, all the new romances, all the new
> *peignes à chignon*, all the new coaches, all the new frocks
> and all the new shop signs. Though he's no police spy,
> he does not fail to notice spots where the pavement needs
> fixing, gambling dens . . . dodgy awnings and flowerpots
> dangerously perched on windowsills.[52]

One day, while sitting in a café listening to the conversation of a group of actors, Bon-Homme decides to keep a journal of all he observes, as a way to relieve his insomnia.[53]

Thereafter the *flâneur* seems to have stayed out of print until the mid-1820s, when he was the subject of two vaudevilles, the one-act *Le Flâneur* (1826) and the four-act *La Journée d'un Flâneur* ('A Flâneur's Day', 1827), performed at the Théâtre de la Porte Saint Martin and the Théâtre des Variétés respectively. In both, the *flâneur* in question is an absent-minded *père de famille*, constantly stopping to observe goings-on around him, and finding himself wrongfully arrested after getting too close to the action.[54] Both comedies begin with scenes set in the street. In *Le Flâneur* the stage instructions call for no less than seven vendors of different kinds to appear on stage, as well as an infantry post, workers passing and so on.[55] 'Long live Paris!' sings the hero of *Le Flâneur*. 'To observant eyes/She is a moving picture.'[56] In 1831 the newspaper *The Figaro* defined the *flâneur* as someone who visited all the free shows, who made the street his living room and all shop windows his furniture.[57] Guides to the city also began taking the *flâneur* as a pseudonym.[58]

Signs and Wonders

From the improbable, enormous, gravity-defying signs of the eighteenth-century city, through posters and placards, to today's vast, neon or digital displays, advertising provides one of the most striking aspects of the modern urban street. Here again Paris and London led the way. Hanging signs shaped to look like massive animals or objects began as a means of advertising that was intelligible to the illiterate and the literate alike. In the period before such signs were common practice, however, these boards had an additional function: to help outsiders and residents establish where they were. Parisians and Londoners were literally lost without them, rendered at once strangers in their own city.[59] In the absence of street numbers, packages and visitors to eighteenth-century London and Paris were addressed or directed to a house 'at the sign of X', or 'by the sign of the Y'.

To take as an example just three common signs, a set of directions might advise one to turn left at the Sleeping Cat, then walk past the World's End until one reached the Stars. As this shows, signs turned even a short walk into something magical, full of bizarre connections and contrasts. Analogies with astrology made it possible to relate time and place in whimsical ways, thanks to the familiar phrase 'to be born under the sign of X', which could apply to where (meaning in which house) as well as when (meaning in which star sign) a person was born. A playful fascination with such signs, regret at their removal and nostalgia for their loss represent another thread linking eighteenth- and nineteenth-century *flâneurs* in Paris and London. Bon-Homme paid careful attention to every new shop sign that appeared on the boulevards, and Baudelaire, too, insisted that the *flâneur* be up to date in his knowledge of them.

Though almost no eighteenth- or even early nineteenth-century signs survive, it is still possible to get a sense of their bizarre nature in London, where many pub signs remain and in some cases (as, for example, The Angel) have come to denote a particular neighbourhood. This aspect of Paris has entirely disappeared. As is demonstrated by the massive projecting signs visible in contemporary Chinese cities, they can represent a significant obstacle to ventilation as well as a safety risk to pedestrians walking below. Such concerns, combined with annoyance at the way signs squeaked in the wind, led the authorities in both capitals to pass laws in 1761, ordering that all hanging signs be removed, or placed flat up against the façade. This was followed in Paris by an ordinance in 1768 on the numbering of houses, intended to create a more rational means of navigating the city. Declaring an ordinance was one thing, actually implementing it another. Numbering was delayed by the aristocracy, who refused to have their *hôtels particuliers* humbled by the attribution of a mere number, just as they refused to have street lights hung from their *hôtels*. In 1799 the ordinance against hanging signs had to be repeated, as did that on numbering in 1805.[60]

The quintessential *flâneur*-artists of eighteenth-century Paris were the brothers Charles-Germain and Gabriel de Saint-Aubin, the sons of a middle-class embroiderer. Although their style was more *galant* than that of Hogarth, they clearly shared an eye for vignettes of everyday street and boulevard life. This is clear from the *Livre de Caricatures* they created for their own amusement, an extraordinary visual palimpsest now in the collection of Waddesdon Manor. The *Livre* is full of diverse design motifs, inventions, political satires and visual puns. One page records the removal of street signs under the police ordinance of 1761 [Fig. 11]. Here one constable staggers, under the weight of a massive sword and a shining sun, towards his colleague, who is busy destroying a massive

FIG. 11: Charles-Germain de Saint-Aubin, 'Bâtir Est beau, mais detruire est Sublime', 1761, in *Livre de Caricatures tant Bonnes que mauvaises*, c. 1740–1775.

boot-shaped sign. That such crude monstrosities should have appealed to the brothers Saint-Aubin, talented artists who spent hours admiring and sketching masters old and new in Paris auction houses and at the annual Salon, indicates that they did not, in fact, think them beneath their aesthetic consideration.

Neither did Bonnell Thornton, a London journalist who in 1762 organized an exhibition of pub and shop signs in Bow Street. On one level this remarkable 'Grand Exhibition of Signpainters' was a sally against connoisseurs, suggesting that they were so blind that they would pay to see an exhibition of anything, provided it was presented as high art, with a catalogue. Such satire may also have reflected English artists' bitterness at the preference shown by their would-be patrons for Italian and French artists. This preference stemmed from the belief that England was too commercial a nation to succeed at a 'polite art'. As the poor sign-painter in Hogarth's *Beer Street* [Fig. 12] reveals, in the absence of better commissions, English artists (including Hogarth) often relied on sign-painting as a means of survival. But the Signpainters Exhibition can also be seen as a celebration of a type of 'street art' that was both 'useful' and 'polite'. The exhibition's organizers and Hogarth himself (who may have been directly involved) certainly held that the English were the finest sign-painters in Europe.[61]

These grotesque signs were often crudely painted, however, and struck many as an obstacle to the creation of *la ville policée*. As a result, critics such as Addison, Mercier and the Saint-Aubin brothers were ambivalent about the removal of signs in both Paris and London. In 1711, Mr Spectator had offered his services to the public as 'Superintendent' of signs, perhaps inspired by a character in Molière's play *Les Fâcheux* (1662).[62] Some signs, Mr Spectator objected, made highly misleading or irreligious connections between very different kinds of people. A prostitute might be found at the sign of The Angel, for example, while other respectable persons might be offended by the depiction of creatures such as mermaids and blue boars that could not be found in nature. Yet it is nonetheless clear that such

FIG. 12: William Hogarth, *Beer Street*, 1751.

devotion to 'police' is ironic, and that Mr Spectator delights in the urban uncanny of the signs.[63]

Parisian efforts to keep signs under control dated back almost a century, to 1666, when the *bureau de la voirie* set a tax on all those hanging them up.[64] More than a century later, however, they were still there in vast numbers, a source of embarrassment to Mercier in his *Tableau de Paris*.[65] He described monstrosities: a boot as big as a barrel; a glove so large that a three-year-old child could be housed in each finger; an arm holding a sword that loomed over the whole street. Without them, Paris had 'a new face, so to speak, clean-shaven and polite'.[66]

But then, as with Addison before him, Mercier also delighted in the semantic slippages and plays on words (as well as plays on images) that these same signs permitted.[67] Just as Hogarth loved to be a *flâneur* in the streets where the sign-painters practised their trade, so Mercier delighted in the second-hand sign shops on the Quai de la Mégisserie.[68] 'There,' he noted, 'all the kings of the earth sleep peacefully with one another: Louis XVI and George III share a fraternal kiss, the King of Prussia sleeps with the Empress of Russia, the Emperor is upon the same footing with the Electors. There, at last, the turban and the tiara [the Papal tiara, i.e. Islam and Christianity] mingle.'[69] Mercier even imagines what these signs would say if they could talk to one another.[70]

The creation around 1820 of a card game based on the signs of Paris and the publication in the mid-1820s of a historical and critical dictionary of the city's signs coincided neatly with the emergence, noted above, in the same decade of the '*flâneur*' (who is named as such).[71] Genuine antiquarian concern for the losses of these emblems led to the creation in 1880 of a city museum in Paris, which we know today as the Musée Carnavalet. By then three famous signs had already been preserved in the Hôtel de Cluny, for want of any more appropriate museum in which to deposit them.[72] In London such street signs survived the Paving Act of 1762. In 1856, George Dodd calculated that London contained no less than 55 Swans, 90 King's Heads, 120 Lions . . . but only one Good Man.[73]

The Sandwich-Man

Where does this leave our hero, the *flâneur*? As he introduces himself in the fourth issue of *The Spectator* (penned by Steele), 'Mr Spectator' strikes a familiar figure, even one that might be called Baudelairean, had it not been written in 1711. Mr Spec is silent, solitary and haunts public places, not to 'make a figure' but simply to gratify his curiosity. He finds solitude among the masses, enjoying a 'Publick sort of Obscurity'. Though he is a familiar presence in the throng, he is referred to, if at all, as 'Mr What-d'ye-call-him'.[74] Like Baudelaire's 'man of the crowd', Mr Spec revels in his anonymity as well as in his eccentricity. He never speaks, yet has an appetite 'to communicate the Fulness of my Heart' when writing for us, his invisible companions. There is even a sense in which the author is gathering himself as he gathers material, and so the *flâneur* erases himself as he writes, unloading the impressions he has lovingly amassed. 'Mr Spec' is resolved 'to Print my self out, if possible, before I die'.[75]

The Spectator also reflected a city with a sense of itself as a cultural entity, as 'the town', a world distinct from the court.[76] Here different ranks, genders and professions could mingle. Entry to this world was secured, not by patents of nobility, but by familiarity with codes of polite behaviour. The seventeenth-century French concept of *honnêteté* had some resemblance to this politeness, in its apparent preference for an easygoing *déshabille* ('undress') over the court's punctilio. *Honnêteté* was an aristocratic costume, however, worn not in the city, but in suburban, socially exclusive festivities such as the *fêtes champêtres* and balls held at St Cloud and Auteuil.[77] This 'world' was still centred on the court, rather than the 'town'.

Of course, the word '*flâneur*' did not exist in the eighteenth century and began to be used only in the 1820s. The *flâneur* did not come of age until later, in 1840–1, with the appearance of a number of works by Edgar Allan Poe, Charles Dickens and Louis Huart, all of which featured solitary walkers, setting the scene for Baudelaire's famous essay of 1845.[78] Most important among them was Huart's *Physiologie du flâneur*, available for just one franc. It played on the fame of Georges Cuvier and other comparative anatomists in adopting the guise of a quasi-scientific or philosophical investigation into the relationship between mankind and other vertebrates. Huart concluded that man's superiority to other animals lay in his ability to be a *flâneur*.[79] His was one among at least seventy such 'physiologies' of urban types to appear in the early 1840s, including one of 'The English in Paris', many of them illustrated with small woodcut illustrations by Honoré Daumier, M.-A. Alophe and Théodore Maurisset.[80] Their text and images having been inspired by Cruikshank prints, these physiologies in turn led Albert Smith and David Bogue to publish the *Physiology of a London Idler* and *Natural History of the Idler upon Town* (both 1848).[81]

The pavements were the *flâneur*'s favourite place to be. 'Sidewalk!' Huart exclaims, 'haven safe from the mud, asylum of the *flâneur*, I salute you! All the happiest moments of my youth transpired on your stones.'[82] He provided one of the clearest accounts demonstrating how the *flâneur*'s viewpoint contrasted with that of the normal pedestrian. Upon seeing a new fabric in a shop window, he explains, a greengrocer would simply remark to himself that it was pretty and might suit his wife – then move on a few moments later. A *flâneur* would be transfixed for two hours, studying the design and colour, considering its place in the history of fashion, as well as the relationship between the manufacturer, his suppliers and retailers. These reflections were a world entirely beyond the ken of the normal passer-by.[83] This is one example of the *flâneur*'s smug sense of being a 'prince' of a realm that, though partly imaginary, is undoubtedly richer than the mundane one the rest of us inhabit.

Though he might be a prince, the *flâneur*'s passage through the city's streets is not without its trials. Just as Mr Spectator notes 'some little Distastes I daily receive', so nineteenth-century *flâneurs* sometimes had to endure a degree of humiliation. Far from suggesting that *flânerie* was impossible, however, if anything the rehearsal of such trials helped to exclude the faint-hearted and uninitiated, to flatter the *flâneur*'s sense of being an omniscient, invisible minority.[84] George Cruikshank's print series *Grievances of London* (1812) visualized the type of sidewalk encounters between dandies and working men (see Fig. 7, p. 62) that awaited inattentive *flâneurs*. Whilst painful, such encounters were celebrated as something that made the city an exciting and colourful place to be.[85]

FIG. 13: Unknown artist, *Flâneur* hit by *volet*, from Louis Huart, *Physiologie du flâneur*, 1841.

The *flâneur* pratfalls depicted by Cruikshank, Daumier and others in the 1820s, 1830s and 1840s were intended to ridicule the *flâneur*'s way of seeing the city as nothing more than a collection of visual impressions. The city has a physical substance, which constantly (and comically) interrupts the *flâneur*'s airy wanderings. This city comes at the *flâneur* from all angles. It is the mud that flies up onto the fine clothes of Mercier; it is the butcher's trestle that pokes out the eye of Cruikshank's dandy; it is the shop shutter that hits Huart's *flâneur* in the face [Fig. 13]; it is the flowerpot that threatens to land on Bon-Homme's head.[86]

The 1820s also saw the appearance of the first sandwich-men, known in French as *hommes affiches* ('poster men') or *affiches ambulantes* ('walking posters'). Here again, London set the pace.[87] Within twenty years such straightforward combinations of two boards linked by leather straps had given way to more ambitious horse-drawn contraptions (enormous coffee mills, Egyptian temples, large cylinders with posters attached) and costumes that entirely obscured the person inside.[88] Instead of carrying or wearing a board printed with the name of a popular brand of blacking, the sandwich-man now became the product. George Scharf's sketch of a

FIG. 14: George Scharf, Blacking tin men (at left), 1834–8.

walking Waren's [*sic*] Blacking tin (1840) [Fig. 14] shows no less than six of these hapless man-tins walking in a line.[89]

Like Huart's *flâneur*, Scharf was fascinated by such men and by posters, which he depicted in all their garish glory. Though initially developed in Germany, lithography was first applied to advertising in London. Those Parisian printers eager to learn the latest techniques of colour lithography, such as Jules Chéret, brought the new technology back to Paris. The results changed not only how Parisian streets looked, but how Paris saw itself. Cheret's posters for Montmartre theatres and music halls provided the lurid colours and sprightly nymphs (called *chérettes*, after their creator) that helped create the 'Gay Paree' considered in Chapter 4.

By the 1840s it was getting hard to tell the *flâneur* and the sign one from the other. An 1849 cartoon shows a Frenchman returning to his London hotel wearing a set of sandwich boards. When asked by the manager why he is attired so oddly, the man explains: 'I saw a lot of English people dressed up like this, so I thought it must be the custom here. I put one on so that nobody would notice me.'[90] Such a disguise certainly afforded people a licence to wander at will through the crowds, although it remains to be seen whether this 'incognito' was a princely one (as Baudelaire had asserted). 'You, *flâneurs!*' Huart wrote in his *Physiologie du flâneur*. 'I would do better to call the *flâneur* a police agent assigned to the sidewalk, the sandwich-man who perambulates public places.'[91] Chapter 5 will consider the *flâneur's* career in assisting the police with their enquiries. For our purposes here, however, it is high time to pause and consider what Mr What-d'ye-call-him has to tell us about the city.

Steele and Mercier, the Saint-Aubin brothers and Hogarth: these figures were among the first to celebrate the urban promenade as a source of delight and mystery in its own right, rather than as an unpleasant passage through the city's monstrously distended body, undertaken only by those unfortunate enough to lack a carriage. The *flâneur* was not a nineteenth-century development. He had emerged in London *and* in Paris, during the previous century, but he remains a peripheral, evanescent and insubstantial figure. An over-deferential reverence for this 'prince' has raised his profile out of all proportion. Under the joint influence of Baudelaire's gravely solipsistic depiction and Benjamin's Marxisant obsession with alienation, the *flâneur's* significance has been wildly exaggerated.[92] Far from being definitive, this particular manifestation of the *flâneur* is actually late, and overlooks the extent to which that philosophical, scientific tone of serious urban analysis was a pose intended to satirize those who made outrageous claims to knowledge.[93] There was a strong hint of irony in their discussion of how to bring order to the chaos of street signage, a knowingness about the limits of expertise and the vanity of seeking a perfect control or 'police'.[94]

Writing about the *flâneur* offers a perspective on paving, transport, shopping, advertising and other facets of urban life that are easily overlooked, as they often have been. But otherwise it may, perhaps, be time to let Mr What-d'ye-call-him do what, by his own account, he most wishes to do – and 'write himself out' of the tales we like to tell about cities.[95]

FIG. 15 : Gault de Saint Germain after Unknown artist, *Entrez Messieurs et Dames,*
C'est le moment ou les Animaux prennent leur Nourriture, 1817.

CHAPTER THREE

The Restaurant

I t seemed that Jean, Duc des Esseintes, had resolved never to leave Fontenay-aux-Roses. A virtual orphan from a young age, at thirty the last of the line of the Floressas des Esseintes, he sold his family's chateau and withdrew to a specially constructed hermitage, cutting off almost all ties to the world. Located just over five miles south of Paris, Fontenay was suburban, but not fashionable. He would be safe from unwanted visitors.

Until this point des Esseintes's life had been a *belle époque* version of the Book of Ecclesiastes. Educated in a Jesuit college, on leaving he had first socialized with a circle of fellow Catholics. Tiring of their hypocrisy, he dropped them to join a group of gambling libertines. His taste for fast company was soon sated and he abandoned them for the company of men of letters. Yet this only increased his contempt for humanity, and he fell victim to an overpowering ennui, which even the most thorough exploration of Parisian vice could not shake.

Finally, on his doctor's advice, he left Paris and retired to Fontenay, where he lived alone, apart from two aged servants. Here he crafted an exquisitely refined cocoon for himself. The shades of the wallpaper, the books and bibelots on the shelves, the colour and intensity of the light and even the perfume of the air – everything was carefully monitored and controlled to provide just the right amount of sensory stimulation. Week by week, des Esseintes treated his various neuroses, while exploring new worlds opened up by Francisco Goya and Gustave Moreau, samples of whose phantasmagoric etchings and paintings he kept close at hand.

One day, after a period during which he had enjoyed perfect health, des Esseintes was attacked by hallucinations of his sense of smell. Trying to match the phantom perfumes, he exhausted all his vaporizers. Determined to break the spell, he tried opening the window, only to pass out cold. A doctor was called, but could offer little remedy. Even Dickens, whose novels normally helped to calm his nerves, succeeded only in filling his head with visions of English life, mingled now with a longing to gather new impressions. After a few days, des Esseintes recovered and ordered his servants to pack his trunks. He was off to London.

The train from Sceaux dropped him at the Porte d'Enfer, where he hailed a cab, planning to buy *Murray's Guide to London* and a toothbrush before leaving Paris. The incessant rain, mud and greasy pavements of the Boulevard d'Enfer seemed to him a foretaste of London, eliciting a shiver of pleasure. Des Esseintes would soon be there, isolated by the fogs and yet caught up in the pitiless commercial machinery grinding down millions of wretched workers. Passing through the Rue de Rivoli, he stopped by a print-shop window, admiring prints by John Leech before entering the shop, where a babble of tourists' voices assailed him.

He then crossed the street to a tavern, where he read the names of various English-brand ports, enjoying a glass while leaning on the corner of a table at which were seated English clergymen, dandies and other visitors. In his mind's eye he picked out various characters, familiar to him from *Bleak House* and *Little Dorrit*. On leaving, he had his cab take him to another tavern on the Rue d'Amsterdam, conveniently close to the Gare du Nord, from whence the Dieppe train left at 8.50 p.m. Once he reached Dieppe, the packet would take him via Newhaven, to arrive in London at exactly 12.30 p.m. the next day.

Settling himself into a booth, des Esseintes surveyed the tavern. Here were sturdy, red-cheeked Englishwomen with buck teeth busy attacking beef pies. His appetite whetted, he ordered oxtail soup, followed by smoked haddock, accompanied by two pints of ale. He then ordered a piece of Stilton and nibbled at a rhubarb tart, washed down with porter. It had been ages since he had eaten so well. Des Esseintes inspected his clothes and was pleased to note that they hardly differed from those worn by the Londoners around him. He was, in this superficial way, a naturalized Londoner. Then he jumped: it was almost time for the train. He called for the bill and, momentarily transfixed by the Englishness of the waiter, managed to pay. He was off.

Des Esseintes is a fictitious figure dreamed up by the novelist Joris-Karl Huysmans, who had been born in Paris to Dutch parents in 1848. Huysmans worked as a civil servant before establishing his reputation as a writer, an admirer of Zola friendly with Arthur Symons, whom we met in the previous two chapters. The hero of *À Rebours* (1884), des Esseintes served as a role model for many an *incroyable* or dandy in *fin-de-siècle* London and Paris. His uncharacteristic feast is set in which would have been a recognizable location: the Austin Bar or English Tavern, located at 24, Rue d'Amsterdam. Baudelaire had rented rooms above it. The Goncourt brothers admired its 'authentic' roast beef. The Symbolist poet Valéry had taken Huysmans and Mallarmé there.

Food in *À Rebours* is more than a matter of taste, an affair of the palate. It is unashamedly visceral, taking in the tongue, of course, but also the lips, the throat, the stomach and the lower organs. To read *À Rebours* is to be surfeited, if not downright disgusted, by the capabilities of one's own body. Des Esseintes is supremely talented at distilling essences and concocting formulas: a gourmet and a scientist, therefore. But he is also a psychologist, well aware of the power of taste to summon up visions that are more than cerebral and more than a case of making connections between different texts, or between texts and visual images. Though he is described as having initially paid little attention to the art of cooking, by the end of *À Rebours* he is pondering a form of 'inverted epicurism'. He suspects his doctor of varying the recipes of the enemas he prescribes like a clever chef, to 'forestall the possibility that the monotony of the dishes would bring on a total loss of appetite'.[1]

Just like any other form of theatre, dining out is about stimulation, about enjoyment and entertainment. From its very beginnings in the eighteenth century, the history of the restaurant is not the history of how hunger was dispelled, but of how appetite is aroused, among a class of people who have never had to wonder where the next meal was coming from. Stimulation can come from the architecture or the decor, from menus or written descriptions, from the waiters, the fellow diners and the social conventions that guide each person's part in the drama. It can come from the exotic and the exceptional; from the local and the genuine; from the 'artificial' and the processed, as much as from the 'natural' and the wholesome. Feasting and dining out have captured the attention of dietitians, anthropologists and sociologists as well as historians.

Des Esseintes's rhubarb-and-porter-filled stomach is a reminder of how closely food is tied up with identity, as well as illustrating how restaurants permit us to travel to other countries without leaving our home city. Dining out is thus another space of crossing between Paris and London. In swopping recipes, chefs, decor and diners, the exchange between these two cities shaped how we eat today. Beginning with the 'restaurants' of pre-revolutionary Paris, this chapter will describe how dining out became a source of pleasurable enjoyment for the middle class. The first establishments to call themselves 'restaurants', these *ancien régime* eateries appeared in the Palais Royal in the same climate of Enlightenment *anglomanie* that inspired Mercier's *Parallèle*. This chapter also considers other places where one could dine out, uncovering what was new about them, as well as the ways in which they simply applied a new name to a style of eating with which Londoners in particular were already familiar.

It can be hard to identify exactly what made a restaurant a restaurant in the eighteenth and early nineteenth centuries. Was it a public stage, or a home away from home? Was it something to do with the food, or how people thought and wrote about it? In observing each other dining out, Londoners and Parisians came to reflect on big questions of domesticity and spectacle, questions already touched on in Chapter 1. As the nineteenth century progressed, the culinary and cultural distinction was forged that marked out the restaurant and made it seem naturally, necessarily Parisian. This was primarily the product of a new genre of gastronomic writing pioneered by Grimod de la Reynière and Jean-Anthelme Brillat-Savarin, as well as the emergence of the celebrity French chef.

The first restaurants (so-called) appeared in London only from the 1860s onwards, part of the rise of the modern chain hotel. This might suggest that they were a late arrival in London, a suggestion positively encouraged by existing historical writing on restaurants and haute cuisine, with its hagiography of great chefs and great gourmands, all of them French. Much writing on the history of dining is coloured by nostalgia for the golden age of this or that great restaurant. Even the founding father of gastronomic literature, Grimod de la Reynière, wallowed in a yearning for the *ancien régime* world of the late-night supper, for the cuisine as well as the free-flowing, witty conversation that supposedly accompanied it. Celebrity chefs eager to lard their menus with grand titles fostered legends of how this or that dish had been invented by some happy accident or stroke of genius – either on their own part or that of their employer, be he Louis XIV or Cambacérès.

The history of dining out has long been told as if it were a revolution. A particularly persistent myth is that the restaurant was unknown in the pre-1789 *ancien régime*. According to this account of the institution's origins, which began with Mercier, it was the execution of Louis XVI and the Terror of 1793 that acted as catalysts.[2] Aristocratic Parisian households collapsed as nobles went into exile or were guillotined, flooding the market with cooks who had no option but to open a new form of establishment aimed at the citizens of the new republic. It was therefore possible for Marxist historians such as Eric Hobsbawm to celebrate the restaurant as a bourgeois institution.[3] Like subscription concerts and theatres, restaurants supposedly involved a new middle class gaining access to a form of entertainment hitherto restricted to the court or a noble elite, and making it into a public stage on which to parade their respectability. Recent work has revealed that restaurants existed in Paris as early as 1766; by the time the Bastille fell, they had become something of an elite fad centred around the Palais Royal. For example, Jean-Baptiste La Barrière left private service in 1779 and set up a restaurant in the Palais Royal in 1782. As an institution, the restaurant was not constructed on the ruins of a noble *hôtel particulier*. Though later historians have been loath to admit it, even Grimod himself was willing to concede the English origin of pre-revolutionary Parisian restaurants.

The Palais Royal

Restaurants were named after the fare they served: restorants, or *restaurants*, that is, bouillons or essences of meat intended to restore the inner balance and good digestion of urban sophisticates. Finding himself unable to consume without nausea even something as plain as strips of toast dipped in a boiled egg, des Esseintes himself has recourse to such a palliative in *À Rebours*, sending a servant hurrying off to Paris to procure a device for making beef essence. This will, he has been promised, help 'to control his anaemia, to arrest the decline of his health, and to conserve what little strength he still possessed'.[4]

Restorants tackled the side effects of overconsumption as well as the ingestion of food that was too highly seasoned or interacted badly with something already eaten. In these cases the natural rhythms of digestion were interrupted, leaving undigested matter festering in the body, where it produced foul miasmas that rose in turn to the head, leading to mental imbalance. Overeating caused too much blood to be produced, requiring blood-letting in some cases. Digestive and circulatory problems such as these also overtaxed the lungs. The Latin motto outside Minet's restaurant in the Rue de Poulies (est. 1767) promised 'tasty sauces to titillate your bland palate; here the effete find healthy chests'.[5]

Restorants were a medical treatment for a condition to which Parisians were felt to be particularly prone, owing to the spicy nature of their meals and the way in which they were prepared and served. In the 1770s restaurants called themselves *maisons de santé* ('emporia of health'). In his *Parallèle*, Mercier noted that in Paris food mainly consisted of soup, which thickened the blood and gave rise to indigestion. Along with 'spicy sauces, seasoned fricassees, stews and the like', all this liquid weakened the body, while the meat gravies served in the finer houses overheated it, again provoking severe illness. Parisian food was so succulent and so artfully prepared that it overstimulated the appetite, making people eat too much. 'Oh, and to top it all one stuffs oneself with bread!' Mercier complained, noting how parents encouraged children to eat it. 'And so the child eats too much, in order to have something to eat along with its bread.'[6]

As the warning against gravy indicates, the restorant did not consist of the juices of the meat, but its pure essence. Although detailed recipes exist for such concoctions, in works such as the *Suite des dons de Comus* (1742), there was a sense in which a restorant was not about simple cuisine so much as anti-cuisine. A restorant might be prepared using onions, turnips, celery, chicken, veal, beef and ham. But it was cooked so slowly, being simmered for many hours, that it served to concentrate these ingredients, enabling one to drink, in effect, a quantity of food that could not possibly be eaten in its original form. Was this an innovation, an unprecedented advance in the technology of food preparation, worthy of an age of progress? Was it a return to a simpler, older way of life? Or was it some worrying combination of the two, a sophisticated prophylactic: allowing jaded sophisticates to continue their unwholesome Parisian lifestyle of overconsumption without suffering any of the natural consequences?

Though they promised to restore the individual's natural balance, restorants could be unsettling. The refinement they represented could smack of a decadent, self-destructive order, rather than an enlightened, healthy society. It was feared that a body used to heavily processed food might become unable to digest plain fare. There were risks, therefore, in turning what should be the simplest of skills into what de Jaucourt referred to in his *Encyclopédie* entry as '*la cuisine par excellence*': an art intended to disguise foodstuffs so as to promote overconsumption.[7] Though the degeneracy of des Esseintes's enfeebled digestion is a century away, even in the age of Rousseau the *philosophes* could view the fad for restorants as a straw in the wind.[8] Rousseau noted that there were Frenchmen who held that France was the only nation where people knew how to eat, but he did not view this positively: 'I would say on the contrary that it is only the French who do not know how to eat, since so special an art is required to make dishes digestible to them.'[9]

The first restaurant (so-called) was established in the Hôtel Aligre, on the Rue St Honoré, a house owned by a leading figure in the Paris *parlement*, Étienne François d'Aligre. As with many early Parisian restaurants, it was probably on the first floor, where the finest rooms of a *hôtel particulier* were usually to be found.[10] It was opened in 1766 by Mathurin Roze de Chantoiseau, the third son of a small landowner and merchant who came to Paris early in the 1760s, at which point he had added the aristocratic-sounding 'de' to his name. Excited by the debate on how France had incurred its massive national debt during the Seven Years War, in 1769 Roze de Chantoiseau published his own ideas in a pamphlet. By then the administration of Louis XVI's chief minister, Choiseul, had grown tired of a debate that it had initially encouraged. Roze de Chantoiseau ended up joining the authors of earlier works in the prison of For-l'Évêque.[11] Among his more successful schemes was that for a universal registry office along the lines of that established in London by John Fielding in 1750, as well as a commercial directory, the *Almanach général*, which appeared regularly for many years.[12]

A concern for healthy circulation ran throughout all these projects. The *Almanach* duly listed Roze de Chantoiseau's own establishment under 'Le Restaurateur', in the section 'Caterers, Innkeepers and Hoteliers'. His entry promised 'fine and delicate meals for 3-6 *livres* per head, in addition to the items expected of a restaurateur'.[13] In his introductory essay he promised that the directory would serve to make all Parisians more mutually serviceable by helping them locate each other and so avail themselves of the increasingly specialized goods and services to hand in the metropolis. The *Almanach* was a microcosm of the city, imposing order on its web of streets and enterprises.

If there was one place that came closest to being a concrete realization of this ordered city or *ville policée*, it was the Palais Royal, which in the 1780s also served as home to several of the city's restaurants, including that run by Jean-Baptiste La Barrière as well as Postal's. It housed Gendron's patisserie, where the great chef Antonin Carême worked in the 1790s. In the early nineteenth century it was the site of Jacques Christophe Naudet's restaurant, and of Véry's, which moved there from the Tuileries in 1805. It also housed Le Grand Véfour, which remains there today. The palace was the home of Louis-Philippe-Joseph, Duc de Chartres, and had extensive gardens, which had served as a kind of public park for local residents. Such open space was hard to find in Paris.

The duke's gardens were internally divided into a number of areas, each the conventionally assigned meeting place of a particular group. Individual walks and even specific trees had been appropriated as their special preserve by circles as various as stock-jobbers, prostitutes, respectable families and other such loose associations. There was an outcry, therefore, when the duke set about redeveloping the gardens in 1781; residents rallied in defence of 'their' gardens. The duke's architect, Victor Louis, had designed a three-sided colonnade of sixty pavilions with a cultivated area at its centre. Seen from the outside, it appeared to be one continuous, impenetrable façade, and its narrow, tunnel-like entrances are easily missed. It must have seemed as if the duke had turned his back on the city's inhabitants, selling their beloved stomping ground from under their feet in order to make a mint from putting up expensive residential blocks accessible to only a few.

That was certainly the view of opponents of the duke's plans. An anonymous pamphleteer published his complaint in the form of a letter from a fictional Englishman resident in Paris to an English lord in London. Its frontispiece showed the trees of the great walk in the process of being chopped down, with two distraught ladies on their knees in front of the prince, one pointing dramatically to the pathetic remnant of a tree. Its author called the redevelopment 'a lesion in public order', drawing attention to the many ways in which the Palais Royal gardens had served to make a cramped city liveable: providing healthy recreation for those poisoned by the capital's noisome atmosphere, as well as a place for the idle to saunter without getting into trouble, where men of business could also meet and make deals. To build on the gardens was to destroy this delicate, inscrutable web of connections and run the risk of very serious consequences. Protected by his anonymity, this 'Englishman in Paris' actually used the French word *révolution*.[14]

In the short term the redevelopment of the Palais Royal in 1781–4 was a resounding success. Though it presented an impassive façade to the outside world, on its opening in April 1784 Parisians found that Victor Louis's colonnades housed a delightful variety of clubs, shops – and restaurants. The old promenaders came back and mightily approved of what they saw. The familiar pleasures of seeing and being seen were still to be had, enriched by the range of new luxuries on offer. Like the massive shopping malls of today's United States, this was a place to exercise, circulate, socialize, eat, drink and shop. 'Themed' boutiques and cafés brought foreign cities to the populace, who could happily spend the whole day there, for everything they might need was on one site.

Mercier wrote that at the Palais Royal 'one person stares at another with a boldness scarcely to be found anywhere outside Paris, or anywhere else in Paris for that matter. One talks loudly, jostles . . . all without causing any offence or any wish to humiliate others.'[15] It was the favourite haunt of the dandy or *petit maître*, who supposedly ordered his evening cup of consommé from one of the restaurants, not because he was actually sick, but because it gave him a fashionable aura of ill health.[16] Such restorants would have appeared on the bill of fare alongside rice puddings, eggs, charcuterie and flavoured creams, all foods that required minimal preparation and could be served quickly.

Restaurants seem to have diversified their offerings quickly – so quickly, in fact, that one wonders how easy it was for them to maintain the veneer of healthy asceticism. For example, in the early 1780s Jean François Vacossin's establishment was serving ray in black butter sauce, fish stews and sauced partridges. While some of his clients ordered only a cucumber salad, green beans and bread, others enjoyed roast mutton and fried calf's ears.[17] A rare 1790s menu from Véry's also features ray with black butter, as well as *blanquette de veau aux champignons, filet de boeuf piqué* with a rather odd-sounding gherkin sauce, and *chorée au jus. Desserts* were relatively simple: cheese or fruit (fresh and as a compote), but no pastries or cream-based sweets.[18]

The clients of these first restaurants seem to have been largely male. Rétif de le Bretonne set one of his fables of modern city women, *Les Contemporaines*, inside a restaurant. In 'La Belle Restauratrice' ('The Beautiful Restaurateur') two noblemen pursue three sisters, two of whom work in such an establishment. Two lose their chastity and are ruined, while the wise one (who is also the prettiest) so impresses the lords with her virtue that, Pamela-like, she ends up marrying one, the Vicomte De-Grand'ville. Rétif describes the advent of the restaurant as testament to 'the weakness of our stomachs, and the premature senescence of our young men'. The waitresses are used to being flirted with by clients, as the restaurant is one of those places 'where only men go'.[19] Respectable women could not, presumably, patronize such an institution without damaging their good names. A 1788 guide claimed that 'honest women, and those of good reputation, never go there'.[20]

In order to select what they wished to eat, diners had to know what was on offer. Hence the invention of the menu. Very few of these survive, although there is evidence that it took diners some time to familiarize themselves with them. Those for Beauvilliers's restaurant at 20, Rue de Richelieu in 1801 carried reminders in bold text that the prices indicated were for single portions only.[21] Patrons also needed to develop a sense of the right order in which dishes were to be consumed, which dishes did not 'go together' and so on, all under the gaze of an expectant waiter. In George Jacques Gatine's print of 1815 from the series *Le Bon Genre*, entitled *L'Embarras du choix*, three ladies in white keep changing their order as one holds the elegant menu, mounted in a refined wooden frame with a handle. The presumption seems to be that they are unable to decide, without a man to order for them, a patronizing view, which has proved remarkably persistent.

It was probably worse for visitors, who clearly found menus intimidating. For their part, Parisians were not entirely sympathetic when these diners hailed from London, understandably enough in the years after the defeat of Napoleon. The two men dining in the 'Rosbif Restaurant' in one print of 1817 (see Fig. 17, p. 90) have clearly fallen into a trap set for English tourists, since this particular establishment doubles as a freak show for passing Parisians. Hawkers stand on a boulevard-style *parade* stage immediately to the left of the restaurant's window. One cries, 'Come in, ladies and gentlemen, you're just in time to see the animals get fed!' Inside the unwitting Englishmen silently eat, while the chef arrives with a freshly cooked cat. Those greedy, stupid English won't know the difference.

The Restaurant's Rivals

In one of a series of tales of *galanterie* pumped out by the prolific Rétif, the setting of 'La Belle Restaurice' can seem something of a stage set, interchangable with the poultry shops, bonnet sellers and other commercial establishments in which the author sets his tales. Given the speed with which restaurants' bills of fare expanded, from the ascetic cup of restorant to the much more varied indulgences we associate with them today, one might well wonder what distinguished the restaurant from other eateries of the eighteenth-century city. Rétif concedes that the first restaurateur did actually serve restorants, but a bunch of *gargotiers* (those who operated a *gargote*, or greasy spoon) had then jumped on the bandwagon, spying an opportunity to charge high prices for food that was tasty enough, yet lacked any restorative value.[22] However, there were important differences.

One striking distinction that made restaurants differ from the other establishments with which middle-class or noble Parisians would have been familiar was the timing of the meal. At a restaurant diners could eat whenever they wanted, in elegant surroundings. A wide range of street food could be consumed at any hour, but had to eaten standing up in the street. Clients could ask a caterer or *traiteur* to send food to their apartment and eat it there, almost as if they had a cook of their own. With cutlery and plates lent by the *traiteur*, they didn't even have to worry about getting someone to wash up. But if they wanted to eat out and be able to sit down in the days before the advent of restaurants their options would have been limited to a *cabaret*, a *guinguette* or a *table d'hôte*. As we shall see, none of these options afforded much by way of choice or quality.

There were around 3,000 *cabarets* in Paris around 1750, which took pride in serving wine 'by the plate' (*à l'assiette*) rather than, as in the case of a *taverne*, 'by pitcher' (*à pot*). Most had two rooms, each with a choice of tables, although customers usually had to share, unless part of a large group. The reference to plates, the presence of kitchen equipment in inventories of *cabaretiers* and other scraps of evidence certainly suggest that wine was served with food. Compared to the constant discussion and comparison of this and that *cabaret*'s wine, however, the subject of the food itself seems hardly to have been addressed at all. We know that salads, fish, artichokes and chickens were occasionally consumed in *cabarets*, but they were in some cases ordered in from another establishment. Food was clearly not the focus at a *cabaret*.[23] The decor was basic, although in 1730 the Chesne Vert in the Rue de Quatre Fils was equipped with copper fountains for rinsing glasses and even a wooden tub for diners to urinate into, to save them having to go out into the street to *lâcher l'eau*.[24]

In spring and summer people could buy food in a market and walk out beyond the city wall, sit at a table in a *guinguette* to eat it and wash it all down with untaxed wine ordered from a waiter. The tax imposed on wine passing through the city's gates or *barrières* was such that a *pinte* of wine (about a litre) that cost eight *sous* inside its perimeter cost only six outside. In 1784 the government quietly set about building a new tax wall further out, threatening to absorb many *guinguettes*, particularly on the capital's northern edge. Riots delayed progress, including one just three days before the storming of the Bastille. An enterprising man named Monier evaded the tax by hurling balloons filled with wine over the wall by night, so that they landed in a property he had bought especially for the purpose. Others laid secret wine pipelines excavated under the wall, or hid bladders under their dresses, in lieu of the 'rumps' that were then fashionable.[25]

Whereas throughout the week most Parisians patronized a dozen or so local *cabarets*, *guinguettes* like Ramponneau's Tambour Royal at Basse Courtille or La Belle Chopine at the Barrière Blanche were the destination for special Sunday or Monday outings, for which customers dressed up specially. There, female company was more welcome than at a *cabaret*, not least because *guinguettes* offered music and dancing. Whereas a visit to a *cabaret* was a routine part of daily life, the *guinguette* was hailed as a supposedly classless utopia removed from the city's daily grind.[26] A painting

FIG. 16: Jean-Baptiste Lesueur, *Famille allant à la guinguette*, 1790s.

in the Carnavalet [Fig. 16] shows a happy family group heading out to a *guinguette*. Besides their children, the couple carry a picnic with them: melons and, in the woman's apron, oysters. While customers were certainly expected to order wine, clearly the operators of these establishments were happy to let patrons bring their own food onto the premises.

Like the *cabaret*, in the years after 1770 the *guinguette* became increasingly disreputable, a place Mercier or other middle-class or elite individuals visited in disguise or out of an anthropological desire to observe the natives having fun, drinking and beating each other up.[27] Mercier found such venues delightful, until the wine went to patrons' heads, whereupon their behaviour disgusted him. 'The shouts and oaths of drunks, backed up by the women and their queasy children, everything betrays a starving people seeking an escape, a chance to drown the sorrows of the week.'[28] Whereas the class make-up of the *guinguette*'s customers had at one time closely matched that of the city as a whole, by the 1770s the elite was abandoning them for the café, whose clientele was more exclusive. Hitherto popular resorts were becoming plebeian.[29]

Though both offered opportunities to dine out, therefore, neither the *cabaret* nor the *guinguette* had much by way of decor. If food was in fact prepared on the premises (rather than brought or ordered in from elsewhere) it does not seem to have elicited much comment or thought. At both the wine was the main attraction. A third form of dining out – the *table d'hôte* or ordinary – bore a stronger resemblance to a restaurant, but offered no choice of either dishes or of serving times. For travellers to Paris unfamiliar with the language, as well as for many middle-class bachelors and young professionals, the *table d'hôte* would nonetheless have been the easiest dining option. Such venues were readily identified by the posters stuck up immediately outside their doors, indicating that food would be served at a certain time for a certain price per head. No menus were posted up externally, however, as there was no menu. People sat at a single communal table. Service was *à la francaise* – that is, several dishes were set down at the same time, from which diners served themselves. When dining in someone's home it was the gentleman's job to serve the ladies, and no one in polite society should sate their own appetite at the expense of other people. A typical *table d'hôte* had its hard core of regulars, who lived and worked in the immediate neighbourhood, their rank matching the cost of the meal.

For visitors and perhaps for us today, the *table d'hôte* sounds rather inviting, an opportunity not only to eat where the locals eat, but to eat with them, at the same table and at the same time. The reality was somewhat different. Visitors were not always served before the regulars. Indeed, visitors or latecomers were unlikely to get a seat anywhere near the end of the table where the serving dishes were placed. Perched below the salt, ignorant, perhaps, of what exactly was being served, unsure of how much of it he was going to get after everyone else had helped themselves, the occasional patron of an unfamiliar *table d'hôte* was in an unenviable position. If diners did not like what had been served or wanted more, there was no opportunity to order either an alternative or an extra helping. One suspects that in *tables d'hôte* where the regulars were well known to one another and the cook endlessly rehearsed the same dishes, the odd visitor provided some much needed variety and entertainment. Arthur Young travelled across France in the late 1780s, and frequently recorded being starved of both conversation and food at a *table d'hôte*. 'The ducks were swept clean so quickly,' he noted of one, 'that I moved from table without half a dinner.'[30]

The situation was very different in London, where it was possible for men to eat out in a variety of different settings, to order what they wanted, when they wanted, and to eat it at their own table. As in Paris there were street vendors specializing in jellied eels, pigs' trotters and other treats. Although these sellers could be found at almost all times of the day or night across the city, on Saturday afternoons they congregated at Tottenham Court Road, to serve labourers who had just been paid their weekly wages. Until the middle of the following century, such vendors pitched themselves on the sidewalks at busy junctions, at which point the eel and pie men retreated to their shops, abandoning their struggle with local police constables for control of the pavement.

While coaching inns provided residents and sometimes non-residents with food, for most Londoners taverns and chop-houses (the two terms were interchangeable) were the commonest places to eat out. These establishments catered to a wide, though still overwhelmingly male clientele, from artisans, apprentices and lawyers' clerks through to benchers and members of the peerage. Although they certainly served beer, ale, porter, wine and punch, taverns were different from alehouses, which, like Parisian *cabarets*, offered little more than snacks. The first coffee house opened in St Michael's Alley, Cornhill, in 1652, starting a coffee boom in the city. But coffee houses served no food, either: only coffee, chocolate, wine and punch.

'Dinner' (which we would now term 'lunch') was the most important meal of the day, and the one Londoners were most likely to eat away from home. Ordinaries first appeared in the early sixteenth century. In May 1667, Pepys attended the ordinary in Covent Garden run by a periwig-maker named Robbins. For his six shillings he got three courses: a mess of pottage, stewed pigeons and beef casserole, all well seasoned.[31] This was expensive for an ordinary in this period: the ordinary at the Blue Posts cost two shillings and sixpence; that at the Eagle just sixpence. In 1690 a French eating house offered an ordinary at three shillings.[32] At a London ordinary, patrons may have had to show up at a fixed time, but rarely had to share a table.

Someone like Mr Robbins, who catered for strangers alongside his main trade, was probably not in a position to offer much choice, nor to serve customers food at other times. But from the late seventeenth century onwards, many taverns in central London could and did serve a range of fare throughout the day. Temple Chop-House had a sign informing passers-by that 'soups and a-la-mode beef [a type of stew], with sallads' were 'always ready'.[33] In the late seventeenth century, chop-houses were also willing to prepare and serve food that customers had brought in. On one occasion Pepys bought a lobster in Fish Street, met some friends who had bought a sturgeon, then retired with them to the Sun Tavern, where the lobster and sturgeon were cooked and served to them.[34] Pepys and his friends were probably seated in a private room rather than in the main dining room. The London Tavern in Bishopsgate could provide fourteen such private rooms in 1786.[35] Rather than being numbered, they were usually named after animals (The Dove, The Hart, The Pye, etc.), with their own signs hanging outside, similar to that of the tavern itself, swinging out in the street. In an age when 'leisure time' as a distinct, carefully guarded preserve was unknown, these were as much places for lobbying patrons and closing deals as a place to 'knock off'.

The chop-house developed from the seventeenth-century cookshops, which served a wide variety of roast meat. The customer simply turned up, indicated how much he wanted from each of the turning spits, and sat down to eat it, accompanied by a bit of mustard, a roll, and perhaps a salad of wilted marigold leaves. Such a meal cost around eight pence in the early eighteenth century. Cookshops were particularly common behind St Martin-in-the-Fields, a neighbourhood known as 'Pottage Island', and at 'Pie Corner', the Smithfield end of Giltspur Street.[36] Having worked up an appetite at Bartholomew Fair, Ned Ward in *London Spy* (1699) found an attractive cookshop, only to be put off by observing the cook wiping his ears, forehead and armpits with the same damp cloth he applied to his pork. 'I had much ado to keep the stuffing of my guts from tumbling into the dripping-pan,' he noted.[37]

By the middle of the eighteenth century, the cookshops' reputation had sunk further and they went underground, literally, continuing to operate from basement dining rooms, to which clients descended by means of a stepladder, straight from the street, as can be seen in Hogarth's sketch of 1746–7 [Fig. 17]. Here a diner could eat at a little table with his or her

FIG. 17: William Hogarth, *Cookshop*, 1746–7.

109

own (dirty) tablecloth for just two or three pence.[38] Cookshops attracted a working-class clientele of hackney coachmen, chairmen (i.e. those who carried sedan chairs) and footmen, who supposedly didn't mind being served 'measly Pork, rusty Bacon, stinking Lamb, rotten Mutton, slinked Veal [that is, from a prematurely-born calf], and Coddled Cow, with yellow Greens, sooty Pottage, and greasy Pudding'.[39] By 1815 these eateries seem to have disappeared; their clientele presumably resorted to establishments like Epp's chain of Ham and Beef Shops, which served ham sandwiches wrapped in cabbage leaves, to take away.[40]

Although the chop-shop or chop-house was a cut above the cookshop, the emphasis was still on convenience and speed, as the alternative name of 'slap bang shop' indicated.[41] Food was eaten at simple tables or booths, with partitions or curtains to provide some separation between groups of diners, each place being supplied with a cruet of sauce and a hook for one's hat. Again the focus was on roast meat. Beans or salad could be ordered, as well as cheese and sweet tarts, but no fish, nothing with a sauce and no fiddly sweet dishes. It hardly comes as a surprise to discover that Samuel Johnson admired their simple fare.[42] While some chop-houses at the pricier end of the spectrum had more ornate decor, with curtains, mirrors and the like, few London eating houses boasted the elegant interiors associated with Parisian cafés and restaurants, with their rococo wooden panelling, marble-topped tables, mirrors and Bohemian crystal chandeliers.[43] Parisians were nonetheless amazed at the easygoing (or simply businesslike) atmosphere in English eateries: 'you walk in as you would into a public space,' one visitor noted in 1786, 'freely and without fuss. Nobody even stops you to ask if you are planning to dine.'[44]

Among the exceptions to this rule in late eighteenth-century London were the confectioners: their bright, sparkling interiors lit by large windows facing onto the street, filled with pastries, creams, bonbons and other delicacies under delicate glass cloches, their contents reflected in gilt-framed mirrors. Clients clearly had to be well dressed to gain

FIG. 18: James Gillray, *Hero's recruiting at Kelsey's*, 1797.

admittance, let alone stay and order something. In James Gillray's print of 1797 [Fig. 18], dandies in military uniform perch daintily on stools, eating sugarplums and jellies. In 1815, Debatt's Pastry Shop in Poultry was known for serving 'sweets, soups and savoury patties' to 'ladies and beaux of delicate stomachs'.[45] These establishments survived well into the nineteenth century, catering in particular to genteel ladies running errands in the city or shopping on their own, even if the sustenance they afforded was limited.

For an unaccompanied lady, a sandwich and a pastry at a confectioner's remained the only respectable option until the 1880s at least. Even then the choices presented by, say, a chain restaurant like a Lyons Corner House still reflected the patronizing commonplace that the female palate preferred light, sweet things to anything more substantial.[46]

As with the restaurant, so in England light soups were held to be conducive to good digestion and particularly appropriate for the sickly or those whose natural appetite had been blunted. In the 1770s the Cornhill confectioner Horton and Birch opened a 'Soup Room', which became the subject of an engraving [Fig. 19]. This establishment, with plasterwork swags on the walls and stars on the ceiling, is relatively crowded, and not only with dandies. There appears to be a group of ladies dining without a male companion, which is striking. Horton's appears here as a going concern seven years after Roze de Chantoiseau's restaurant opened on the Rue St Honoré; it was still functioning in the early twentieth century.[47] In 1793, Francis Saulieu set up as a 'restaurateur' in Nassau Street (now Gerrard Place), serving 'boulli' in his 'salle à manger, or eating-room'.[48] The emergence of a new form of dining experience in London, involving

FIG. 19: Anon., *Mr Horton's Soup Room*, 1770.

consumption of restorative soup at separate tables in elegant surroundings, elicited concerns about the emasculating and appetite-sapping effects of luxury on 'macaronies' (that is, dandies) that are remarkably similar to those evident in the Parisian discussion of *petits maîtres*.

Soup rooms did not catch on in London as restaurants had in Paris. That is not, one suspects, because Englishmen were uninterested in dining out on well-prepared food. On the contrary, they already had plenty of cookshops, chop-shops, inns and taverns in which they could do so. That, however, was not the case in Paris before the appearance of Roze de Chantoiseau. Though the working class and lower middle class had their *cabarets* and *guinguettes*, these establishments were mainly for drinking and did not offer separate tables or much choice in the way of dishes. As we have seen, in the closing decades of the eighteenth century they were becoming off limits to middle-class and elite patrons. There are several indications that Parisians were aware of this difference, including the fact that early restaurants could market themselves as fashionably English. In October 1769, Duclos, who had taken over Roze de Chantoiseau's establishment in the Hôtel d'Aligre, advertised his restaurant as providing *nouvelle cuisine à la mode anglaise*.[49] In the 1770s restaurants were associated with the fad for pleasure gardens or 'Wauxhalls', such as the Colisée on the Champs Elysées and the Wauxhall in the Rue des Grands Augustins, modelled on the famous London pleasure garden of Vauxhall.[50] When Antoine Beauvilliers opened his renowned restaurant in the Rue de Richelieu in 1782, he chose to call it La Grande Taverne de Londres.[51]

With little more information to go on, one has to speculate as to what was 'English' about Duclos's and Beauvilliers's establishments. It could have been the simplicity with which the food was prepared, in line with the simple *redingotes* (riding coats) that were a mainstay of 'English' fashion at the time. It might have been the way in which it was served: that is, on demand and at separate tables. Duclos's advertisement promises that the customer will find 'all kinds of dishes as tasty as they are wholesome, available at all hours'. His prices were modest 'so that anyone can keep within his budget'.[52] Either way, it is clear that Anglomania played a role in the evolution of the restaurant as a spectacle of consumption. Although Grimod himself admitted this influence, it has otherwise been largely overlooked by recent historical writing on the restaurant.[53]

Why did these kinds of eateries take so long to appear in Paris? The persistence of the guild system until its abolition in 1791 is partly to blame. Guilds protected individual trades, operating in the interests of incumbents against newcomers or anyone proposing to introduce 'innovations' (itself a pejorative term, in both English and French, until the nineteenth century). A guild controlled the number of individuals who could practise a certain trade in a particular place by regulating entry to the trade, through the system of binding apprentices to an individual master for a fixed amount of time, and by prohibiting anyone from practising their trade without acquiring or purchasing a mastership in the guild. Members of a guild took pride in the 'mystery' of their trade, and went to great lengths to preserve its position among its fellow guilds, by processions and other rituals, many of which centred on the guild's patron saint, and the feast days and churches associated with them.

Chartered in 1482, the Worshipful Company of Cooks of London survives to this day, formed by the union of two much older guilds, the Cooks of Eastcheap and the Cooks of Bread Street. The Company had powers to search premises, seize illegal victuals and burn them in front of the pillory, into which the illegal cook had first been inserted. It could also levy fines. These powers to police cookshops and similar establishments were gradually eroded in the late sixteenth and early seventeenth centuries. There were complaints that taverns were illegally 'victualling', as well as an attempt in 1670 to prevent bakers from producing pies, puddings and other baked meats 'properly belonging to the Cooks Trade', but these had little effect.[54] When the guild proved unable to compel practitioners to bind their apprentices despite an Act of Parliament in 1753, confirming the guild's rights, its income slumped, forcing it to cut back on its ceremonial dinners and bringing it close to bankruptcy.

Individuals who did bother to complete apprenticeships and become Freemen resented the fact that this did not protect them from foreign interlopers who had not 'served their time'. In 1773, 'An Injured Freeman' wrote to the Company, complaining that he and his friends had been refused work by a Master of the Company who employed non-British cooks at higher wages. 'At this time six of the most capital shops employ foreigners and give them better wages than Freemen,' he noted. By rights a Master could employ immigrants only if he could swear that unemployed Freemen could not be found.[55] The Company failed to stem this tide of foreign 'interlopers'. Its motto, 'Vulnerati non victi' ('Wounded, but not vanquished'), speaks of a long and ultimately unsuccessful attempt to contain Londoners' appetites for new ways of eating.

In Paris there were separate guilds for cook-caterers (*traiteurs*), poultry-men (*volailleurs*), roast-meat sellers (*rôtisseurs*), ham and pork sellers (*charcutiers*), pastry-cooks (*pâtissiers*) and so on. How could one sell a chop and not be a master *charcutier*? According to one 1782 account, the *traiteurs* brought legal charges against Boulanger, a *restaurateur* who had presumed to sell sheep's trotters in white sauce. This dish was a ragout, they insisted, not a restorant.[56] It was recognized that it was difficult to determine where one such trade ended and another began. Many master *traiteurs* held masterships in both the pastry-cooks' and the *rôtisseurs'* guilds, making the distinction moot. Jacques Minet of the restaurant in the Rue de Poulies was elected to office within the *traiteurs*, something that suggests that the guilds did not see restaurateurs as their sworn enemies.

In 1768, Roze de Chantoiseau paid 1,600 *livres* for the privilege of being appointed *traiteur auprès de la cour*, that is, a caterer enjoying royal exemption from Parisian guild regulations. Jean François Vacossin, Nicolet Berger and Anne Bellot followed suit.[57] Berger used this special status to argue that restaurants should be exempt from the ten o'clock curfew (eleven in summer) and from the surveillance of the city constabulary or *garde*, which broke up fights in *cabarets* and threw out patrons at closing time. Patrons of Després's restaurant in the Rue de Grenelle, as well as those of another restaurant on the Boulevard des Italiens, clearly felt themselves to be above such manhandling: the restaurant was not just another *cabaret*. A nameless member of the military order of St Louis told an officer of the watch on 22 April 1784 that he had no right to enter Després's restaurant, adding that he should 'go fuck himself and not come back'. Tensions were eased somewhat when, in 1786, the Paris *parlement* ruled that restaurants be allowed to stay open one extra hour.[58]

Dining Alone

Mercier complained in 1798 that restaurants had done for those family meals that had provided the great set-pieces of *fraternité* during the heady early years of the Revolution.[59] State-promoted feasts of brotherhood, in which fellow citizens were supposed to drag tables out into the street and dine with their neighbours *en plein air*, had met with mixed success, as nobody could work out who was going to pay the bill.[60] Though Grimod and Brillat-Savarin certainly expressed a similar nostalgia, theirs was for the *ancien régime*. A noble cuisine could not be separated from the social system that had given birth to it, and was unimaginable without the clergy, tax-farmers and nobility who knew how to eat well.[61]

The *corps diplomatique* did its best, bemoaned Paul Vermond in 1835, but even there signs of decay were evident. Talleyrand, the greatest diplomat and gourmand of them all and the patron of Carême, was too old to play his part, prompting the observation: 'Talleyrand, our Lucullus, is reduced to eating puree.'[62] Like Grimod before him, Vermond bewailed the disappearance of supper, a meal that had been served later in the evening than dinner, and that differed in not having a soup course.[63] Its disappearance was just another case of the bourgeoisie making life dull. And dull meant English: in the very next sentence Vermond observes that 'we borrowed the beefsteak from England at the same time as the *frac* [a simple coat]'. As far as he was concerned, the restaurants had been built on the ruins of the *souper* and gastronomy itself.[64]

The son of a well-to-do tax-farmer, Alexandre Balthazar Laurent Grimod de la Reynière had first come to the Parisian public's attention in February 1783, when he staged an elaborate dinner party with a coffin as its centrepiece. Born with deformed hands, the young Grimod seems to have harboured a strong resentment against his father, which may have encouraged him to court a scandalous reputation, as well as to socialize with *philosophes* and employ his legal training in defence of poor peasants. Invitations to the 1783 dinner took the form of burial announcements, and Grimod's seventeen guests were subjected to a succession of inspections by actors dressed up as Romans, monks and lawyers. Painstakingly choreographed, solipsistic and misanthropic, this ritual repast was worthy of Huysmans and des Esseintes. Members of the public were admitted to a viewing gallery, as if Grimod were royalty. This custom of royal eating in public had been practised by James I and Charles I, but fell into disuse in England after the Civil War.[65] It continued in France, however, and eighteenth-century visitors to Versailles could gain access to such spectacles with an ease that seems incredible today.

Banished from Paris by a royal warrant, Grimod moved to Lyons, where he set up shop as a food retailer and *parfumier*, experimenting with what were then new ways of doing business, such as fixed prices. These experiments were not a success and he eventually returned to Paris, where he set up a new theatre review and his renowned *Almanach des Gourmands* (1803–10). The best-selling *Almanach* included the world's first restaurant reviews as well as pieces critiquing different brands of mustard. It was larded with anecdotes of the *ancien régime*, great cooks, their patrons and their meals. Though most of the restaurants covered were in Paris, in discussing where to source the finest ingredients the *Almanach* ranged across France and beyond, helping to construct a national gastronomic map with the city as its heart or, rather, its mouth. A 'Gastronomic Map of France' later appeared as the frontispiece to Charles Louis Cadet de Gassicourt's *Course in Gastronomy* (1809), one of a number of guides published in the wake of the *Almanach*. These included Honoré Blanc's one-volume *Guide des dîneurs de Paris* (1815) as well as Ralph Rylance's short-lived *The Epicure's Almanack* (1815), a guide to 650 London eateries.[66] Yet another was the great *La Physiologie du Goût* (1825), by the judge and gourmand, Jean-Anthelme Brillat-Savarin, which featured a history of cooking from the discovery of fire onwards, along with anecdotes of his periods in exile, recipes and musings on the relationship between diet, sleep and obesity.

The influence of Grimod and Brillat-Savarin on later gastronomy writers is clear, evident in a shared tendency to wallow in nostalgia. Yet Grimod was a son of the Enlightenment as well as a scion of the aristocracy, interested in how science could be harnessed to improve the technology of food preparation. For example, he noted the potential value of electricity as a means of humanely dispatching animals. Such were the wonders of electricity that it not only killed the beast but tenderized its meat at the same time.[67] Grimod's greatest legacy was to make gourmandizing acceptable. In the 1750s the Saint Aubin brothers had viewed the very idea of court nobles experimenting with cooking as inexplicable, ludicrous and a sign of the incurable decadence of Versailles.[68] Grimod did not just make such attention to food acceptable, he made it fashionable and refined. Fifty years on, Brillat-Savarin could note with some accuracy that 'nowadays everyone understands the difference between gourmandism and gluttony'.[69]

Like the *flâneur*, the gourmand defied clear categorization by class and rank. There was the same arrogant pose: of consuming a spectacle that the vulgar rich could never buy, which was accessible only to a select few initiates 'in the know'. The *Almanach's* success made Grimod France's 'Minister of the Gob' (*ministre de la gueule*), and restaurants as well as manufacturers courted his endorsements or *légitimations*. British travellers writing for the improvement of fellow Britons devoured his descriptions, emulated his style or simply plagiarized him. These authors were perhaps guilty of overlooking the note of deliberate self-parody in Grimod, of taking him and his commandments as gospel truths that were supposedly self-evident to any Frenchman. These gastronomic texts were mined for illustrations of the decadent, fussy Parisian character, which could invent fifty different flavours of vinegar, yet remain a stranger to any notion of family values or decency. For the English the restaurant became a place to go not only to enjoy fine food, but to reflect on the societal costs that apparently went with such devotion to cuisine. Chief among them was a total disregard for domesticity and for privacy, which countless observers yoked together with the absence of a French equivalent for the word 'home'.

The Parisian female spent so much time outside her apartment that any sense of a distinction between 'being out' and 'being at home' was lost. A Parisian lady studying her reflection in one of the many mirrors lining a restaurant's main dining room could thus be described in one 1844 account as doing so with as much 'nonchalance' as if she were in her own dressing room.[70] Parisians were 'at home' in the restaurant precisely because they did not have any notion of what a real 'home' was.[71] The paradox should have been clear, but it wasn't. Nor was it noted that many of those sitting in the restaurant's main dining room would have been American or British tourists in search of some 'local colour'. The Parisian habit of dining in private rooms or *cabinets particuliers* within restaurants, rather than in this main room, makes it difficult to categorize the institution as either a 'second home' or a 'public place'.

Cabinets varied in size from the intimate, intended for two, to large rooms able to accommodate a dozen. In 1810, Jacques Christophe Naudet's restaurant in the Palais Royal had four such *cabinets*, on the third floor. Similar to the small rooms found in seventeenth- and eighteenth-century taverns, each was numbered and contained a table, chairs, a mirror and in many cases a chaise longue. These *cabinets* were a gift to the authors of vaudeville farces such as Boniface Xavier, Félix-Auguste Duvert, and Eugène Labiche in the 1850s, allowing quick entrances and exits, secret assignations and mistaken identities.[72] Such was their reputation for adulterous encounters that *cabinets* could not be patronized by respectable women, or at least not openly. Gavarni's scenes played on these associations, one showing a young husband who has been on the trail of his wife. The waiter has described a woman matching her description leaving this *cabinet particulier*, but the duped husband cannot make out the signature (on the bill) of the man who accompanied his spouse. He confides in his old friend Anatole, but his loyal comrade's pose of befuddled introspection is itself suspicious, suggesting that he, too, has been enjoying the woman's favours and is equally upset, having discovered that he is not her only adulterous liaison.[73] Jean Louis Forain's lithographs of fifty years later show how little the decor of the *cabinet* had changed, even if the use of such spaces for prostitution is more clearly evoked.[74]

Though Parisians were candid enough to admit the restaurant as a potential adjunct to illicit behaviour, this was not the same as treating it as a public place. Back in 1769, Duclos's restaurant explicitly stated that its rooms were perfectly arranged 'for those who have no wish to dine in public'.[75]

As with the myth of the Revolution flooding Paris with unemployed chefs, here again the restaurant fails to fit with a narrative of *embourgeoisement*, with a belief that the restaurant was a stage on which a triumphant middle class could perform. Thus a bourgeois restaurant regular like Louis Véron, physician and editor, could write that a restaurant offered the pleasure of experiencing 'silence and solitude in the middle of a crowd'.[76]

Instead one is struck by the continuities across the revolutionary period and, indeed, across the Channel. If the restaurant is defined by its ability to offer patrons a selection of food at separate, cloth-covered tables at a time to suit them, then it must be conceded that there were restaurants in both Paris and London before Roze de Chantoiseau opened his establishment in 1766. In Paris the *cabaret*'s offerings were limited, admittedly, and guild restrictions caused complications. London's taverns and chop-houses offered a wider choice, at least until the mid nineteenth century. As the *cabaret*'s reputation declined, new forms of eatery appeared in the nineteenth century, able to cater to the majority of Parisians who could never afford renowned, high-class restaurants like Véry's.

They included establishments providing food in the style of *la France profonde*, such as the Trois Frères Provençaux in the Palais Royal, a breed of restaurant that Vermond, for one, sneered at. There were also the fast-food outlets or *bouillons*, large enterprises with branches across the city, able to serve huge crowds with beef or *poulet rôti* (often with *pommes de terre frites*) at long tables, something Vermond dubbed 'nomad cuisine'. Baptiste-Adolphe Duval opened the first of his chain of *bouillons* in the Rue de la Monnaie in 1854. His establishments were staffed with female waitresses ('*bonnes*') in an effort to make ordering less intimidating.[77] There were also English-style taverns and restaurants, which offered all-you-can-eat roast beef to be washed down with ale and porter, 'just like in the novels of Walter Scott'.[78]

The Celebrity Chef

The cult of the celebrity chef as a mercurial, temperamental, virtuoso performer further entrenched the idea of Paris as the home of fine cuisine, simply because all such celebrities were Paris-trained. Grimod and others viewed François Vatel as the first entrant in a French Valhalla of cooks. The seventeenth-century *maître d'hôtel* to the financier Nicolas Fouquet and to Louis, Le Grand Condé, Vatel is reputedly the inventor of *crème Chantilly*, named after the residence of the Grand Condé. It was at Chantilly in 1671 that Vatel committed suicide by sword, distraught at a delayed delivery of fish. Their tardiness would, he feared, compromise his princely host in front of his guest, Louis XIV.

Vatel was a secular martyr to the chef's art. With the exception of John Townshend of the Greyhound in Greenwich and other London tavern cooks, who had enjoyed enough of a reputation to publish their own cookbooks in the 1770s, British cooks had no one of the renown of Vatel.[79] As demonstrated by the complaint mentioned above, of an anonymous Freeman of the Cooks Company, even at that time London's finer eateries preferred to pay higher wages to foreign chefs than comply with rules mandating a preference for the native sons of England.

London continues today to prove an attractive place for French chefs to establish a reputation and build their careers as impresarios who write as well as cook. This trend began in the early nineteenth century with the arrival of several Paris-trained chefs in royal or noble households, but especially in the new purpose-built gentlemen's clubs that sprang up along Pall Mall and Piccadilly in the thirty years after Waterloo. Chief among them was the Reform, associated with the Whig or Liberal end of the political spectrum, but they also included the Conservative club, the Carlton, as well as forces clubs such as the United Service, and gambling clubs like Crockfords. Designed by Charles Barry in Italianate style, the Reform Club's palazzo opened in 1841, in close proximity to the Travellers, the Athenaeum and, on the opposite side of Waterloo Place, the United Service, itself built in the mid 1820s to designs by John Nash.

As befitted an age of reform, the clubs gradually took on many of the functions previously filled by Holland House (owned by the Fox family) and other grand London houses owned by landed party grandees, in hosting salons at which the leading political, literary and artistic figures gathered in a climate of aristocratic deference and clientage. If any institution could serve as a monument to the rising bourgeoisie, it was the gentleman's club, an affordable substitute for the nobleman's town house, a home away from home for MPs serving the new parliamentary constituencies created by the 1832 Reform Act, a comfortable refuge for professionals and men of business and, later, for members of the civil service created by the reforms of the 1860s, in which merit replaced personal connections as the criterion for entry.

The clubs quickly established a reputation for fine cuisine, largely thanks to the publicity-hungry chefs they hired, but perhaps also to the food served to members. The first of these celebrity chefs, Louis Eustache Ude, had served his time in the kitchens of Louis XVI, where he followed his father. He subsequently came to England, where he spent twenty years as chef to the 2nd Earl of Sefton at Croxteth Hall in Liverpool. He published his own cookbook in 1813 and moved to London, working for Frederick, Duke of York until his death in 1827, when he was hired by Crockfords Club at the princely salary of 1,000 guineas – reputedly the same sum the Prince Regent paid his French chef, Antonin Carême. Unsatisfied by his salary arrangements, he decamped in 1839 to the United Service, where he remained. Two years earlier, another Parisian chef, Alexis Soyer, had arrived further down Pall Mall, at the Reform.

Soyer's work for the club is commemorated by his signature dish: *côtelettes de mouton à la Reform*, consisting of lamb cutlets rolled in egg, breadcrumbs and finely chopped ham.[80] Soyer's energy was such that it was regularly diverted into other projects, all of which added to his fame, even if they had little to do with restaurants or fine cuisine. Soyer became a very Victorian 'improver', combining an appetite for solving large-scale engineering challenges with an equally Victorian concern for the health and well-being of the poor. He made the Reform's steam-powered kitchens [Fig. 20] a showpiece of what we today would recognize as 'just-in-time' logistics. He applied the same inventiveness and attention to detail to soup kitchens during the Irish Famine, to the reorganization of the British army's kitchens in the Crimean War, and to the diffusion of

FIG. 20: G. B. Moore after W. Radclyffe, *Reform Club. The Kitchen*, 1840s.

nourishing recipes to the lower middle classes. His *Shilling Cookery for the People* appeared in 1854.

As the celebrity chefs' frequent changes of employer reveal, their status had yet to be determined, even as they gained in prestige as masters of a culinary art form. Vatel and his peers in the age of Louis XIV had not actually been called 'cooks', but carried grander titles (and even swords) as *écuyer de cuisine* or *maître d'hôtel*. Some may even have been poor relations of their employers. Antonin Carême originated, or at least codified, many of the building blocks of French cuisine in his five-volume *L'Art de la cuisine française au XIXe siècle* (1843–7), which was left incomplete at his death. He had experience both of aristocratic service and of running his own businesses. As his memoirs indicate, Carême felt that haute cuisine belonged in private households, yet insisted that those who employed him and his peers should not treat cooks as if they were servants.[81]

At a club the chef was usually placed under the authority of a committee rather than of a single individual, an arrangement chefs seem to have found tolerable. Soyer's Reform Club was of course inaccessible to non-members, except if invited in as the guest of a member, and was entirely barred to women. Although in Paris he had worked in the Grignon and been head chef in the Boulevard des Italiens, in London the closest thing to a restaurant Soyer ever operated was a temporary one intended to serve visitors to the 1851 Great Exhibition. In December 1849, he signed a fifteen-month lease for Gore House, a large mansion with an extensive park right on the edge of Hyde Park, close to the site of Joseph Paxton's glass-and-iron 'Crystal Palace', which began construction in the autumn of 1850. Here he opened Soyer's Universal Symposium of All Nations, a cross between a pleasure garden, a theme park and a restaurant.

Gore House was lavishly appointed, with a somewhat louche reputation, thanks to the previous tenant, Lady Blessington, a *bon vivante* notorious for her relationship with her adopted son Alfred, Count d'Orsay. With the help of stage designers and the journalist George Augustus Sala (then an impecunious artist), Soyer constructed a series of themed dining spaces, multi-media environments whose statuary, frescoes and magic lantern effects magically transported visitors to exotic locales like the Alhambra, the North Pole and the Peruvian rainforest. Two steel-and-glass dining halls were erected in the grounds: a 'Baronial Hall', seating 500, and 'The Encampment of All Nations', seating 1,500. According to Soyer's own guide, the Symposium was intended to 'triumph over geographical limits, and laugh the restrictions of space to scorn', offering hospitality and wonderment in equal measure to the Great Exhibition's visitors, 'civilised or uncivilised'.[82] The Hall of Architectural Wonders contained models and paintings of landmark structures from across the world, allowing a virtual Grand Tour to be completed in minutes.

The complex also included an American-style cocktail saloon, the Washington Refreshment Room. Here Soyer capitalized on Vauxhall's introduction of 'American drinks' such as mint juleps and cobblers, one of a series of American-themed entertainments (ten-pin bowling, the 'Ethiopian Serenaders' and the body-popping dancer Juba being among them) offered by that pleasure garden in the late 1840s.[83] Although the American bar was a roaring success, overall the venture was a failure, opening to the public two weeks late and racking up losses of £7,000. Given its proximity to an attraction that drew an astonishing 6 million visitors in five months, this may be considered an achievement. Soyer could not have accomplished all he had without a head for numbers, so perhaps it was simply his inability to focus on one project consistently for long periods that led to the Symposium's financial problems. Having lavished so much attention and money on the fittings and on a series of press and charitable dinners, one of them attended by Karl Marx, Soyer seems to have neglected the average punters, who resented paying two shillings and sixpence (in the Encampment, a meal in the Baronial Hall cost double that) for cold food and slow, rude service.[84]

The Symposium gave many Londoners and visitors to the Exhibition their first taste of a Parisian chef's dishes. As a 'monster' temporary structure designed to feed 4,000–5,000 a day (only 1,000 showed up), it smacked more of logistics than of gourmandizing: a culinary version of one of Isambard Kingdom Brunel's tunnels, down which poured vast quantities of chicken, ham and beer. Soyer's audience seemed more interested in cooing over the Disney-like special effects or engineering challenges (the 307-foot long tablecloth used in the Encampment, for example, or the daily roasting of an entire ox by gas) than in discussing the finer points of this or that sauce, let alone eating.[85] That said, the food served at the Symposium was better and more varied than that available inside the Exhibition, which was catered by Mr Schweppes. Generally speaking, however, the Great Exhibition was not about gastronomy, whose moment came instead at the 1867 Exposition Universelle in Paris, where the cuisines of all nations could be enjoyed, cheek by jowl, on the Champ de Mars, complete with staff in national costume.

For all they contributed to the aura of Parisian cuisine and the cult of the chef, private clubs and Soyer's 'Symposium' can seem marginal to the history of the restaurant. It was only in the 1860s that restaurants (so-called) came to London, thanks to the St James's Hotel, for example, and Epitaux's in Pall Mall, although these remained rare exceptions. In the decades around mid-century the world of pie shops, chop-shops and taverns had continued to turn. The livery and various clubs still had their turtle soup, and excursions to enjoy whitebait suppers at Greenwich remained popular. The Cheshire Cheese in Fleet Street (for rump-steak pudding), Pimm's in Poultry (for oysters) and Simpson's in the Strand (for venison) seemed set in a British aspic and would remain so well into the twentieth century.[86] Such establishments clung to a tradition that was already starting to look a little fusty in the mid nineteenth century, its memories of Samuel Johnson a cod-Georgian *rechauffé*.

In his *Epicure's Year Book* for 1868, Blanchard Jerrold drew a clear distinction between establishments that offered 'good plain dinners', and the few French-operated ones, which served '*cuisine*'. At the latter, he noted, 'when the diner orders beforehand, and shows that he can distinguish between good and bad cookery, he may be tolerably confident that the result will be respectable.'[87] This was certainly an improvement on the situation in the previous decade. The 1853 edition of Abraham Hayward's *The Art of Dining, or, Gastronomy and Gastronomers* included a history of cookery and Parisian restaurants, extracts from Grimod's *Almanach* and biographical sketches of famous French chefs who had practised in London. But there was no advice on where to eat in the capital, apart from an account of clubs and noble households, as well as advice on how to put together a menu for a dinner party at home, a practice more common in London than it was in Paris.[88]

Gatti's on Westminster Bridge Road and the Café Royal off Regent Street were the most famous of this first generation of Parisian-style restaurants. Among the host of nineteenth-century restaurateurs and hoteliers who hailed from the Italian-speaking Ticino in Switzerland were Carlo and Giovanni Gatti. Their family came to London via Paris and engaged in a number of businesses besides cafés and restaurants, most importantly as ice-cream manufacturers and organizers of promenade concerts at Covent Garden. Before moving west to Victoria, in the 1850s they had operated two

'Swiss café restaurants' in Hungerford Market and Holborn Hill.[89] As with the Café Royal, opened in 1865 by Daniel Nicols (originally Thévenon), Gatti's differed from its rivals not so much in the food it served as in the decor: plate-glass windows, mirrors, panelling and red upholstered seats. As with the Criterion (est. 1874), here orchestras played behind palm trees in spacious dining rooms. Themed rooms, in particular grill rooms, allowed diners to enjoy different levels of formality and, in some cases price, all under one roof. The most famous of these, such as the Domino Room at the Café Royal, would attract their own coterie of bohemian regulars in the 1890s.[90]

Though restaurants in London were few, Jerrold noted, it was there that grand Parisian cuisine reigned rather than in Paris itself. In the French capital, standards had slipped, as restaurants began to rest on their laurels, apparently secure in the knowledge that their fame would continue to attract diners and especially tourists. This observation might be dismissed as patriotic prejudice, but Jerrold pinned the blame squarely on English tourists, on 'Madame Manchester', who did not recognize a good *foie gras aux truffes* when it was put in front of her. Jerrold's comment echoes a common complaint regularly rehearsed in the 1840s and 1850s by Parisian gastronomes, including the Count d'Orsay and Balzac. The loss of the famous seafood restaurant on the Rue Montorgueil, Le Rocher de Cancale, Grimod's 'eighth wonder of the gourmet world', was particularly felt.[91]

Hotels were one beachhead for haute cuisine in London, beginning with the St James's Hotel and continuing on into the Edwardian period with the Savoy and the Ritz. The St James's reputation for fine food was made by Charles Elmé Francatelli, head chef from 1863 to 1870. Francatelli trained under Carême in Paris and had worked for various English aristocrats, as well as at the Melton Club, Crockford's (where he followed Ude) and the Reform (where he followed Soyer). He had briefly worked for Queen Victoria, but only for a year, owing to her preference for plain fare. Ude had reviled English cuisine as ludicrous, claiming that the English knew no sauce but melted butter. Francatelli's *The Modern Cook* (1845) included

English recipes for lark pudding *à la Melton Mowbray* alongside French ones, encouraging English cooks to develop and refine their own tradition.[92]

The 'Epicure's Dinner' served in November 1867 indicates just what the St James's Hotel and Francatelli were capable of. It opened as French tradition dictated with a soup, then a fish course (*purée de gibier à la chasseur* and *épigrammes de rougets à la Bordelaise*), followed by the entrées: *mauviettes à la Troienza*, cutlets *à la duchesse*, its very own *médaillons de perdreaux à la St James* and roast mutton, rendered as *selle de mouton rôtie*. This was followed by truffled pheasant, a *mayonnaise de crevettes, choufleurs au parmesan* and a *charlotte de pommes*. Dessert was a *gateau à la Cerito* [sic], named after the Italian dancer Fanny Cerito, whose performances at the Haymarket Theatre in the 1840s had enthralled Soyer, who finally succeeded in marrying her in a low-key ceremony held in Paris in 1857.[93] Along with *Cerito's* [sic] *Sultane Sylphe à la Fille de l'Orage* and *Bomba alla Cerito*, the former created by Soyer, the *gâteau à la Cerito* joined a host of nineteenth-century dishes, usually desserts, named after famous singers, dancers and actresses.[94] Escoffier's peach dessert in honour of the Australian soprano Nellie Melba would follow in 1892.

Although large hotels had been built at railway termini in the 1830s and 1840s, the 1860s saw a step-change, both in size as well as in architectural pretension and level of service. Chief among this new generation were the Westminster Palace (1861), the Langham (1865) on Regent Street and the Midland Grand (1873) on Euston Road. Designed by George Gilbert Scott, this Gothic Revival palace at St Pancras boasted a one hundred-foot coffee room, 'ascending rooms' (i.e. lifts) and even a Ladies Smoking Room. The upper storeys were given over to rooms for the valets and other servants accompanying the guests. Though the clientele was elite, it did not enjoy en suite facilities. Even at the Victoria Hotel (1887) only four of the 500 bedrooms had private bathrooms.[95] Electric light arrived only with the Savoy, which opened in 1889, linked to the theatre of the same name (1881), which had been the first building in London lit by electricity. In

1889 its owner, Richard D'Oyly Carte, brought in Auguste Escoffier and César Ritz to manage his new hotel, Ritz having established his first hotel in the Place Vendôme two years earlier.

The reputation of their kitchens drew Londoners as well as travellers to these hotels, which became increasingly international in the 1890s and 1900s. Though London's Savoy set the pace, the ramifications of this golden age of hotels reached far beyond London and Paris. Escoffier and Ritz travelled across Europe, drawing on a body of investors as cosmopolitan as they were. In the era of the Grand Tour, Frederick Augustus Hervey, 4th Earl of Bristol and Bishop of Derry, had lent his name to a panoply of Italian and French inns, including a hotel in the Place Vendôme, making the name 'Bristol' a mark of quality in the early nineteenth century. However, Bristol's name had been appropriated by unaffiliated establishments without his permission, whereas the 'Ritz' was an international brand, managed by the Ritz Development Company. In the Edwardian period, 'Ritz' supplanted 'Bristol' as a byword for quality.

Escoffier made navigating the menu easier for his English clients by offering a *prix fixe*. He dispensed with the architectural and largely inedible *pièces montées* or centrepieces that had obsessed Carême, and cut back on the heavy sauces.[96] He nonetheless revelled in bespoke menus, such as that ordered by a party of young men who requested a meal entirely in red, paid for with the sum they had won betting (on red) at Monte Carlo. At the Savoy, Escoffier duly served them a *selle d'agneau aux tomates à la Provençale* with a *purée de haricots rouges*, a *parfait de foie gras en gelée au paprika doux à la Hongroise* washed down with rosé champagne.[97]

Dining options for women in late nineteenth-century London and Paris remained limited, as they had been in the previous century, when a woman seen in a Parisian *cabaret* or eating anywhere in London other than a confectioner's was likely to be considered a prostitute.[98] The author of *London at Dinner* (1858) described the lack of places 'where strangers of the gentler sex may be taken to dine' as 'one evil of long standing', though females could be taken to Epitaux's in Pall Mall and Verey's in Regent Street.[99] When women took themselves out, however, restaurateurs became nervous. The staff at the Trocadero were under instructions to contact the Superintendent whenever any unfamiliar ladies arrived unescorted. Once approved, the party would be placed at certain smaller tables in inconspicuous corners, 'the object being that in case of misbehaviour we can screen the <u>table</u> off'.[100] For many women the only option remained what *The Lady* in 1888 referred to as 'a scrambled meal, probably taken standing up in a pastry-cook's'.[101]

Given this climate, it is perhaps unsurprising that women-only dining rooms, restaurants and clubs sprang up in the 1880s and 1890s, to cater both to the growing number of female office workers as well as shoppers. Some hotels, such as the Hotel Providence in Leicester Square, had separate dining rooms for ladies, something entirely unknown in Paris.[102] In 1888 a former Girton graduate opened a women-only restaurant in Mortimer Street, The Dorothy.[103] With their simple menus and female waiters (known as 'nippies'), the chain of Lyons Tea Houses that began appearing across London in the 1890s were clearly aimed at women. The great West End department stores of the Edwardian period did not just offer respectable ladies a place to shop, they made a day in town possible, by providing dining as well as toilet facilities.[104]

'Tell me what you eat,' Brillat-Savarin famously observed in his *La Physiologie du Goût* (1825), 'and I will tell you what you are.'[105] As a place of performance, the restaurant afforded Londoners and Parisians a space in which to consume national stereotypes. It would continue to be commonplace to claim that the French live to eat, while the English eat to live. Indeed, some have taken the crudity of English cuisine as a badge of honour, something worth protecting from the French.[106] As early as 1570, Londoners were accusing migrant French cooks employed in noble households of corrupting Britain's taste for solid, wholesome fare.[107]

If British food was 'well dress'd' rather than 'well sauc'd', at least there was plenty of it to go around. Thus while the 'Frenchman in London' prints, discussed in the introduction, usually showed him as foppishly dressed and thin, prints of Englishmen in Paris caricatured them as massive, martyrs to halitosis and flatulence.[108] As Mercier noted, such clichés often served to maintain the status quo on both sides of the Channel. As with several of the clichés touched on in the course of this book, a closer look reveals a more complex picture. By observing one another eating in restaurants, Londoners and Parisians reflected not only on diet and taste, but on attitudes towards domesticity, a debate discussed in Chapter 1. Yet the establishments discussed here defy easy categorizing as either public or private, or even as British or French.

This chapter has considered a wide variety of eateries across several centuries, most of which were not known as 'restaurants'. One might well ask whether the restaurant was in fact 'invented' in Paris by Roze de Chantoiseau. As we have seen, the first Parisian 'restaurants' peddled a kind of anti-cuisine, while many of the things that made such eating houses stand out in Paris were already common in London, and may well have been borrowed: separate tables, service on demand, bills of fare. What exactly makes a restaurant a restaurant? Is it the service and the setting, the food, the way in which we talk about it – or a mixture of all three?

The restaurant is bound up with an attentiveness to the actual craft and technique of food preparation as well as with a self-conscious stageyness.[109] Patrons of seventeenth- and eighteenth-century venues in Paris and London do not seem to have had a vocabulary or genre of writing able to describe the food or its preparation in detail. It was either 'well dress'd' or it wasn't. Dining out was such a part of everyday life, associated with both business and pleasure, that what was on the plate probably did not seem much worth thinking or writing about. It was Grimod and, later, Brillat-Savarin who made the ingredients, their preparation and those who prepared them appear a world in themselves, something to take seriously. Building on the original restaurant's enlightened concern for diet and rational consumption (perhaps seen as fashionably 'English'), these writers created gastronomy: a dense structure of myth, history and geography, which impressed and intimidated observers, not least the English.

Together with the cult of the celebrity *émigré* (French) chef, this Paris-focussed cuisine arguably stopped English cuisine from developing further in the nineteenth century.[110] Though this had the advantage of making London remarkably receptive to foreign cuisines in the nineteenth and twentieth centuries, a tradition was lost, only fragments of which can possibly be recovered. Perhaps it harmed French cuisine too. The haute cuisine of 1900 was not very different from that of 1825, giving the lie to Brillat-Savarin's predictions of dishes new to science, 'mineral esculences perhaps, liqueurs distilled from a hundred atmospheres'.[111] As with the invention of 'Gay Paree', considered in Chapter 4, so here the two cities developed a mutually reinforcing set of stereotypes. Despite the strength and persistence of those stereotypes, they should not blind us to the roots of the restaurant in a dialogue between Paris and London.

And what about des Esseintes, whom we left in the Rue d'Amsterdam, on the point of leaving the Austin Bar to catch the boat train from the Gare du Nord? Having paid the waiter and stood up from the table, he found himself suddenly rooted to the spot.

> He kept telling himself: 'Come on now, on your feet, you must hurry'; but instantly there would be objections to gainsay his commands. What was the point of moving, when one could travel so splendidly just sitting in a chair? Wasn't he in London now, surrounded by London's smells, atmosphere, inhabitants, food, utensils? . . . He looked at his watch, 'It's time I went home.'[112]

Des Esseintes never did go to London.

FIG. 21: Henri de Toulouse-Lautrec, *The Englishman at the Moulin Rouge*, 1892.

CHAPTER FOUR

The Dance

In 1860 the *Mémoires* of the dancer known as Rigolboche appeared, ghosted by none other than Louis Huart, author of *La Physiologie du flâneur*, in tandem with the playwright Ernest Blum. A derisory piece of hackwork, Rigolboche's memoirs were one of a number of such reminiscences to appear in the 1860s, a sub-genre that traced its origins back to Céleste Mogador's best-selling *Adieux au Monde* (*Goodbye World*, 1854). The opening pages of *Mémoires de Rigolboche* struck a characteristically shrill, arrogant note. 'Come on, you gents, make some room, if you please! I am enlisted in the sacred batallion of celebrities, I am your equal in renown, I am qualified to address you by *tu* and use the pronoun "us" when speaking of the glories of Paris.' As if sensing that such vanity might grate, Rigolboche then stops to address the reader directly. 'This is beginning to sound a bit funny to you, right? But that's just the way it is; this is how it's done in the age of advertising!'[1]

Such memoirs at least had the virtue of being short. 'What more do you expect?' asks 'Rigolboche': 'I'm only eighteen!'[2] In this combination of sob-storytelling, denigration of would-be imitators and smug self-satisfaction at the author's fame, Huart was well aware of their hackneyed nature.[3] Despite some witty asides ('I believe in the Devil – he's done so much for me!'), the rest of Huart's text does little to break with convention, not least in its celebration of Rigolboche's signature dance. 'The cancan is a quintessentially French dance,' it insists. 'It has become the national dance. It's the embodiment of the Parisian imagination.'[4] 'Rigolboche' describes how the melody gradually takes control of her body, causing her to shake all over. She frightens herself, feeling the same emotions that a somnambulist feels when she is magnetized. 'The music condenses in my stomach and rises to my brain like champagne.'[5]

Today the cancan is synonymous with Paris, or rather with 'Gay Paree'. Every world city has its well-worn tourist itinerary, a set of sites that is also a series of rituals to be performed. Inhabitants sneer and avoid such 'tourist traps', to the extent that never having climbed the Empire State Building becomes the badge of a real New Yorker. In most cities the tourist trail and the resident's routine rarely cross, and the former is viewed with bemused detachment by those who know 'the real city', or who want to claim that they do. Arthur Symons knew to take a Baudelairean 'bath of multitude' on his first trip to Paris, but also what to avoid. 'We did not go up the Eiffel Tower,' he reported home, 'though I have a sort of recollection of having seen it about somewhere.'[6]

In some cases, however, the residents can begin to feel that their city is under threat, or even that they are strangers or revenants in someone else's theme park. This mood is certainly present in the classic mid-nineteenth-century work of Baudelaire, bemoaning the alienating and disorientating effects of Haussmannization. The cult of *vieux Paris* ('old Paris') that emerged is clearly related. Although it would be foolish to generalize, many Parisians are painfully aware of the appropriation of their city by tourists, more so, perhaps, than Londoners.

Parisians blame the 'Disneyfication' of their capital on the Americans. The composers Cole Porter, Yip Harburg and George Gershwin certainly have much to answer for, creating songs set in or about Paris that were later transformed into films such as *An American in Paris* (1951). In fact 'Gay

Paree' had already been invented by the time the Americans got to it. It was a product of the variety theatre and the music hall: a building type as well as a style of performance that was developed in 1850s and 1860s London and then exported to Paris, where new 'music halls' (the English word was retained) such as the Folies Bergères were constructed along the lines of London's Alhambra. Music halls thrived on the kind of intercity exchange outlined here, even as they often demonized such an exchange in deference to their audience's fierce patriotism. Upon closer inspection, quintessentially Parisian or London figures appear anything but. Even if people didn't always like to admit it, the dialogue between the two cities put the 'Champagne' in 'Champagne Charlie' and the 'Jane' (an English name) in 'Jane Avril'.

This chapter is about the cancan, a dance that began life as France's 'national dance' around 1830 only to become a byword for 'Gay Paree' at its most tacky sixty years later. By 1890 the high kicks, the frenzied movement of skirts and the teasing flash of foaming petticoats *were* Paris for many visitors, and for a surprising number of residents, too. Although it suited both sides to insist that the cancan was Parisian *pur sang* (pure blood or thoroughbred), in fact the familiar form of the dance had a more complex pedigree. The dance known in France today as 'French cancan' (again, the English word is employed) was a fusion of Parisian cancan and London skirt dancing, evolving as performers travelled between the two cities, adapting their routines to suit what they thought were local tastes.

The *Chahut*

Its name deriving from a sixteenth-century word meaning a din or racket, the cancan emerged in Paris following the 1830 Revolution, a mutation of the *chahut*, that 'indecent' dance that the famous police spy Vidocq (whom we shall meet in Chapter 5) observed being danced around 1810 at Guillotin's, a smoky dive of a *cabaret* near the *barrière* of Courtille.[7] Both were based on the quadrille, a type of *contredanse* or country dancing imported from England in the previous century, usually performed in groups made up of four couples. Up until 1855 the cancan was a dance of the people, the kicking part being largely reserved for the men. With the exception of an unsuccessful attempt to introduce it to London's Vauxhall Gardens in 1845 and to Cremorne Gardens in 1852, the cancan did not stray outside Paris's dance halls or *bals publics*.[8] It was mainly to be seen south of the river, at the Grand Chaumière and the Closerie de Lilas (also known as the Bal Bullier) on the Boulevard Montparnasse.

These were developments of the eighteenth-century *guinguettes*: the commercially operated café-cum-dance halls located outside the city wall, described in the previous chapter. George Cruikshank's 1822 print [Fig. 22] shows the fictional Regency buck 'Dick Wildfire' busy 'quadrilling it' in one close to the Champs Elysées. Consisting of a series of ramshackle buildings open to the elements, these were summertime resorts, modelled on the pleasure gardens found in the suburbs of London. The Chaumière had started as a series of thatched sheds erected in 1788 by an Englishman named Tinkson.[9] *Guinguettes* catered to working-class families looking for somewhere to drink, eat, dance and generally blow off steam on a Sunday, before the weekly grind began all over again. Whereas the mid nineteenth century would see the advent of dances for single couples (like the waltz and the polka), at the *guinguette* people danced in large groups, as in square- or line-dancing. A quadrille required at least four couples and consisted of no less than five 'figures' or parts, which together lasted around fifteen minutes. The 'band' consisted of three or four performers, whom Mercier describes as regularly squabbling with dancers over what music should be played. 'The violin player and the dancer finish up by getting plastered and fighting each other, then everyone sleeps and works until the following Sunday.'[10]

Despite their name, the *bals publics* of the 1820s and 1830s bore a stronger resemblance to the *guinguette* than to the famous balls organized at the Opéra.[11] Each of the 230 *bals* operating in the early 1830s could accommodate between 50 and 300 patrons, and opened on weekdays as well as Sundays.[12] The majority were the preserve of a particular neighbourhood or trade, which would have made them less accessible to outsiders than their cheapness and easygoing aura might otherwise suggest.[13] Those that were the preserve of the petit bourgeoisie did not welcome outbreaks of cancan, although others positively encouraged it. This was certainly the case of the *bals* that catered for clerks, students and their *grisettes*, the same *bals* patronized by the down-at-heel writers who made these establishments synonymous with Parisian 'bohemia' in the 1840s.

FIG. 22: George Cruikshank, *'Life' on Tip-toe, or Dick Wildfire Quadrilling it, in the Salon de Mars in the Champs Elysées*, 1822.

Supposedly named after the grey cloth she wore, the *grisette* of *Bohème* typically lived alone, sending back to her parents in the country what money she could scrimp from her labours as a semi-skilled worker.[14] As Théophile Gautier noted in 1846, most of these *grisettes* were 'students' (*étudiantes*, as in companions of students), 'even though nobody has yet been able to establish what discipline they are studying – they work little, dance a lot, sustain themselves on biscuits and beer'.[15] For their male patrons *grisettes* were, like the *bals* themselves, a guilty pleasure: a form of safe 'slumming' to be enjoyed for a few years before settling down with a respectable bourgeois wife. For the *grisette* there was always the hope that, against all odds, she might become that wife.

Although many had covered halls for bad weather, the *bals publics* were primarily intended for summer use; in winter customers danced at indoor *bals d'hiver* (winter balls) or *jardins d'hiver* (winter gardens), which were more centrally located. Entry was usually free, but clients paid between twenty and thirty centimes for the slip of paper or *cachet* that entitled them to a single dance. The larger *bals* like the Bal Favié in Belleville were run by dancing masters, who kept a weather eye on their young clients. Though the students at the Chaumière were studying law or medicine rather than dancing, the master of ceremonies, 'Père' Lahire, knew 'his' students by name and corrected them when they fell out of line. A trusted confidant, 'Father' Lahire proudly displayed the 108 dissertations that had been dedicated to him over the years.[16]

The *bals publics* were also surveyed by an officer of the *garde municipale*. For reasons that remain unclear, the cancan was perceived by the authorities as an expression of resistance to the July Monarchy, the constitutional monarchy of Louis-Philippe, which lasted from the July Revolution of 1830 until 1848. The 1831 edition of the police manual advised *sergents de ville* to order those dancing the *chahut* or cancan to desist. If they disobeyed, they were to be arrested and brought before the magistrate, charged under Article 330 of the penal code (as an offence against public decency). One view of the *bal* at Asnières shows a *municipal* shouldering through the crowd, arm outstretched, ready to throw out a man capering in front of two ladies.[17] As this image indicates, the cancan was a masculine display, performed as a *cavalier seul* (male solo) within the quadrille. The band encouraged such strutting by repeating the theme for this part of the quadrille, giving men more time to experiment with novel *galibes*, *gambades* and other forms of capering.

The first generation of cancan stars were talented male amateurs who practised respectable trades by day only to metamorphosize into kicking celebrities by night, known merely by *noms de guerre* such as 'Chicard' and 'Brididi'. Chicard could be found during daylight hours in the Rue St Denis, where he was a leather merchant named Alexandre Lévêque; Brididi was a florist in the Rue de Ponceau. The cancan was not really a step or dance in the traditional sense, but rather a sort of exaggerated, bow-legged stepping or body-popping performed for the admiration of the man's female partner or the intimidation of rival males. If it was intended as a form of political protest, it was a playful form.

Compared to the enthusiastic reaction to the arrival of the polka in the winter of 1844, the cancan does not seem to have excited much comment. Enforcement of the ban seems to have been weak. Each *municipal* had several establishments on his beat, all of whose owners kept him discreetly if well plied with complimentary drink. Once thrown out of a dance hall, offenders seem to have been able to return quickly and reoffend. When cases went to court, defendants defended the cancan as a means of self-expression. 'I made that step up just the other day, all by myself,' one told the court in September 1837. 'I didn't pick it up from the Opéra, not me, I dance my own way, that's the way I am.'[18] Nobody found the cancan titillating. Amusing, perhaps; the reference to the Opéra suggests that it was partly intended as a parody of the stars of the Opéra ballet. An optional addition to the quadrille, it was not associated with any particular melody, rhythm or time signature.

The decade after 1855 saw the dance shift, however, from amateur to professional, from male to female and, most importantly, from participation to voyeurism. The Bal Mabille played a key role in all these changes, helping several girls kick their way out of the working class, starting with Rigolboche. They performed the cancan solo on the dance floor, starting and stopping apparently at random, rather than forming part of a programme of entertainments arranged beforehand with the Mabille's manager or its orchestra. Once they got going other dancers would rush to form rings around them, joined by those who had come with no intention of dancing themselves, but rather to admire those who did. As Pierre Véron noted in *Paris s'amuse* (1861), Parisians went to *bals* to promenade, to dine, to gossip, to ruin themselves . . . but not to dance.[19]

Spectators were of a higher social class than dancers. One newspaper account of 1867 noted that the Mabille's 'indigenous population, the lowest of the low, the plebs, the *tiers état*', were the only ones to dance. The rest of the clientele consisted of well-dressed prostitutes and the tourists on whom they preyed. Whereas the Englishman had once been easy game, he was now, the journalist reported, more cautious than the Parisian himself.[20] Thanks to the 1867 Exposition Universelle, which drew over 8 million visitors to Paris, there were plenty of tourists of other nationalities at the Mabille.

Mabille Senior had launched his *bal* in 1840, but it did not make a name for itself until April 1844, when it reopened after being redesigned by his sons Victor and Charles, who also increased the admission charge from fifty centimes to three francs. In the new Mabille coloured gaslights hung like exotic glowing fruit from artificial palm trees whose trunks were bronze and whose leaves were zinc.[21] This was no longer a resort for down-at-heel students and their cheap dates. The spectacular use of a new technology not only allowed the Mabille to operate late into the night, but made dancing a spectacle of light that proved immensely appealing. In 1851, Victor Mabille took over Ranelag (named after London's Ranelagh pleasure garden) in the west of the city and made it into a more respectable version of the original. He thus revived the fortunes of a resort that had somehow managed to weather various crises, a survivor of the original 1770s fad for English-style 'Wauxhalls' that had managed to cling on as a kind of luxury *guinguette*.[22]

Their patriotism spurred, perhaps, by the arrival of the visitors, hack writers who penned pamphlets or memoirs of such *bals* now began to write about the cancan. They insisted that it was *the* national dance, and began to construct its past, as well as offering tenuous explanations for why it so suited the French people. 'The cancan is preeminently French,' explained Paul Mahalin in his *Mémoires du Bal Mabille*. 'Among a people like us, as light in spirit as in body the cancan must be and is more of a physical need than a passing sensation, more passion than science – an art.'[23] The novelists Théophile Gautier, Eugène Sue and Alexandre Dumas *père* were among the regulars at the Mabille.

A semi-professional *habituée* of the Mabille could supplement her income by asking admirers for a drink, dinner or simply fifty centimes for a drink. Some went on to become kept mistresses, while the most talented and ambitious performers turned professional, able in a few cases to support themselves entirely by means of their dancing, on the stages of variety theatres or as a 'turn' in performances put on as interludes at Ranelag and the Jardin d'Hiver. Such performances contributed to what might be called the 'theatricalization' of the cancan already noted. Dancers who were not so successful became housekeepers, street-sweepers or *ouvreuses* (i.e. ushers who let theatre patrons into their boxes). There were doubtless many *ouvreuses* who had hoped to follow Mogador's example and end up a celebrity and a countess at thirty, with carriages and servants.[24]

Compared to the memoirs of her great rival Rigolboche, those of another famous cancan dancer, Finette, seem to present a more rounded portrait. Whereas Rigolboche and her partner La Goulue rarely let their slightly superior smirks slip, photographs of Finette seem to suggest a more playfully self-aware personality. She was also somewhat less critical of her rivals than they had been of her. 'Finette smokes, Finette gets drunk, her language is vulgar, she beats her maid from morning to night,' Rigolboche had sniped in her memoirs. 'They say Finette writes charming letters. She doesn't even know how to write her own name and only reads magazines . . . she gets her piano teacher to do her writing for her.'[25]

A Creole born on the Île Bourbon (the old name for La Réunion, east of Madagascar), Finette was brought to Bordeaux by her mother. Josephine Durwend (her real name) was apprenticed to a dyer at fifteen and raped by a friend of the family at sixteen. After the attack she went into hospital, where she met a doctor who made her his mistress, setting her up in a house. Determined to make it to Paris, she soon left him for a cashmere merchant, then passed – via the Armenian attaché to the Turkish embassy – into the ballet. After completing her training she left the Opéra for a series of bit parts, including a tour with an acting troupe. Several well-known cancan and skirt dancers came unstuck when they mistakenly imagined they had a calling for the stage. Finette realized she did not and managed to support herself dancing solo or as part of a troupe of four led by a Mademoiselle Colonna. The account of her several *ménages* is sober and unsentimental. As she herself observed, everyone thinks her sort will sell anything for money, 'but I never said "I love you" without meaning it'.[26]

Unfortunately her memoirs were published just before her 1867 trip to London, which played such an important role in the development of 'French cancan'. They do, however, cover the period in which she contributed two important additions to the cancan: the splits and the hat trick. The former provided a somewhat inchoate dance with a dramatic finish: the dancer simply dropped to the floor. The latter involved a well-aimed kick to knock a spectator's top hat off his head. Her first attempt was at the Opéra, in response to a British admirer supposedly betting her 1,500 francs that she couldn't do it. Finette was mainly to be found in the variety theatres that sprang up in the 1860s. These gave the emerging stars of the Mabille and other summertime *bals* a chance to appear in more ambitious staged revues, to build up a following and to support themselves all year round. Together with the Ba-Ta-Clan on the Boulevard du Prince Eugène (now Voltaire) and the Théâtre des Délassements Comiques on the Boulevard du Temple, the Eldorado on the Boulevard de Strasbourg played an important role here.

Established in 1858, the Eldorado opened every evening at seven, offering a programme of airs, duets, cantatas, comic scenes, overtures, waltzes and quadrilles that lasted until eleven. For the 1867 Exposition crowd, the Eldorado staged an operetta titled *Le Beau Paris*, alongside a nightly performance of cancan, or rather 'the grand eye-kicking quadrille', danced by Clodoche, Flageolet, the Comet and Normande. Entry was free, but refreshments were priced differently in various parts of the auditorium. Here Finette, Rigolboche and other female dancers performed the cancan in calf-length skirts, with their legs fully encased from their boots right up to their *pantalons* (trouser-like undergarments) in thick satin tights. There were no petticoats, nor garters, nor suspenders. No one touched or lifted their skirts. All that would have to wait until Finette and the cancan reached London's music halls.

A Champagne Swell

The music hall was born in 1850s London, as a series of publicans hired local builders to build large rooms over their beer gardens or to enlarge existing back rooms. One of the earliest still surviving, Wilton's in Wellclose Square, dates from 1859 and is typical of the first generation. Tacked onto the back of a pub in Tower Hamlets, it consists of a long room with a narrow proscenium arch and a shallow stage. Performers and audience were obliged to mingle: there was only one way onto the stage (walking through the audience), no wings in which to hide and no flies, making all but the most rudimentary stage scenery impossible. Columns supported a creaky gallery, with little sense of separation between those up in the gallery and those below or on the stage. Wilton's was also typical in having tables and chairs (since removed) set at right angles to the stage, with a sort of high table nearest the stage for the chairman. This master of ceremonies announced the acts and kept a weather eye on the audience. A shaving mirror set before him enabled him to see what was happening on the stage behind him. Even in a small hall like Wilton's, those at or near the chairman's table would have been expected to consume food and drink on a scale befitting their exalted position.

The musical forces available at Wilton's were probably limited to a piano, perhaps supplemented on occasion by a couple of violins, a cornet, a flute and a double bass. The songs were simple, usually based on just two or three chords, the melody rarely modulating into another key. Recollecting a career during which he claimed to have composed more than 17,000 songs, Joseph Tabrir described his working methods in an 1894 interview for *The Era*, the trade paper for the entertainment industry. 'Think of a catchy refrain – Think of the d[amne]d silliest words that will rhyme anyhow. Think of a haunting pretty melody – and there you are,' he explained, adding somewhat bitterly, 'the fortune of your publisher is made.'[27]

Many of the lyrics and even more of the tunes would have been taken from eighteenth-century catch and glee clubs, the music and lyrics having been kept alive by performances at early nineteenth-century pleasure gardens and at their working-class equivalents, the 'gaffs'. A number of famed character singers, such as Sam Cowell and Harry Clifton, as well as minstrel groups such as the Aethiopian Serenaders got their start in the basement supper rooms off the Strand, such as Evans's, which had their heyday in the 1840s. Here the audience was exclusively male, dining on devilled kidneys and porter in stuffy conviviality. At supper rooms and the early music halls, the chorus would have been sung by soloists and audience alike, who exercised considerable discretion over the evening's programme, cutting off singers deemed insufficiently talented and demanding encores from those they admired (a practice known as 'chirruping').

Although both types of music hall operated in parallel for several decades, the opening of Charles Morton's Canterbury Hall in Lambeth in December 1856 marked a shift in gear, towards purpose-built music halls. These benefited from deeper and better equipped stages, larger auditoria, orchestras, multiple bars, a promenade, lavishly decorated foyers and saloons and even, in some cases, picture galleries. The Canterbury could accommodate 2,000, with much clearer distinctions between different classes of customer. A low barrier separated the expensive, relatively spaced-out tables in the part of the hall closest to the stage from those set further back, which were crowded together. Music halls had previously been restricted to the less desirable East End and districts south of the river. Several of the most impressive second-generation halls opened in the heart of the West End, in particular around Leicester Square. Weston's Music Hall (later renamed the Holborn Empire) opened in 1857 and Morton opened a second hall, the Oxford, on the corner of Tottenham Court Road and Oxford Street in 1861.

The gallery was clearly a separate realm, beginning a process of elevation that would climax in Sickert's haunting etchings of the Edwardian halls, where the denizens of the gallery peer down like caged animals glimpsed through grilles, their cloth caps picked out by the footlights' glare. Some of the most irritatingly persistent refrains, those that still spark associations today, took as their theme this yawning gulf between gallery and stage or between gallery and 'stalls': Nellie Power's 'The Boy I Love is up in the Gallery' and Nellie Farren's 'What Cheer "Ria"' (shortened to 'wotcher'). The heroine of 'What Cheer' splurges on a ticket to the stalls only to discover that despite her best efforts she is unable to enjoy herself properly. In part this is because her friends in the gallery expose her as an interloper, by shouting questions down at her as she squirms uncomfortably in borrowed finery. Music halls were not the 'hail fellow well met' equalizers they are sometimes held to be.

The 1860s also saw the arrival of the music-hall star system. Professional performers adopted a particular character, song or motto as their signature, and then flogged it to death. Music publishers brought out sheet music, enabling those possessed of that symbol of middle-class respectability, the upright piano, to take these songs home. Song covers were enlivened by chromolithographs by the likes of Alfred Concanen, featuring the singer, as well as vignettes illustrating particular verses. Costing between two shillings and sixpence and four shillings, many of these illustrated the japes of the 'swell', the well-dressed, enviable man about town, or poked fun at wannabes who had the will but not quite the means to carry off this role. There were transvestite 'swells' like Nellie Power, who performed in male costume, and songs that celebrated independent working girls who supplemented their income (from typing or sewing) by fleecing foolish admirers. Power's 'The City Toff' made fun of the eponymous 'Toff': 'He is something in an office' but his 'Paris diamonds' are clearly paste, and 'the little barmaids titter,/At his sausage, [a suggestive gesture would doubtless have been inserted at this point] and his bitter'.[28]

The greatest swell of them all was the Champagne Swell, Champagne Charlie, a character created by George Leybourne in 1866. Born in Gateshead in 1842, Leybourne worked as an engine fitter before he entered the halls, moving to London in 1864. Alfred Lee's lyrics presented him as rich, single and generous, leading a life of idle luxury: 'A noise all night in bed all day and swimming in champagne.' 'For Champagne Charlie is my name' explained the chorus, 'Good for any game at night, boys./Who'll come and join me in a spree?'

> From coffee and from supper rooms from Poplar to Pall Mall,
> The girls on seeing me exclaim, 'Oh! What a champagne
>   swell!'

The notion it is of everyone, if it were not my name,
And causing so much to be drunk, they'd never make
    champagne.
The way I gained my title's by a hobby which I've got
Of never letting others pay, however long the shot.
Whoever drinks at my expense are treated all the same.
From dukes and lords to cabmen down, I make them drink
    champagne.

With the crowd trained to shout 'Yes!' at the end of each line of the chorus and Leybourne's bottle primed to explode at the end of the song (using a trigger mechanism), the song celebrated both conspicuous consumption and concupiscence.

As well as generosity and a cast-iron stomach, Charlie also had brand loyalty. 'Some epicures like burgundy, hock, claret and moselle,' he sang. 'But Moët's vintage only satisfies this champagne swell.'[29] He carried a bottle of Moët while on stage and his contract committed him to drinking nothing else while in public, as well as to driving a coach with two postilions at all times. Moët's rivals soon realized they needed their own promoters. Alfred Peck Stevens ('The Great Vance') was Veuve Cliquot's champion. 'Cliquot! Cliquot!' sang Stevens. 'That's the wine for me.' A 'Cliquot Galop' was published, which cheekily claimed to be composed by 'Champagne Charlie'. Along with Victorian slang words like 'crib' (meaning 'home'), the ostentatious quaffing of 'Mo' (Moët) would be borrowed by American rap artists of the late twentieth century, as refugees from another type of ghetto doused the flames of class war by celebrating their own arrival among the rich and famous.[30]

Though Charlie claimed that he was responsible for making everybody drink champagne, in reality some credit must go to the Liberal Chancellor of the Exchequer and future prime minister William Ewart Gladstone. Gladstone enjoyed drinking a quart of champagne at lunch and felt that such moderate consumption of a refreshing stimulant would help wean the British working class off their binge-drinking of gin. A freer trade would improve morals by encouraging the working man to put quality before quantity. Whereas the import duty on champagne had been set at five shillings and sixpence since 1831, in the wake of the January 1860 tariff treaty with France (named after the radical free-trader Richard Cobden, who led the negotiations), Gladstone's budget that year reduced it to three shillings. As a result, British consumption of French wines more than doubled in the space of twelve months, from 547,000 gallons to 1.1 million. It doubled again the next year (1861) to 2.2 million; in 1862, Gladstone decreased the duty further to two shillings and sixpence; consumption kept on rising, to 4.5 million in 1868. Unfortunately there was no sign that these measures also brought about a change in tastes. As Gladstone's opponents among the Victorian Temperance movement suspected, rather than leading to a change in taste, consumption of *all* forms of intoxicants increased.[31]

Whilst the trend would take several years to trickle down to the music halls, 'Champagne William' (as he might be called) undoubtedly contributed to the creation of a phenomenon. Champagne in the 1860s was much sweeter than it is today, which certainly helped as well. Unfortunately the Franco-Prussian War disrupted supplies in 1870–1, and thereafter champagne houses began producing drier vintage champagne, pushing up prices against the swells.[32] The song and the pose persisted into the next century, however, yoking Paris and fizzy drinks together in the popular imagination. Listeners to songs like 'Our Lively Neighbours' would have had no trouble understanding what the tenor performer was on about when he spoke of Paris as 'whizzing, fizzing wine uncorking'. Though far less dramatic, the lowering of duties also facilitated exchange in the other direction, most notably in the case of Bass Brewery, which launched their bottled beer in the 1860s. Bass Pale Ale and champagne sit side by side on Parisian music-hall menus, as well as on the counter in Edouard Manet's famous painting *Bar at the Folies Bergères* (1882).

Finette

Music-hall impresarios like Charles Morton always kept an eye out for new acts. The establishment of the first booking agency for music-hall artistes in 1858 certainly made this easier, but enterprising managers like the Alhambra's John Hollingshead were soon looking further afield. A former commercial traveller turned journalist, Hollingshead had made a name for himself producing lurid exposés of 'underground London', as well as by campaigning for the loosening of theatre licensing laws and the removal of paper duties, the so-called 'taxes on knowledge'. Hollingshead served as the Alhambra's manager from 1865 to 1868, taking on a theatre that had originally opened as the Panopticon of Science and Art in 1854. Located on the north side of Leicester Square, this complex of laboratories and lecture rooms intended for the diffusion of 'useful knowledge' had been converted into an auditorium seating 3,000. In 1864 the new leaseholder, Frederick Strange, added a forty-foot 'Torrent Cascade' with 'real water' to the foyer.

In Hollingshead, Strange had hit upon a manager who combined outstanding business sense with a healthy disrespect for the Lord Chamberlain and his regulatory powers over London's theatres. In January 1867, Hollingshead staged a pantomime with several spoken lines, even though the Alhambra was licensed to stage only burlesques: single-scene, silent assemblages of pratfalls and clowning with characters drawn from Italian *commedia dell'arte*. The title of the pantomime (which was also the first line spoken in it), *Where's the Police?*, was clearly intended to provoke the authorities. Hollingshead was duly summoned before the magistrates in Marlborough Street, where he was fined £240. By that point several other unlicensed theatres had made common cause with him, and with their support he declared his intention to appeal against the decision.

That same year Hollingshead and the Alhambra's ballet master, Mr Milano, travelled to Paris in search of new acts. At the Café de Herder

FIG. 23: Finette from, *The Censor*, 20 June 1868.

they came across Finette, recently returned from a tour of Germany. Hollingshead hired her to perform in London the following summer, initially at the Royal Lyceum (in Wellington Street), under E. T. Smith's management. On 11 May she was at the Alhambra, performing a 'Parisian Carnival Quadrille, with new variation' in an 'Anglo-French ballet' called *Mabille in London*.[33] The first rumblings of discontent appeared in *The*

Censor for 20 June 1868, alongside an engraved portrait showing Finette in mid-kick [Fig. 23], her wanton locks suggestive of Satanic horns, trampling on 'Beauty', 'Sense', 'Decency', 'Grace' and 'Honour'. Her left hand waves a flag with the motto 'To Destruction', clearly indicating where this Parisian Pied Piper was leading the nation's youth.

Finette was, *The Censor* claimed, a sign of the decadence of the times. Was it not troubling that thousands of Englishmen, including boys and young girls, were applauding a woman performing 'lewd antics and lascivious movements, which even in Paris are banished to such exceptional places of resort as the Mabille'? There was nothing graceful about Finette, the article insisted, who wriggled and threw her legs about, not as a dancer, 'but as a votary of Aphrodite Pandemos'. The item concluded by censuring E. T. Smith for introducing underage swells to what the author sarcastically hailed as the era's most advanced and 'progressive' pleasure: drinking champagne with ballet-girls in the Lyceum's cellar bar.[34]

By 1869 this clamour had finally induced the Lord Chamberlain, Viscount Sydney, to take action. Having gone himself to view the show, he sent all theatre managers a shot across the bows. Finette's season at the Lyceum had not been interrupted, however, so Hollingshead judged it safe enough to bring the cancan to the Gaiety and the Alhambra in October 1870. There Finette appeared as part of Mlle Colonna's troupe in a short 'water ballet and spectacle' titled *Les Nations, or the Grand Cascades*, which lasted an hour, from 10.15 p.m. to 11.20 p.m. Joining the troupe on the programme were the Royal Tycoon's Private Troup of Japanese and the marvellous monkeys from the Cirque L'Imperatrice.[35] By this point the Franco-Prussian War had broken out, and Finette was presumably content to remain in London. The only way back to Paris would have been via balloon. The city was besieged.

On 8 October, Police Superintendent Dunlop of C Division sent in plain-clothes officers to observe Finette. Inspector J. E. Perry and Sergeant John Pope had their tickets paid for by the Met. If the report they submitted two days later is anything to go by, they did not appear to have had a very good time:

> We beg to report having attended the Alhambra Palace Music Hall on the 8th inst, when the ballet *Les Nations* was performed, in the which Mdlle. Colonne [sic] and *troupe* (four in all) appeared, and danced the Parisienne quadrille, or ordinary 'can-can'. Two of them personated men, dressed in bodices and trunks to match, and flesh-coloured hose; the others as females, dressed as ordinary ballet girls, except more of the thigh was visible in consequence of [their] having very scanty drawers. The dance, on the whole, is indecent, especially on the part of one dressed as a female, who raises her foot higher than her head several times towards the public, and which was much applauded. There was a large influx of visitors shortly before the ballet commenced, but which was decreased immediately after. The other performances were carried on principally by females dressed as males, but there was nothing objectionable observed.

The police waited until Frederick Strange applied to Marlborough Street for renewal of the Alhambra's music and dancing licence, and then submitted their report along with an engraving from *The Day's Doings*, a periodical for men who liked to 'go it'.

Hollingshead by this point had moved on, and his replacement, a Mr Poland, was hard put to defend Finette. He argued that the engraving could not be admitted as evidence as it came from a paper known for exaggeration, and he pointed out that Finette had danced the cancan for a whole season at the Lyceum without anyone objecting (he did not subscribe to *The Censor*, clearly). Finally, Poland had recourse to an argument that would be wheeled out by many a theatre manager in the years that followed. If the Alhambra's licence was *not* renewed, 450 people would be thrown out of work. Two hundred of them were girls, he later added, the implication being that if these young ladies had kept to the straight and narrow up until that point, they would not be able to continue to do so without the regular income (around twenty shillings a week for the less important performers) provided by Mr Strange. Despite his pleas, the magistrates voted 7–2 not to grant a licence.[36]

Strange fought back, hiring a slightly disreputable QC named Digby Seymour who seems to have bullied the magistrates into rehearing the case. Seymour argued that the cancan they danced was not the Parisian quadrille of that name, but a sanitized version. The Alhambra would never, he insisted, have asked British magistrates to license the cancan, which was nothing more than a 'harlots' quadrille'. He promised that the altered version would never be danced again. Though temporarily cowed, the magistrates were eventually rallied by one of their number, Pownall, who asked them whether 'we in this country [are] to revert to scenes which are patronised in a neighbouring capital'.[37] Their decision stood. When Strange's licence ran out in early November, he switched to staging concerts of Gounod and Strauss, performed by a monster orchestra of 150.

Given these hazy and conflicting accounts, it is difficult to determine what Finette was in fact doing. But we can be sure of what she was wearing, from her publicity photographs and the matching description in her memoirs. These make it clear that she was wearing a man's or boy's costume, specifically that of a fisherman. In her memoirs Finette explained that she had thought up this costume of black, red and gold embroidered shorts herself.[38] Though she was wearing shorts, Finette's thighs would not, contrary to the Met's plain-clothes officers, have been visible. White sheer tights covered her legs entirely. Her costume was little different from that worn by female leads playing the parts of boys in the popular parodies that borrowed plots and titles from high drama (Goethe's *Faust*, for example) and translated them into incongruous or ridiculous settings (resulting in *Young Doctor Faust*, in this case). As Hollingshead himself put it, Finette was dressed 'a little more decently than a burlesque prince'.[39] Her drawers hid more of her thighs than the *caleçon* (skirt) worn in *ballets d'action* in the 1840s, the age of Carlotta Grisi.[40]

For the police and the magistrates, the obscenity lay not in the costume but in what Finette was doing, and perhaps what the audience were doing as well. Perry and Pope were especially shocked by the height and direction of Finette's kicks: 'higher than her head' and 'towards the public'. They were also struck by the 'influx of visitors' just before her appearance, and the coincidence of her high kicks and those visitors' applause. The indecent implication was that these visitors had timed their arrival around Finette, and specifically around her high kicks. The constables did, however, describe her performance as a 'dance'. This is interesting, as many had interpreted the cancan as the opposite of dancing. Writing in 1854, Bayle St John called it 'a violent kind of gymnastics, in which genteel young men [sic] kick up their legs, wag their heads, distort their bodies, and scatter their arms, elbows, and hands'.[41] Although Finette and her three colleagues divided into two couples for the other parts of the quadrille, one half dressed as women and the other as men, Finette was the star. She took centre stage at the climax of what one might call a 'turn', one focussing on her limber contortions.

In 1872 an all-male cancan troupe from Paris, Les Clodoches, had a run at the Cambridge. As a music hall the Cambridge did not have a licence for dancing, so those resorts that did have dancing licences paid the comedian Robert Young to attend the Cambridge over four nights and then prosecute the Cambridge's manager, Mr Nugent, in the Court of Common Pleas. The trial turned on the question of whether the cancan was a dance or, as one witness put it, 'more of contortion business'. Young described how the Clodoches danced 'the French "can-can" Quadrilles, and were encored'. Their performance lasted twelve minutes, and on one of the four nights they sang as well as danced. The men dressed as women also did the 'splits'.

The Cambridge's lawyer submitted that the Clodoches were capering rather than dancing, only to have the judge point out that 'to caper' was to 'dance as if he were a goat'. This rather flummoxed the defence. 'Judge and jury' shows had been a popular form of entertainment in the 1840s, and more than one member of the jury in *Young vs. Nugent* must have struggled to take the case entirely seriously, as witness after witness gave up trying to put the cancan into words and began miming it in the witness box, to 'loud laughter' from all present. The jury found for the defendant, apparently agreeing that the cancan was 'a kind of pantomimic action . . . getting into curious positions'. Performed by men as well as women, the cancan was ludicrous, not licentious. Although it was enacted with a musical accompaniment, which may (the evidence in court was conflicting) have been taken from Jacques Offenbach's *Grande Duchesse de Gérolstein* (not, apparently, his *Orphée aux Enfers*, where the cancan tune we all know appears), the cancan was not performed *to* music. This confirmed that it was not a dance.[42]

Skirt Dancing

The story of cancan might have stopped there, around 1870. An early form of break dancing, born in Parisian *guinguettes* and *bals publics* fifty years earlier, had been developed by a few flexible professionals (male as well as female) from the Mabille, eventually turning into a contortionist act performed on the variety and music-hall stages of Paris and London. All with nary a lacy petticoat in sight. That the cancan survived was thanks to a British dancer, Kate Vaughan, [Fig. 24] inventor of a new type of dance known as skirt dancing and, crucially, the first performer to flash her lace petticoats on stage. Although Vaughan's own tour to

FIG. 24: William Downey, Kate Vaughan as Lalla Rookh at the
Novelty Theatre, 1884.

Paris in February 1876 was not a success (she was booed off the stage), Parisian stars like Finette, and especially the slightly younger generation of La Goulue and Grille d'Egout, copied Vaughan's dress and skirt manipulation. Combining it with the high kicks of gymnastic cancan, they in turn created French cancan.

Kate Vaughan, like Finette, had received training in ballet technique, in her case from Madame Conquest, ballet mistress of the Grecian Theatre, where her father was in the orchestra. Kate and her sister Susie formed the Vaughan Troupe with two other female dancers, specializing in 'black dance', that is, the 'Negro national dances' of the kind Juba (William Henry Lane) had performed at Vauxhall in 1848: the 'Virginny Breakdown', 'Alabama Kick-up' and 'Tennessee Double-Shuffle'.[43] The Troupe performed at Cremorne in the late 1860s, when the ubiquitous E. T. Smith was the lessee. Cremorne's pagoda dance floor had hosted London's first experiments with cancan in 1852; Vaughan now incorporated kicks into her routines, which included cancan under the label 'Parisian quadrille'. Hollingshead spotted her and brought her to the Gaiety, where she became the first of a series of 'Gaiety Girls', from 1877 performing alongside Nellie Farren in a new foursome with the comedians and burlesque harlequins Edward Terry and Teddy Royce. Their troupe topped the bill at the Gaiety up until Vaughan's ill-advised decision in 1883 to drop dancing in favour of acting.

Her style of dancing consisted of performing traditional dance figures, usually the waltz, with both hands clutching and moving her skirt in time to the music. Wearing a long skirt facilitated such movements, which in turn revealed what Vaughan was wearing under her skirt: several lace-fringed petticoats with gold-spangled black tights underneath, descending to a pair of leather ankle boots.[44] Vaughan also wore long black gloves over bare arms and adopted a vacant expression doubtless intended to allure. Like Finette, Vaughan posed for many publicity photographs, including one of her recumbent, looking slightly less lively than the stuffed macaw ogling her. Although it is unclear whether she invented skirt dancing herself, or was instructed by John D'Auban, ballet master at the Gaiety, Vaughan certainly found many admirers. The art critic John Ruskin was fascinated by her. He and the Pre-Raphaelite painter Edward Burne-Jones fell into each other's arms when they discovered their shared appreciation of Vaughan.[45]

Vaughan does not appear to have lifted her skirt very high or to have performed high kicks, but she clearly succeeded in creating the impression that she might do so at any moment. Her somewhat detached or possibly demure expression and her relatively slow movements seemed to split her into two halves. Rigolboche and other Parisian cancan dancers may have described the spirit of the dance as invading their bodies and taking them over, but in Vaughan's case the conflict was externalized. Audiences were hooked not because she was lifting up her skirt, but because she seemed to be struggling unsuccessfully to keep her skirt down. The skirt seemed to have a will of its own. As the title of her first skirt dancing routine – 'Ain't She Very Shy?' – indicates, Vaughan and her managers were well aware of this teasing quality. Unlike Finette, Vaughan seemed an unwilling, reluctant or even repentant performer. Male observers got an added frisson out of that, as well as from the flash of lace, which revealed nothing and suggested everything.

Although we have no images of Vaughan dancing, we do have images of her less talented imitators that show them lifting their skirts over their heads. Her partner Nellie Farren was famous for dancing the waltz while leaning her torso backwards. In this position she did not have to kick very high to reveal her lacy petticoats. Vaughan's successors at the Gaiety, Connie Gilchrist, Lettie Lind and Alice Lethbridge, were probably no different, even if other stages hosted more exuberant skirt dancers such as Sally Collins, known as 'Wiry Sal' or 'Sal the Kicker'. In 1891, Lottie Collins made her debut in her show-stopping number 'Ta-Ra-Ra-Boom-Di-Ay'. Though the kick Collins delivered on the 'B' of the 'boom' as well as her vocal projection would have shocked Vaughan (who did not have much of a voice), Collins nonetheless stuck to the spirit of the skirt dance in dividing the act into two halves: 'demure' (refrain) and 'wild' (chorus).

Before Kate Vaughan, cancan had been a solo dance for male or female performers involving challenging contortions, the most demanding of which (the high kicks and splits) were either reserved for male dancers like the Clodoches or for female dancers in boy's costume. Photographs of Rigolboche and Finette rarely show them in skirts, and when they do it is clear that underneath they wore only plain white leggings without pantaloons, petticoats or Valenciennes lace. The invention of skirt dancing – and in particular Vaughan's apparently unsuccessful tour to Paris – inspired the generation of Parisian dancers that followed Finette to dress differently as well as to grab hold of their skirts and wave them around. Photographs from the the 1880s of La Goulue (Louise Weber) and Grille d'Egout are strikingly different: the dancers are holding up their skirts to reveal a much more tantalizing display of white petticoats or *jupons.*

Their legs are encased in black silk tights, but are visible up to just below the knee, where the white frilly *pantalons* (essentially a pair of short trousers) begin. Later photographs of the pair with Nini Pattes-en-l'air and Sauterelle show them in pumps with *pantalons* that end just above the knee [Fig. 25]. Though it is hard for us to imagine the cancan without thinking of suspender belts, here they are absent.[46]

During the 1870s, while Finette and the Clodoches were tangling with the courts and Vaughan was developing her skirt dancing, 'le music hall' arrived in Paris. New types of theatre appeared in the French capital, closely modelled on London's Alhambra, while *bals publics* like the Mabille and the Casino-Cadet closed. In May 1869 the Folies Bergères opened in a former furniture warehouse on the Rue Richer, known as Les Colonnes d'Hercule. It struggled initially and only really got going after the Franco-Prussian War, when Léon Sari took over the management, having previously managed the Théâtre des Délassements Comiques. In 1875 he had the Folies enlarged, putting in a London-style promenade or *promenoir.*

FIG. 25: Unknown artist, Nini Pattes-en-l'air, la Sauterelle, Grille d'Egout and, in front of them, La Goulue at the Moulin Rouge, 1900.

Paintings such as Manet's *Bar at the Folies Bergères* fully exploited the scopic effects made possible for the first time by this juxtaposition of spaces for drinking, ogling, circulating and performing. Though few scores survive, the titles of the songs popularized by Yvette Guilbert and others around this time tackled topics similar to those addressed in London music halls: 'Ah qu'c'est drole un amoureux' ('Oh, What a Funny Thing a Sweetheart is'), 'Je Suis Pocharde' ('I'm Tipsy'), and so on.[47]

For some reason, at the end of the 1880 season Sari decided to fire the staff and convert the Folies into a concert hall, only to change it back when the *concert de grand musique* failed to take off – at which point he was declared bankrupt. Only under the next lessees, M. and Mme Allemand, did the Folies introduce a full programme of music-hall variety. In October 1889 the Moulin Rouge was opened by Charles Zidler and Joseph Oller, on a site at the foot of the Butte Montmartre previously occupied by a *bal*, La Reine Blanche. This featured a large ballroom made of iron, with an orchestra at one end and a second stage outside in a small garden, itself dominated by a large elephant in which private performances of belly dancing were given by 'la belle Fathma'.[48]

At the Folies Bergères and the Moulin Rouge, the London influence was obvious, encompassing the performers as well as the general ambience, as shown in work by Henri de Toulouse-Lautrec (who moved to Montmartre in 1886) and in written accounts by Symons and Huysmans.[49] The former's lithograph *The Englishman at the Moulin Rouge* (1892) [Fig. 21, p. 134] shows a moustachioed gent chatting up two ladies. Huysmans visited the Folies Bergères in 1879, describing his visit in his *Parisian Sketches* (1880). He admired the theatre for its boulevard air, found it both ugly and superb, in 'exquisitely good and outrageously bad taste', and relished the English humour of the Hanlon–Lees double act. Little Tich (Harry Relph) also clowned at the Folies Bergères. Indeed, he was such a hit that he was made an officier of the Academie Française in 1910.[50] Meanwhile at the Moulin Rouge, 'Les Ecossais' (The Scotsmen) delighted female audiences by swinging overhead on trapezes while wearing kilts.[51]

At the Moulin Rouge and the Folies Bergères, the cancan was performed not on a stage, as Vaughan and Finette had danced it in London, but in the old Mabille way: on the dance floor, surrounded by circles of male and female spectators. It was now all about the dizzying, fizzing effects of skirts and petticoats, a multicoloured, hazy blur. Jane Avril developed a three-stage cancan, which she danced both solo and as part of the Troupe de Mademoiselle Eglantine. This began with 'the mill', in which the dancer lifted her skirt and raised one leg, hopping on the other leg and spinning the raised foot in a circle. After changing legs, the dancer lowered her skirt slightly and began a series of side-to-side movements redolent of the

163

gambades originally performed by men in the days of the Grand Chaumière. The final phase consisted of high kicks and the adoption of well-known poses, such as the *porte d'armes* (with the leg held back against the shoulder, like a rifle), the *gitarre* (where one leg is held diagonally across the body, like a guitar) and the *grand écart* (the 'splits').

In May 1891 the gentleman's magazine *Gil Blas* issued a supplement devoted to 'eccentricities of dance' by 'Rodrigues', that is, the bibliophile and collector Eugène Rodrigues-Henriques. He gave a heady description of the cancan at its zenith, as performed by La Goulue, a dance as collective orgasm. He described how that 'piece of pink flesh' above her garter 'spurts molten steel over the panting spectators' until, eventually, 'a dark stain indicates that most intimate of efflorescences, and a similar thrill seizes the watching men and women.'[52]

La Goulue's partner, Grille d'Egout, saw the same dance very differently, providing a glimpse of the mundane reality that lay behind those curtains of lace: the world where dancers had to save up their meagre wages to keep themselves in the expensive undergarments that were gradually eclipsing their individuality. Asked by *Gil Blas* to describe how she saw the cancan, she wrote her own article:

> One must have pretty knickers. They're indispensable.
> Without nice knickers, no cancan. Me, I prefer white
> knickers, long petticoats with fine lace, and *pantalons*
> furnished with lots of ruffles. It is possible to wear coloured
> knickers, but they should be pale. Tights must be black,
> the better to stand out against the white . . . When you're
> dressed like this you can raise your legs without any worry.
> I must nonetheless add that I never dance without first
> attaching the bottom edge of my *pantalons* to my stockings
> with pins. Women who show their flesh, that's disgusting.

As with Finette's account, this account has a ring of truth to it entirely lacking from the one penned by 'Rodrigues'. Although there is some photographic evidence that La Goulue did reveal a 'patch of skin', it seems that in fact this was rare before 1914, and certainly before 1900. 'Sure, they call me Grille d'Egout [Sewer Grate] – I'm no duchess –,' her article continues, 'but I don't like scandalous things – I'm not some kind of lout, oh, no.'[53]

Gay Paree

In the 1890s Charles Godfrey was at the top of his game as a variety performer. Born Paul Lacey in 1851, Godfrey had started out as an actor before leaving the theatre for the music hall. Forty years later he topped the 'Grand Christmas Programme' from the Tivoli Theatre of Varieties in the Strand, his name appearing alongside seasoned stars such as Arthur Lloyd as well as the high-kicking Lottie Collins. Although he never achieved similar fame, Godfrey did have a secure position in the second rank, specializing in songs about fashionable men about town. He achieved considerable success with 'The Masher King' and similar numbers celebrating the sort of high-rolling lifestyle first eulogized by George Leybourne.

Another of Godfrey's hits was 'Gay Paree', composed by Edward Jonghmans to words by Richard Morton, describing a trip to Paris with three friends (Tom, Dick and Harry). Having stuffed a trunk with their clothes, the four set out and are soon strolling down the *'Shongs Elizer'*. Dick spots four girls he claims to know and invites them to join his friends. The four proceed to tease their delectable companions with references to frogs and disdainful comments on the Eiffel Tower, which had opened in March 1889. One of the 'tasty' girls takes offence at being chucked under the chin and called 'Yummiest of Totties!', at which point the gendarmes intervene. Fisticuffs and a short chase up the 'Rue de Something' end in them being bailed by a weary British consul and sent 'Back again to London town!'[54]

Songs about gangs of men roaming London streets getting drunk, harrassing women and tangling with the police were nothing new in the 1890s. Compared to the japes of George Leybourne's 'Champagne swells', the supposedly harmless antics of the 1880s and 1890s 'masher' have a more violent feel. Songs like J. H. Milburn's 'Come Along Boys, Let's Make a Noise' came close to promoting hooliganism. 'Bill Smith, Tom Jones and Johnson and myself went out last night to have a spree', Charles Waterfield sang in 'We All Had One', 'which ended just as usual with a fight.'[55]

While punch-ups could happily be found anywhere, Godfrey sang of a city with much more to offer. As the chorus put it:

> Through Gay Par-ee! Gay Par-ee!
> Four silly Britishers out upon the spree!
> Promenading – Boulevarding,
> Simply on the spree!
> Dainty damsels, tasty ma'amsells,
> May I kiss you? – *Oui!*
> I and Tom, and Dick, and Harry,
> Out in Par-ee, good old Par-ee! Gay Par-ee![56]

Femmes fatales, flânerie, dodgy French and (mock) remorse all appear in 'Gay Paree' songs of the 1890s and early 1900s. Another 'Four gay Englishmen with lots of L. S. D. [pounds, shillings and pence]' hit 'Pareé' [sic] in the Charles Deane song 'Four Englishmen in Paree', and ramble through the boulevards, 'looking for something choice'. The rest of their trip is exactly the same as Tom, Dick and Harry's, except they manage to punch out the girls' madam as well as 'the silly frog' waiter.[57]

Those listening to Godfrey at the Tivoli did not have to travel far to enquire about arrangements for their own spree: the South East and Chatham Railway advertised their 'Paris and Back for 30s' package in the programme itself. Thirty shillings secured a third-class, fourteen-day open return via Folkestone and Boulogne. (First class returns cost fifty-eight shillings.) Passengers had a choice of two departures a day, and the journey took just nine hours. At roughly £85 in today's money, it was considerably cheaper than a flexible return on Eurostar (£250).[58] Even before factoring in accommodation and other costs, however, thirty shillings was nonetheless a significant sum of money, and most of Godfrey's audience would have had to content themselves with experiencing 'Gay Paree' in song or in displays of cancan on London stages.

When the cancan returned to London in 1896, transformed again, the response was mixed. Nini Pattes-en-l'air [Nini Feet in the Air] played at the Alhambra and other music halls as part of the Eglantine Troupe. Those in the know recognized that, this time around, the Parisian visitors were dressed differently, in skirts instead of shorts. But there was also a sense that what they were offering was nothing new for London audiences. As the music-hall correspondent to the weekly review *St Paul's*, 'Powder-Puff', noted: 'when Nini Patte en l'Air [*sic*] first came to us, her style of dancing was novel to those of us who knew not our Paris. But since she was here last, acrobatic dancers have ceased to be strangers to us.'[59] Although Arthur Symons had noted somewhat breathlessly of the *chahut* that 'even in Paris you must be somewhat ultra-modern to appreciate it', in reality by the mid 1890s the cancan was no longer scandalous.[60] This was not due to any lack of would-be censors. The English social reformer Laura Ormiston Chant and her lobbyists were chivvying the newly established London County Council to take a more active role in regulating London stages. But they were more exercised by suggestive music-hall lyrics and especially by 'poses plastiques': shows in which women encased entirely in fleshings posed silently, their bodies immobile.[61]

Meanwhile in Paris the success of 'le music hall' attracted opposition from those who feared that it was eclipsing the style of music and performance found at *cabarets* and *cafés-concerts* or *caf'concs*, the intimate summertime resorts that took on the slightly soiled mantle of the *guinguettes*, as places where bohemians could mingle with the working class.[62] Whereas resorts such as the Grand Chaumière and Mabille had initially catered to similar appetites, in the 1860s they were cleaned up for a more self-consciously polite audience, as well as for the tourists, who demanded better food and a more navigable programme, as well as a clearer divide between the professionals, who performed, and the spectators, who simply watched. By the 1880s, *cabarets* had become a studied counter-cultural alternative to 'le music hall', which seemed in contrast overly slick, commercial and tacky. In 1869 the musical newspaper *Le Calino* noted the tendency to make the Eldorado and its ilk a scapegoat. The public should not, it continued, be thought fools if they deserted older venues in favour of the new variety stages, whose only sin was to try to move with the times rather than serve up entertainments that harked back to the *parades* (ramshackle fairground-style theatres) of the Champs Elysées in the previous century.[63]

This parting of the ways drew a clear line between *chanson* and variety, and arguably condemned them equally to a sort of living death. Rather than spawning new developments, the combative performance style of the singer Aristide Bruant was carefully protected as a more 'genuine' Parisian art form than music hall, even though Bruant's *cabaret artistique*, Le Chat Noir, was just a short walk from the Moulin Rouge.[64] Toulouse-Lautrec could find dynamism in both, but to a younger generation the slicker electric spectacle of the music hall held a greater appeal: it was commercial, yes, but as a hearty embrace of modernity rather than a nostalgic straitjacket. On his arrival in Paris in 1900, Picasso initially haunted the Lapin Agile *cabaret*, but soon abandoned it for the Olympia music hall, as his early Cubist collages indicate.[65]

By then the cancan celebrity as a breed was on her last legs. Solo performers or small troupes of two or four had been eclipsed by the arrival of larger troupes who would make cancan synonymous with fixed smiles and chorus-line monotony. The apparently random steps and kicks of the cancan had perhaps made this inevitable, by implying a separation between the upper and lower halves of the body, as if the movements of the cancan represented the mindless, spasmodic breakdown of a dancing machine. In the 1830s amateur cancan dancers had celebrated their steps as reflections of their own individuality. Unfortunately journalists as well as professionals like Rigolboche tended to describe 'their' cancan in terms of hysteria, hypnosis or electrification, as if it were a case of individual dancers being 'out of control', like runaway automata.[66]

Larger troupes came on the scene, either from London (the Tiller Girls) or, increasingly, from the United States (such the Sherry Girls and the Barrison Sisters). This meant that individual performers could be swopped in or out almost at whim, without the act suffering or changing in any way.[67] The viewer's focus seems to have moved from the face down to the legs. La Goulue (which loosely translates as 'Glug-Glug') and Bouffe Toujours ('Always Munching') took their names from the semi-amateur phase of cancan, when dancers being entertained by customers had to drink or eat fast and frequently, before the men who were footing the bill lost their enthusiasm. The names of Grille d'Egout ('Sewer Grate') and Nini Belle Dents ('Nini Nice Gnashers') were inspired by their teeth.

In the 1890s nicknames like Peau de Satin ('Satin Skin') or Nini La Belle En Cuisse ('Nini Pretty Thighs') became more common. The focus had changed from personal habits or facial features to parts of the body newly rendered visible by ever higher kicks. For all we or her contemporaries knew, Nini Belle Dents might have had pretty thighs as well. But nobody would have seen them when she was dancing, back in the 1860s. As cancan dancers revealed more of themselves, they lost their identity, becoming just elements in a line-up of what twentieth-century Parisian audiences simply called *les girls*. By 1900 the celebrity *danseuse* was gone. In 1902 the Moulin Rouge closed.

However, this iconic venue reopened in the 1920s, creating that combination of dining and spectating that has lingered into the twenty-first century. It went on rehashing the *revue à grand spectacle* of the sort that had been pioneered at the Folies Bergères back in 1886, but which did not become a regular feature there until 1902. Revues with titles like *Place aux Jeunes* (1886), *Plaisirs de Paris* (1889), *Vive Paris!* (1906) and *Paris Qui Danse* (1919) were quickly reduced to tired formulaic exercises that continue to this day, for the benefit of tourists and the modern business traveller.

Patriotic myths have led us to overlook the role of Anglo-French dialogue in the creation of 'French cancan'. Moral stereotypes and a commercial eye for the 'exotic' further encouraged both sides of this exchange to deny that they had learned anything from the other. London theatre managers like Hollingshead and decency campaigners like Lady Ormiston Chant agreed on one point: the British could never, ever have dreamed up something so risqué, or so fascinatingly seductive as the cancan. In 1874 the editor of *Vanity Fair*, Thomas Gibson Bowles, went so far as to claim that 'the word can-can cannot be translated into English without indecency . . . the dance is suggestive of the most indecent acts'.[68] Parisians for their part were happy enough to stable this cash-cow in Montmartre, secure in the knowledge that the so-called *vieux Montmartre* of Bruant was preserved, albeit in aspic, behind the electric glare of the Place Blanche.[69]

The fact that Parisians continue to refer to cancan as 'French cancan' (not *cancan français*) serves to underline the convoluted pedigree of this most 'Parisian' of dances, as well as the divide between Paris and Paree. The cancan is French, but not *français*. The label is, apparently, applied by and for non-Parisians. Thus London and Paris blamed each other: Paris was at fault for misdirecting London's youth with its 'harlots' quadrille';

London for turning the French 'national dance' into tourist schlock. They were both right. In just fifty years they had constructed an invisible city, one that was as seductive, glamorous and romantic as it was mechanized, commercial and high-tech. *Paris Qui Danse* – 'Gay Paree'.

FIG. 26: Unknown photographer, *Quai des Orfèvres/Rue de Jérusalem, c.* 1900.

CHAPTER FIVE

The Underworld

In 1878, Henry Vizetelly returned to London after an eventful sojourn in Paris as correspondent for the *Illustrated London News*. In addition to becoming an authority on French wine, Vizetelly had opted to remain in the French capital for the duration of the Franco-Prussian War, filing his stories by 'balloon post' during the siege of Paris. Vizetelly, who came from a family of London printers, had enjoyed great success as a newspaper and novel publisher in the 1850s. Now in London, he returned to publishing, and in 1880 launched a new series of 'Popular French Novels', which he translated himself, with the help of his son. Henry took pains to inform his readers in advance that, in addition to selecting the very best and newest French novels, he would also be careful to include 'only those works of an unobjectionable character'.[1] As we saw in Chapter 1, Vizetelly's translations of Zola in 1888 would land him in serious trouble, but for now Vizetelly focussed on French crime fiction. In 1880 he had issued a translation of Adolphe Belot's *Le Drame de la Rue de la Paix* (1868).

Belot's novel opens with the discovery of a violent murder, an apparently guilty spouse and a secretary at the *commissaire de police*, Vibert, who is convinced of the woman's innocence. Vibert has become tired of his desk

173

job and wants his patron, the Marquis de X, to get him transferred to the 'detective force'. He pictures himself out in the streets, hunting down criminals, wearing a disguise, a pair of handcuffs in his pocket. 'I run, I climb, I tumble down, I ride in carriages, or behind them, I go ten leagues in every direction, or I stop for twelve hours in the same place with my eyes riveted on a front door. Ah, what incomparable happiness!'[2]

Having gone to some expense having Vibert trained up for an honourable profession, the marquis is disappointed in his protégé. As far as he is concerned the only reason anyone would wish to become a detective would be as a means of practising vice while hypocritically pretending to combat it.[3] Yet he has put in a good word with the Prefect of Police, who has already agreed to transfer Vibert. The marquis will have nothing by way of thanks. Even as he consigns Vibert to life in the Rue de Jérusalem, where the headquarters of the Paris police was located, the marquis's mask of aristocratic hauteur slips slightly. He wants to be kept abreast of developments in the Rue de la Paix case. 'Adieu, dweller in the Rue de Jérusalem!' he signs off. 'Put yourself on the scent, hasten to discover the trail. I await your report.'[4]

Belot's was one of a raft of detective novels to be published in Paris in the 1860s. A playwright who turned to fiction late in his career, Belot did not specialize in the genre as did such authors as Émile Gaboriau and Fortuné du Boisgobey (the *nom de plume* of Fortuné Hippolyte Auguste Abraham-Dubois). It was Gaboriau above all who made the genre his own, creating the fictional detectives Tabaret and Monsieur Lecoq in *L'Affaire Lerouge* (1863). Lecoq went on to star in several more novels. Written at a blistering pace, Gaboriau's novels enjoyed a phenomenal success. Though the Franco-Prussian War was a serious blow to Lecoq's fortunes, in the 1860s his name was all over Paris – quite literally, thanks to an unprecedentedly aggressive teaser campaign on the part of his publisher. With Vizetelly's help, Lecoq arrived in London in 1881, the focus of a new series of 'Gaboriau's Sensational Novels', later expanded into 'Gaboriau and Du Boisgobey's Sensational Novels'.

Available for a shilling, novels like *The Slaves of Paris* and *The Severed*

Hand were 'railway fiction', bound in lurid red paper with a portrait of Gaboriau and a (reassuring?) endorsement from Prince Bismarck. *The Standard* positively gushed: 'The romances of Gaboriau and Du Boisgobey picture the marvellous Lecoq and other wonders of shrewdness, who piece together the elaborate details of the most complicated crimes, as Professor Owen, with the smallest bone as a foundation, could re-construct the most extraordinary animals.'[5] Gaboriau's name became synonymous with a new genre: 'detective fiction'.[6] Among Gaboriau's fans was a Scottish doctor struggling to find clients for his new practice in Portsmouth. In early 1884, Arthur Conan Doyle made a small study of best-selling thrillers to determine what the market wanted, before making his own contribution to the literature. The market wanted an English Lecoq. In 1886, in *Beeton's Christmas Annual*, they got Sherlock Holmes.

Holmes is, of course, much more than a fictional character. Indeed, many of his fans insist, as knowing or 'ironic believers', that he is not a fictional character at all.[7] He is synonymous with London, a city he left reluctantly, on the rare occasions that his sidekick Dr Watson persuaded him to pass the summer in the countryside for the good of his health. Outside the capital, Holmes was not himself. Nor was London London without its resident consulting detective. Yet the fictional detective emerged on the other side of the Channel: from earlier journalism and writing by Rétif de la Bretonne as well as from the works of hacks who penned the sensational memoirs of Vidocq, sometime criminal as well as head of the French secret police. Holmes's methodology and mannerisms, as well as many of the conventions observed in Dr Watson's reports of his cases, drew heavily on such Parisian precedents, which were scientific as well as literary. In exploring the birth of detective fiction in eighteenth- and nineteenth-century Paris and London, this chapter reconnects the calculating machine that is Holmes with what Watson called his 'Bohemian soul'.[8] It also traces the transformation of the city night from a menacing miasma haunted by prostitutes, students and other undesirables into a world of enchantment and thrilling adventure.

The Spectator-Owl

There has never been the rank of 'detective' in the French police. The word entered the French language (from the English) only in the 1870s.[9] Yet there are good reasons for tracing the origins of the detective story back to eighteenth-century Paris, to Rétif de la Bretonne, a remarkably prolific journalist whose work, like that of Gaboriau, is almost entirely forgotten today.[10] In 1788, on the eve of the Revolution, Rétif published *Les Nuits de Paris, ou la spectateur nocturne* (*Paris Nights, or the Nocturnal Spectator*), a series of short sketches describing the narrator's nocturnal adventures over 363 nights. Each chapter gives a detailed account of his wanderings through the city, in sufficient detail for us to trace the exact route taken by the 'Spectator-Owl' [Fig. 27]. Night by night he wanders at random, recording observations that slowly, but only partly, resolve into stories of crime, disorder, errant children and amorous intrigue. Rétif would later add two more volumes, entitled *La Semaine Nocturne: Sept Nuits de Paris* (*The Nocturnal Week: Seven Nights in Paris*), to the original fourteen.[11]

As the 'Spectator' moniker indicates, Rétif was an Anglophile familiar with Addison's *Spectator* and other works of English literature, a genre that was highly admired in the decades before the Revolution.[12] *Les Nuits de Paris* may have been published in London.[13] The idea of organizing the text by numbered nights echoes Edward Young's poem *The Complaint: or, Night-Thoughts on Life, Death and Immortality*, which was published in a French translation by Pierre Le Tourneur in 1769. *Les Nuits de Paris* was in prose, rather than verse, however, and though it certainly dwelled on mortality at times, it ranged much more widely.

As the introduction made plain, the Spectator-Owl saw himself as a guardian of the public, wandering alone through the shadows of the immense city, the unrecognized protector of the common interest. Whilst the narrator is certainly a police detective, this is 'police' in the eighteenth-century sense, which is explored in the introduction. There are rants

FIG. 27: Anon., Frontispiece to Rétif de la Bretonne, *Les Nuits de Paris*, 1789.

against tax-farmers, carriages, the lack of public conveniences and the demoralizing effects on young girls of *parades*. But the writer's wonder at the city's variety and size, at its pull on country-dwellers, his sensitivity to lighting effects and the way in which an observation made one night illuminates one made several nights later, all create a mood of urban mystery that is entirely novel. Although the 'Spectator-Owl' poses as a disinterested bourgeois, it has been suggested that Rétif himself may have been a police spy (or *mouchard*). Whatever the case, like Mercier and, later, Holmes, the Spectator-Owl is a supreme observer, a 'meddler', a 'busybody'.[14]

There is a sense of vicarious suffering common to all detectives. The detective confronts scenes we feel we too ought by rights to confront, because we acknowledge that those scenes are the flip- or night-side of that web of exchange that serves our every need.[15] At the very least we recognize that because we are citizens (*concitoyens*), it is incumbent on us to do something about the evil that threatens to ensnare our fellow men. Where we should act ourselves, we send the detective to observe and to act on our behalf. Like Vibert's jaded marquis, these are facets of urban life that we avoid as morally or physically harmful. But we long to know the truth behind the mystery before everybody else.

In Rétif this vicarious suffering is imbued with the enlightened idealism familiar from the first three years of the Revolution. He is appealing to us as *concitoyens*. Thus he argues that it would be better if law-abiding local residents got up their own nightly patrols, rather than leave the city to the mercy of criminals, prostitutes and corrupt professional constables (*exempts*).[16] Though he can rely on us, as good bourgeois, all of us are perched on the volcano of a dangerous underclass. The Spectator-Owl knows this class better than anybody else can. Whereas their employers see only their public faces, 'I live among them and hear them just as they speak among themselves. Hence I know how important it is to stop any display of excitement, however innocent or noble its cause may seem to be, and never to let the common people [*peuple*] act.'[17] *Les Nuits de*

Paris was printed in early November 1788. In less than a year the Bastille would be stormed.

As Mercier had noted playfully in his *Parallèle*, the Parisian could never really enjoy the political debate that formed such a big part of London's coffee-house culture because he always suspected that there was a *mouchard* listening in who might be taking notes of what he said.[18] The police spy cast a long shadow in Paris in the three decades before the Revolution. Though much more organized and militarized than the patchwork of parish watch committees that maintained public order in London, the forces controlled by Lieutenant-General of Police Sartine and his successor Lenoir (in office 1759–74 and 1774–90 respectively) were not massive. Spies like Jean-Baptiste Meusnier certainly existed, but were nowhere near as powerful as people imagined.[19]

As in the German Democratic Republic, so in *ancien régime* France, individuals never knew whether the person who struck up a conversation with them in a *cabaret* or a *guinguette* was a spy or whether their mail was being intercepted. Attempts by the Paris police to organize the rendition of a rogue French diplomat from London in 1768 ensured that the Paris police and the Bastille prison enjoyed almost as terrible a reputation in the English capital as they did in the French.[20] Far from seeking to quell such scaremongering, Lenoir admitted that he positively encouraged it.[21] Phantom *mouchards* were a welcome addition to his force: they did not require salaries and could not be bribed.

Such surveillance helped keep Paris stable, in the short term. In the long term, popular fears of the spy, of the Bastille and of *lettres de cachet* (royal warrants ordering the exile or incarceration of an individual) undermined the regime. Even genuine attempts at reform of the monarchy were widely misconstrued as a result of the suspicion sown by such police measures. Attempts to liberalize the grain trade led to rumours of a 'famine pact', with the king supposedly scheming to starve his own subjects. In such a climate it was impossible for Rétif's Spectator-Owl to present himself to his readers as an actual member of Lenoir's secret police. Only after the Revolution could the city's inhabitants imagine themselves cheering on a member of the Paris police. Even then, this support came about in a very strange manner.

Making the Night Visible

Rétif was nonetheless ahead of his time in the way he celebrated the city night in aesthetic terms. He noted how newly installed street lamps or *réverbères* 'shape, but do not eliminate these shadows, they make them even more striking: it's the chiaroscuro of the Old Masters!'[22] Literary or artistic representations of the city streets at night are very rare in the eighteenth century. There were firework displays, of course, but these were restricted to royal or ecclesiastic festivities until the 1760s when the 'Wauxhalls' described in the previous chapter brought them to a new public.[23] Accidental incinerations of theatres or other large buildings were spectacles of a different kind, but no less memorable and worthy of depiction, as with the fire at the Hôtel-Dieu in 1772.[24] These were exceptional events and disasters, however. For the most part the urban night wasn't just stygian, it was invisible. It wasn't that city-dwellers feared the interval between dusk and dawn (though some did); it simply did not exist for them. It was dead time, a void. One of the great untold stories of metropolitan life is its colonization of the hours of darkness, a story that can be touched on only in passing here.[25] This was not, as Rétif acknowledged, a case of improvements in street lighting eliminating the darkness. Quite the contrary.

Lighting made the nocturnal visible for the first time, and not just for *flâneurs* and detectives. By 1710, Steele could already see how London's night was being appropriated by the 'polite' world, with its routs, masquerades and glittering pleasure gardens, even if people feared being attacked by thugs or 'mohocks' on the way home.[26] Two years later it was possible for *The Spectator* to give an extended account of a twenty-four-hour *flânerie* undertaken by Mr Spectator. In 1738, William Hogarth published a series of engravings entitled *The Times of Day* [Fig. 28], celebrating London as a city that never sleeps.[27] Parisians by contrast did not see much worth depicting in their streets – at least, they didn't in 1738.[28] Yet illustrations of this kind would not have been possible without the street lights that were initially installed in the late seventeenth century and steadily improved over the course of the eighteenth.

FIG. 28: William Hogarth, *Night* from *The Times of the Day*, 1738.

If the result of improvements in street lighting was to make the urban night both visible and pleasurable rather than invisible and frightening, these effects were partly unplanned. City-wide street lighting was originally intended to make it easier for the night watch to patrol and enforce the nine o'clock curfew (ten o'clock in summer). The curfew, which had been in place since at least the thirteenth century, was signalled in medieval London and Paris by the ringing of a bell, whereupon taverns and *cabarets* were supposed to close. Householders were duty-bound to hang a candle in a lanthorn by their door (in London) or above their first-floor windows (in Paris) on moonless winter nights.[29] As the name suggests, these devices were made, not of glass, but of horn. They shed little light and did not last more than a few hours. Nor did they need to, being designed to help people find their way home in the hours between dusk and curfew.[30]

Previously the city night had been the preserve of students, apprentices and prostitutes, the first two groups providing the last with much of their custom.[31] Their nocturnal activity confirmed these young men's position on the edge of an otherwise regimented society. Although the hours of darkness could seem more tolerant and even democratic, this distinction was marginal, and 'night walking' was a crime. There was always the risk of running into the watch, who were likely to pick up anyone found out after curfew without a lantern and a good story to explain themselves.[32] While male night walkers could talk themselves out of trouble, females walking the streets were assumed to be prostitutes. They were likely to be brought before a magistrate for further examination and possibly incarceration: in the prison of the Châtelet (in Paris) or in one of five night prisons or compters (in London).[33]

Though the rules were similar, the level and means of enforcement differed in the two capitals. In Paris the watch was an armed paramilitary force, the *guet*, which in 1719 consisted of 139 archers (one hundred on foot, the remainder mounted). The Garde de Paris (forty-three horse, at least initially) was established in 1666, and was also charged with patrolling the streets at night.[34] The night watch of London was a civilian force, unmounted and unarmed, apart from some rusty halberds, which few actually possessed.[35] Whereas the *guet* was paid by the king, London's night watch was made up of householders following a rota (like jury service): each night, citizens met at a pre-arranged spot to patrol their own neighbourhoods, wearing their own clothes. In addition to rounding up night walkers, the watch checked that doors of houses and shops were shut, and also cried the hours. The contrast between militarized Paris and free London seems sharp enough. Whereas the curfew remained in force in eighteenth-century Paris, in London it was widely flouted. In 1660 many shops were open until 10 p.m., and many taverns even later.[36]

On closer inspection, however, the picture becomes more complicated. The Parisian authorities tried using a plain-clothes force. In 1740, Police Lieutenant d'Argenson experimented with patrols of fifteen plain-clothes men led by an inspector; 1775 saw the introduction of *patrouilles grises*, made up of a sergeant from the Châtelet and *gardes* in civilian clothes.[37] Far from being model citizens, in the late seventeenth century the vast majority of Londoners were paying substitutes to carry out their duties for them. In 1696 only one of the City's wards could claim to have the stipulated number of watchmen on duty. Those who had showed up were 'decrepit, superannuated wretches' (according to Daniel Defoe), who knocked off early.[38] Though Acts of 1735–6 affecting the cities of both London and Westminster raised levels of pay, the stock image of the watchman or 'charley' as a dopey old codger survived up to the creation of the Metropolitan Police in 1829. The Regency bucks of Piers Egan's *Life in London* (1821) seem to have found knocking over their watch-stands (with 'charley' inside) was as much fun as the 'mohocks' had a century before.[39]

Breaking street lights was another popular way such dandies could reclaim the night, a source of nocturnal amusement that dates back to the first city-wide lighting schemes. In 1667 the ordinance that established the *Lieutenance de police* in Paris ordered the setting up of 3,000 candle lanterns.

This system was funded by the *taxe des boues et lanternes* (which funded street cleaning as well as lighting). The new lights were suspended from ropes above the middle of the street, being lowered by pulleys for lighting and cleaning. They were to remain lit until 2 a.m. between 20 October and 31 March (i.e. Michaelmas to Lady Day). The number of lanterns had increased to more than 5,700 by 1729 and were just shy of 7,000 in 1770.[40] Single candles shed little light, however, and often blew out.[41] Since the 1670s, London 'projectors' like Richard Reeves and Samuel Hutchinson had been hawking designs for more powerful oil lamps. In 1695 the Corporation of London agreed to sell to the Light Royal Company (for £600) exclusive rights to put up oil lights within the City of London, for twenty-one years. Lamps were to be no more than thirty yards apart on main streets, thirty-five on lesser ones, and the Company was empowered to collect fines from householders who did not light up. Around 1,000 Light Royals were installed in the City, which encouraged neighbourhoods in Westminster to adopt similar lamps. The Lighting Act of 1736 added a rating scheme based on the assessed value of all houses, extending the hours of lighting and narrowing the prescribed distance between lamps.[42] In 1739 there were 4,825 lamps in the City's twenty-six wards, maintained by seventeen contractors.

The twenty years after 1765 saw Paris make the switch from wax to oil, with the introduction of oil-powered reflector lamps or *réverbères*, one of the most talked-about municipal improvements in the capital during the eighteenth century.[43] Powered by smelly tripe oil and hung over the middle of the street thirty *toises* (about 200 feet) apart, the hexagonal *réverbères* had between two and four wicks. There was a commissioner and an inspector in each *quartier* to check that they were working properly, which was not very often.[44] By 1790 there were 3,783 of them, rising slowly to 5,123 in 1828.[45] In both London and Paris, 'link-boys' or *porte-falots* continued to make a good living by carrying torches or lanterns with which to light the inhabitants' way home. That these urchins continued working well into the nineteenth century suggests that the illumination of the city was far from complete.[46] The *réverbères* nonetheless inspired the first depictions ever made of the city at night.

Two paintings of Paris streets illumined during the hours of darkness, by the Lille artist Henri Joseph Van Blarenberghe, allow us to see some of the effects of the *réverbères*. One shows a police raid on a brothel located in a street without *réverbères*; the other (incomplete) shows a scene in the Rue St Honoré, lit by *réverbères*, where there are prostitutes out on the sidewalks. The paintings are almost the same size, and may have been intended as an ironic comment on the effect (or, rather, the lack of effect) of the new lighting on the Parisian sex trade. In the raid scene [Fig. 29] we see few people apart from the police archers in blue, the officials in black and red and the coachmen. It is so dark that the only other vehicle out on

FIG. 29: Henri Joseph van Blarenberghe, *Descente de police la nuit*, c. 1780.

the streets (dimly visible in the background) is preceded by a man carrying a torch (just out of sight), who leads one of the two horses by the bridle. Were it not for the raid, there would be nothing to see.

Nothing nearly so dramatic has happened in the scene with the *réverbères* [Fig. 30], and yet there is plenty going on, with a real sense of people and vehicles flowing through the scene, rather than collecting around a rare and surprising interruption to the stillness of the city night. Several of the residents of the surrounding apartments are awake (in the raid scene they have been awoken by the ruckus outside, and still wear their nightcaps). Men and women are walking along the Rue St Honoré, and no less than four coaches travel down it; it is bright enough for the horses not to need anyone leading them. The buildings in the two scenes hardly differ, but a change has come over the city. Even if nobody stops to stare, the Paris night has become visible for the first time.

FIG. 30: Henri Joseph van Blarenberghe, *Scène de rue, c.* 1780.

The arrival of gas lighting in London in 1807 elicited many of the same responses as had the arrival of the *réverbères*: wonder, as well as ironic complaints that they would be bad for prostitutes. 'If this light is not put a stop to,' wails one trollop in Thomas Rowlandson's 1809 print, *A Peep at the Gas Lights*, 'we must give up our business. We may as well shut up shop.'[47] Unfortunately Rowlandson has made no attempt to depict the resulting light effects, as Blarenberghe had. Instead he shows the lights during the day, when, of course, they were not lit. With the notable exception of pleasure gardens, there are few depictions of London at night from this period.

With the advent of gas London streets became brighter; by 1815 thirty miles of gas pipes had been laid. The first commercial attempt to install gaslights in Paris came a cropper in 1819; it was only ten years later that the Rue de la Paix and the Rue de Castiglione became the first streets there to be gaslit.[48] As we have seen, however, the perception and the use of the city night had surprisingly little to do with the actual level of illumination achieved at any given point in time. Almost a century passed before anyone attempted to match the night walking escapades of Mr Spectator and the Spectator-Owl. In 1851, George Augustus Sala wrote 'The Key of the Street', which appeared in Dickens's popular middle-class periodical *Household Words*. Sala's account of how he passed the hours in London between midnight and 8 a.m. launched his career as a journalist, and inspired later works on the nocturnal city, such as his *Twice Round the Clock* (1858) and *Gaslight and Daylight* (1859). In Paris, Gérard de Nerval decided to see what would happen if he tried to spend the night out on the streets, if he could write about his own city the same way Sala had about London. Published as *Les Nuits d'Octobre* ('October Nights', 1852), the experiment was far from successful. The narrator and a friend struggle to work out where they can go that is open late. The two start reminiscing about the splendour of London nights, and wondering why their capital can't be more like its fellow. 'But why,' the narrator asks in despair, 'isn't it here like it is in London. A great capital city should never sleep, right?'[49]

Vidocq, the French Police Spy

François-Eugène Vidocq was born in Arras, the son of a baker, in 1775. According to his memoirs, from a young age he showed a proclivity for thievery and double-dealing, funding wild debauches by stealing from the till of his humble family's bread shop. Confined for a short period at his father's request in the prison of Les Baudets, Vidocq (that of his *Mémoires*, at least) spurns this opportunity to reflect and mend his ways. Set free, he lures his mother out of the house on a pretext, robs the family home and runs away. He plans to sail for the New World, only to be robbed himself. Penniless, he joins a circus. Starting off as a mere lamplighter, he subsequently secures permission to train as an acrobat. When he shows too little aptitude for tumbling, however, he is given the job of playing a 'South Sea cannibal'. Vidocq refuses to carry out the show-stopping finale, in which the 'cannibal' eats a live cockerel, and is dismissed. At this point the Prodigal Son returns home to a surprisingly warm welcome.

Old habits die hard, however. After several binges Vidocq joins the Bourbon Regiment. He deserts, but only after having fought nobly under General Dumouriez against the Austrians at the Battle of Jémappes (6 November 1792). After the battle Vidocq crosses over to the Austrian side, feigns illness and is invalided to Louvain, where he becomes a fencing master. He then returns to Arras, a city now caught up in the bloody patriotic fervour of Revolution. Incarcerated in Les Baudets for a second time, he now finds himself in the company of aristocrats and suspected confederates of the Austrians. Arras, after all, is perilously close to the front line. It seems that Vidocq's happy-go-lucky career might be at an end, but he survives. His career now takes him on a tour of various prisons, starting with St Peter's Tower in Lille, ending in La Force (in Paris) and taking in the hulks at Brest along the way. Time after time he climbs, jumps or tunnels his way to freedom. Pressed into the Dutch navy, Vidocq is one moment being charged with plotting a mutiny and the next promoted to bombardier. Having escaped the galleys, he successfully traverses a battle-scarred landscape dressed as a nun.

This abridged account gives something of the flavour of Vidocq's flamboyant persona, even if many details ring hollow. In the absence of documentation or scholarly attention, our main source for Vidocq's life is his four-volume *Mémoires*, published in 1828–9.[50] Although the details are not clear, Vidocq's publisher, Tenon, had another writer, Émile Morice, work up volume one from notes and information supplied by Vidocq.[51] Morice's Vidocq rarely pauses to reflect on his actions; he and all the other characters have little depth. Morice was clearly borrowing from the picaresque novel tradition, and the English reader is repeatedly reminded of the equally incredible adventures of Tobias Smollett's heroes, such as Roderick Random, or the real-life thief-taker Jonathan Wild.[52] French precedents could be found for the tales of daring heists that built up around the highwayman Cartouche and Louis Mandrin, who led a small army of smugglers in the 1750s. But whereas Wild was hanged and both Cartouche and Mandrin were broken on the wheel, Vidocq died in his bed in 1857, aged eighty-two.

Louis-François L'Héritier took over for the later volumes. A hack writer who wrote a novel and play adaptations as well as works of military and revolutionary history, L'Héritier made Vidocq's memoirs a runaway success.[53] The *Mémoires* nonetheless have a disjointed feel. The first fifteen chapters are fast-paced and racy, with constant changes of scene. Though they form a significant part of the *Mémoires*, ultimately these adventures are a back story to Vidocq's career in the Sûreté, where he made his name as a poacher-turned-gamekeeper. Officially established in 1812 as a branch of the Préfecture de Police (itself established in 1800), the Sûreté was renamed a year later by Napoleon as the state security service, the Sûreté Nationale. Vidocq led a squad of ex-convict detectives within the Sûreté from 1812 to 1827, based at 6, Rue de St-Anne, a building behind, but distinct from, the

Préfecture in the Rue de Jérusalem. In 1832 he returned to head what was now officially known as the Brigade de Sûreté.[54]

Vidocq was not above the law, however, and he spent several periods in prison. Just a few months after his return in 1832, he was forced to resign his commission and the Sûreté was reorganized. Between August 1842 and July 1843 he was held in the prison of the Conciergerie, charged and then convicted of extortion, having been arrested during a massive raid on Sûreté headquarters by the police. (The conviction was quashed on appeal, in a trial that lasted a matter of minutes.) This episode does not seem to have harmed his reputation, and Vidocq is still celebrated as the first detective, the father of modern criminology, immortalized in his own lifetime by his friend Honoré de Balzac as Vautrin in the novel *Le Père Goriot* (1834–5). Vautrin was himself the subject of an 1840 melodrama staged on the Boulevard du Temple, one of a series of melodramas centred around bloody tales of murder, whose popularity helped make the avenue into the 'Boulevard du Crime'. Vidocq even wrote a melodrama himself.

In contrast to the paper-thin characterization of the first volume, L'Héritier's Vidocq of the later volumes is a somewhat more rounded and sympathetic figure. Having escaped from yet another prison (in Douai), Vidocq sets himself up as a shopkeeper in Paris, only to find himself pushed into fencing goods for his underworld friends, who were apparently blackmailing him. Dragged back into a life of crime, Vidocq goes into hiding in the capital, before a dramatic rooftop arrest in the Rue Tiquetonne leads to yet another spell in La Force. Vidocq turns informer, making good use of his considerable fame and popularity among the inmates of Parisian prisons as well as among the thieves' dens of the Barrières de la Courtille, du Combart and Menilmontant.

In the words L'Héritier put in Vidocq's mouth we can recognize the voice of Rétif's Spectator-Owl, of the detective. The scene in which Vidocq describes how he infiltrated the dankest criminal dens is characteristic, lauding his own skill at worming his way into the confidence of 'this herd of wretches'. They inform him of their plans in advance, allowing him to arrange for their arrest.[55] Vidocq initially works alone. Impressed by his results, however, by 1812 senior police commissioners have placed three inspectors under his command. Vidocq now begins to go after the big fish. The final volume of the *Mémoires* sees him adopt a more scientific approach, gathering the fruits of his years of experience into an analysis of distinct classes of criminal.

Even as the number of men under his command increases (to twelve by 1817), Vidocq continues to run with the hare and hunt with the hounds, regularly disguising himself as a petty thief in order to join criminals in their nightly exploits. The text is larded with passages of dialogue in thieves' argot, something readers clearly found fascinating. Argot dictionaries for bourgeois readers appeared hot on the heels of Vidocq's *Mémoires*, in rather the same way they had in the wake of John Gay's *The Beggar's Opera* a century earlier. Helpfully, Vidocq's own two-volume *Dictionnaire Argotique* had both a French–argot and an argot–French dictionary.[56] Armed with such knowledge, readers could imagine themselves befriending a party of low-lifes in a *guinguette* as smoothly as Vidocq does in his *Mémoires,* cursing the 'pigs' in fluent argot.[57]

Like Rétif, Vidocq's position as narrator and detective is ambivalent. Taken for criminals, both men are deeply shocked and offended at the slur on their characters, yet neither wishes to be yoked together with the authorities. Indeed, both men characterize the authorities as plodding, lazy and compromised by political clientage. Though they may complain about it (and complain they do), ultimately they wish to hunt alone. As we have noted, this tendency confirmed the traditional association of the Paris police with the Bastille, with political repression under the *ancien régime,* under the Terror, the Empire and the post-1815 Restoration. Almost a century after Mercier, Gaboriau's Parisian still imagines the police spy or *mouchard* lingering half asleep in the corner of a café, listening to the conversation going on around him.[58]

Much of Vidocq's work in the *Mémoires* is not strictly speaking detective work, as the omniscient hero knows the details of the crime before it is committed, rather than having to work it out afterwards.[59] Where he does come across a crime whose origins he does not know, Vidocq's methods and tools are surprisingly rudimentary, considering his reputation as the father of criminology. Vidocq captures the thief Hotot by his boots, linking them with footprints found at the scene of the crime, for example.[60] Such acts are exceptional, however. Vidocq's extraordinary powers are a product of his own courage and of his ability to disguise himself as a criminal. Of course, one might well conclude that Vidocq's mastery of this disguise was nothing of the kind: that the mask he wore was that of the detective, not the criminal. As his reputation grew, members of the public nonetheless flocked to him for advice, to the point that, after his second dismissal in 1832, Vidocq set up a private detective business, the Bureau des Renseignements Universels.[61]

Vidocq's memoirs appeared in English translation in 1828, the same year they were published in French. They were translated by William Maginn, an impecunious, inebriate Irish journalist and Tory pamphleteer.[62] In 1828, Maginn was in Paris working as correspondent for *The Representative,* a short-lived Tory newspaper. He was also hiding from his debtors. Though he remained there only a few years, Maginn clearly threw himself into the city's literary life. In addition to his work on Vidocq, he translated *La Physiologie du Goût,* Jean-Anthelme Brillat-Savarin's famous work of gastronomy, discussed in Chapter 3. He took pride in having learned Parisian thieves' argot during his stay, and his interest in crime clearly embraced London as well as Paris. The same year as his Vidocq translation, Maginn penned *The Red Barn* (1828), an anonymous account of the murder in 1827 of Maria Marten by her common-law husband, William Corder. This case was renowned because the location of Marten's hidden body (the barn) was supposedly revealed by means of a recurring dream.[63]

Causes célèbres like the Marten murder were grist to the literary mill in

1820s London, where eight- or sixteen-page 'penny-bloods' (blood-soaked 'true stories' of crime) offered a way for aspiring journalists and writers like George Augustus Sala to make a living. Maginn's Vidocq translation and his *Red Barn* were much longer works, but titillated the same appetite for horror. Even if the London public was hungry for a hero capable of tracking down those behind such outrages, it was hard to imagine such a figure operating in their city. There were admittedly the 'Bow Street Runners', set up by magistrate Henry Fielding in the winter of 1748/9, who enjoyed a small amount of funding from central government. Under Henry's successor and half-brother John, in the 1770s the Bow Street court collected and distributed information on criminals and their dens across the capital and much of Britain.

The 'Runners' continued to operate until 1839, but they were a small force of between six and a dozen volunteers: freelancers and former criminals. In the early years they struggled to distinguish themselves from semi-criminal thief-takers like Jonathan Wild, who were notorious for 'peaching' on fellow criminals in order to pocket the £40 reward (around £3,000 today) offered for convictions of burglars, coiners and highwaymen.[64] The Metropolitan Police Act of 1829 established the Metropolitan Police, but there were no equivalents to Vidocq in the London force, which consisted of five divisions with 144 constables in each. Only in 1842 was a 'Detective Department' of two inspectors and six sergeants created under Commissioner Sir Richard Mayne, manned by working-class men who had risen through the ranks. These detectives had a low profile until the 1890s, when several published their memoirs.[65]

The detective was thus primarily a Parisian figure. Maginn's translation spawned two melodramas that celebrated Vidocq. In 1829, Douglas William Jerrold's *Vidocq! the French Police Spy* was staged at the Coburg Theatre, where Jerrold was house dramatist. This two-act melodrama competed with the Surrey Theatre's production of *Vidocq, the French Police Spy*, by J. B. Buckstone. Both featured choruses of cheery galley slaves, lovelorn Parisian baker-boys and striking end-of-act tableaus in which everyone on stage is at daggers drawn. They present Vidocq as a French equivalent to Macheath, the hero of Gay's *The Beggar's Opera*, a lovable adventurer and reluctant bigamist.[66] Such was the success of these dramas that Vidocq travelled to London to exhibit himself in person, alongside a collection of chains and other criminal memorabilia, at the Cosmorama, Regent Street, in 1845–6.[67]

Cuvier's Anatomy of Crime

One of the few places Nerval can find company on his nocturnal wanderings in *Les Nuits d'Octobre* is on the Butte Montmartre. Here, long after the cafés have closed in the city below, he can find old quarrymen gathered around a bonfire. They tell him stories of helping the great natural historian Georges Cuvier in his geological researches, of the mysterious fossil creatures they have brought up from the bowels of the earth, silent witnesses of past 'revolutions'.[68] Author of the *Discours sur les révolutions de la surface du globe* (1825), Cuvier had been appointed Professor at the Musée d'Histoire Naturelle in the Jardin des Plantes in 1802. There he busied himself reconstructing fossil mammals. His job was rendered all the more challenging by these new creatures being dug out of local quarries. How were all these primordial victims to be classified into species, genus and all the other categories and subcategories of the Linnaean system? How could order be introduced in these chaotic, primeval catacombs?

Cuvier noted that his fellow palaeontologists had largely overlooked fossilized quadrupeds, preferring to classify shelled creatures and fishes, because they tended to be preserved in their entirety in fossil beds. The bones of quadruped mammals, in contrast, were usually scattered, the result of being eaten by predators or picked clean by scavengers. Confronted with a collection of bones jumbled together, palaeontologists could never be sure whether they had a complete skeleton. One way in which Cuvier simplified his task was by positing that nature was not a cloud of life without any structure, but organized around a limited number of basic blueprints. There were creatures designed around a backbone ('vertebrata'), or around a circular or radial plan ('radiata', like anemones) and so on. Each classificatory group had a central form or archetype.

It was believed that no creature could stray too far from this ideal form or type. Though this archetype might or might not be present as an actual species, like planets orbiting around a sun, all creatures were supposedly held in the gravitational pull of 'their' archetype. That mysterious, unsettling force that multiplied nature's forms, the origin of new species was confined within certain bounds. This apparent balance would prove ever harder to maintain, as creatures were dug up that refused to stay in their orbits. Dismissed as 'sports' (that is, mutant forms), these comets streaked across the tidy constellations of Cuvier's comparative anatomy. Though Charles Darwin would write the first sketches of his theory of speciation by natural selection in 1838, such was the strength of the static Cuvierite consensus that Darwin refrained from publishing his heresies until 1859.

In addition to archetypes Cuvier also made his classificatory job easier by positing that the organs, bones and musculature of any creature were connected by a series of relationships. These allowed the whole to be reconstructed from any one part. In 1825 he presented to his colleagues his 'principle of the correlation of forms' as a useful tool that would help unravel the mystery shrouding complex forms of extinct life.[69] Cuvier's principle and his powers of imaginary reconstruction of long-extinct life forms established his reputation. It was claimed that he could reconstruct an entire creature from a single bone or tooth. At his death in 1832, Cuvier was considered one of Europe's greatest men of science, even as his approach to the history of life on earth was coming under attack from the biologist Geoffroy Saint-Hilaire and the geologist Charles Lyell.

Whichever position one took, it was clear in the 1820s that Paris was the home of comparative anatomy and palaeontology. Compared to the Musée d'Histoire Naturelle, the dusty omnium gatherum of the British Museum and the chaotic Hunterian collection of the Royal College of Surgeons were a disgrace. In the face of a campaign for reform led by the radical editor of *The Lancet*, Thomas Wakley, the RCS set about putting its house in order. In 1827 it hired one of its youngest members, Richard Owen, aged just twenty-three, to bring to completion the long-awaited catalogue of the collection.[70] Over the following decade Owen established himself as a comparative anatomist, gradually abandoning his original plans to go to sea as a naval surgeon or set up in private practice. Appointed Hunterian Professor of Comparative Anatomy in 1836, Owen moved to the BM twenty years later, taking up the new post of superintendent of its natural history collections. By then Owen's status as 'the English Cuvier' was beyond question.

This excursus into comparative anatomy may appear tangential. Yet Cuvierite comparative anatomy, and particularly the principle of correlation of parts, provided the foundation for the science of detection as it was developed by Vidocq, by Gaboriau and, eventually, by Conan Doyle. 'It has frequently been the case,' Vidocq observed, 'that, by inspecting a single article of clothing, I was able to divine a thief's entire appearance, from head to foot, quicker than our celebrated Cuvier could have recognized an antideluvian animal (even a fossilized man) from two maxilla and a half-dozen vertebra.'[71] As *The Standard* noted, Gaboriau's Lecoq reconstructed crimes 'as Professor Owen, with the smallest bone as a foundation, could re-construct the most extraordinary animals'.[72] It is clear that Holmes is familiar with the work of Cuvier and other French men of science.[73] At one point he propounds a theory of human development similar to one developed by the embryologist Étienne Serres in the 1820s.[74]

Whenever Lecoq or Holmes reconstructs a criminal from his footprint, they are drawing on Cuvier's method. In his *Recherches sur les ossemens fossiles* (1812), Cuvier even described how the comparative anatomist could reconstruct an entire creature from nothing more than a footprint: that is, without having even the proverbial single tooth or bone.[75] Whether it was transmitted via Owen in London or via Conan Doyle's professor at Edinburgh University, the surgeon Joseph Bell, this science of detection was Parisian in origin.[76] This is why Edgar Allan Poe based his fictional detective, C. Auguste Dupin, in Paris, a city he never visited, rather than London, which he knew well.

Dupin is introduced in 'The Murders in the Rue Morgue' (1841) as a young man of reclusive, bookish habits with a private income, the last of what was once a wealthy line. The narrator proposes that the two take rooms together in the Faubourg St Germain, where they pass the days in reading and conversing behind closed shutters. They venture out only at night, on long walks, 'seeking amid the wild light and shadows of the populous city, that infinity of mental excitement which quiet observation can afford'.[77] Dupin is not a member of the police, though the Prefect of Police does consult him. Nor, apparently, does he work for money. Poe, who had clearly read Vidocq's *Memoirs*, has Dupin gently patronize Vidocq as 'a good guesser, and a persevering man'.[78]

Though the methodology advanced by Dupin is fascinating, the tales are very loosely structured. The city that forms the backdrop to these tales is barely sketched out. Around the same time French writers such as Eugène Sue and Paul Féval were rather more successful at creating a sense of the city as one criss-crossed with secret conspiracies that transcend boundaries of profession and class. Sue's *Les Mystères de Paris* (1842–3) was the most commercially successful of these, spawning a raft of imitators. These included *Les Mystères de Londres* (1844) by Féval, which successfully creates a mood of urban menace, presenting the city as a wilderness stalked by urban 'pathfinders': a conscious borrowing from Fenimore Cooper's *The Last of the Mohicans* and other popular novels of 'Red Indians'.[79]

Though these works did not feature detectives, professional or amateur, they did create certain narrative tropes that would survive into the second half of the century, as well as shaping how the city itself was represented in the works of Gaboriau and Conan Doyle. The overall mood is captured by the frontispiece to the 1845 English edition of *Mystères de Paris*, with its wizened wizard pulling back a curtain to reveal the moonlit metropolis. There are certainly parallels between the figures deployed by the French writers Féval, Sue and Alexandre Dumas in his *Mohicans de Paris* (1854) and those found in works of a similar vintage by Reynolds and Dickens.[80] In all these novels the denizens of the urban underworld are roughly divided into three classes. At one end are the redeemable elite, who so often turn out to be well-born victims of kidnappings. At the other lie an irredeemably evil minority who are rarely sketched out in any detail, but who can, in a few cases, take on a life of their own, as in the cases of Dickens's Daniel Quilp and Féval's Marquis de Rio-Santo.

The rest are stock figures. Their redemption is feasible, but the consistency with which, like parasites, they thrive off the respectable lends them such a charm that the narrator is content to take (and leave) them as he finds them. Sue's La Chourineur falls into this category. Plots are not character driven. Instead, characters are bounced around as circumstance (and the exigencies of writing in instalments, with audience reaction having its effect 'in real time') dictate. They have been described, justly, as urban fairy tales, and the contemporary reader cannot help but be struck by their insipidity.[81] Fabulous lost inheritances, chirpy street arabs and chases through gloomy streets would all find their place in the world of Holmes and, before him, Lecoq – together with, happily, much more promising material.[82]

'Monsieur Lecoq!'

On Wednesday, 15 April 1868, lurid posters began appearing on walls across Paris. These featured the name 'Monsieur Lecoq!' repeated three times, each iteration adding another exclamation mark. The following Tuesday large advertisements started to feature in the newspapers, with the same curious inscription. Since the 1840s, songs with a relentlessly repeated final syllable to every line had been driving Parisians to distraction. The repeated syllable or *scie* (as in 'saw') grated on the ear in an inane fashion, like the babbling of a child. In May a Lecoq song appeared, which took the '-oq/oc' sound as its *scie*.

Quel est donc ce Monsieur Lecoq?	Who is this Monsieur Lecoq?
Dit le buveur devant son bock	Asks the drinker with his bock
Ou le laboureur sur son soc,	The peasant behind his plow
Le matelot sur son grand foc	The sailor sitting on the jib
Ou le capucin sous son froc . . .	And the capuchin in his habit . . .[83]

Monsieur Lecoq was a fictional detective, and the posters, advertisement and song were part of a unprecedented campaign intended to create a buzz about Lecoq's adventures, which were about to be serialized in a Parisian newspaper. The promised date for the first chapter came, and went, without Lecoq appearing. Suspense was ramped up further. It was all a ruse, of course, intended to sell more copies of the newspaper in which Gaboriau's novel was to be published.

Born in 1832, Émile Gaboriau [Fig. 31] worked as a legal clerk and had a short military career before moving to Paris to live by his pen. As secretary to Féval, Gaboriau served his apprenticeship with a master of the school of *mystères*, but, unlike the older generation of writers, he chose to place a detective at the heart of his works.[84] His first novel, *L'Affaire Lerouge*, introduced two detectives: the elderly, independent consultant Tabaret and his pupil of twenty-five, Lecoq, a junior officer of the police, whose unusual methods regularly make him the butt of his colleagues' patronizing humour. Written in 1864, *L'Affaire Lerouge* was serialized in Moïse Millaud's *Le Soleil* between April and July 1866.

FIG. 31: Gillot, *Émile Gaboriau*, 1873.

Gaboriau's next five novels all took the younger Lecoq as their hero, starting with *Le Crime d'Orcival*, a mystery set in the Auvergne, which was serialized between the end of October 1866 and February 1867. The third novel, *Le Dossier No. 113*, began to appear the day after *Le Crime d'Orcival* finished. The fourth novel, *Les Esclaves de Paris*, started in *Le Soleil* in July 1867. A triple-decker, its third part finished in March 1868. Harried by Millaud, in twenty-four months Gaboriau had written four novels: three of them in two volumes, one in three. In 1869 he also wrote *Monsieur Lecoq*. It was a fearsome pace to sustain. Millaud was a consummate businessman, and now that Lecoq had established a following, he took the opportunity to serialize *L'Affaire Lerouge* all over again in 1869, this time in *Le Petit Journal*, complete with illustrations. Circulation shot up to 470,000, a record for the *Journal*. This is all the more impressive given that *L'Affaire Lerouge* had since been published as a book by Edouard Dentu. As Doyle would do later, Gaboriau took advantage of the fame of his crime fiction to cajole his publisher into taking on earlier work that he himself considered of greater literary merit. He was so fed up with Millaud's constant badgering, however, that he may even have welcomed the Franco-Prussian War, which brought the series to a halt.

By then novels featuring Lecoq had already been translated into German and published in Vienna and Berlin. A contract for an English translation was drawn up, but was not signed, again, one suspects, because of the war. Even so, at Gaboriau's death in 1873 there were a number of works remaining in manuscript, such as *La Corde au Cou* (in which the detective is a lawyer, Manuel Folgat) and several works in other genres. Several shorter pieces were published in 1876 as *Le Petit Vieux des Batignolles*.[85] Lecoq outlived his creator, with Fortuné Du Boisgobey's *La Vieillesse du M. Lecoq* appearing in 1878, again published by Dentu.

Out in the field Lecoq's skill at reconstructing events at a crime scene is remarkable. In *Monsieur Lecoq* the junior officer is left alone at a low *cabaret* in the fields beyond the Barrière d'Italie, where a Sûreté patrol has stumbled across the scene of a shoot-out that has left three dead. It is winter, and Lecoq takes advantage of the snow to identify who else was in the *cabaret*. To him the blanket of snow is a white page on which the guilty have written their crimes. From a man's footprints Lecoq establishes his age, dress and the fact that he wears a wedding ring.[86] Confronted with this and other examples of his 'long chains' of 'subtle observations', colleagues are incredulous, then bemused. Lecoq often strikes a lonely figure, as when he gazes out over the city of Paris, teeming with life under 'a slight haze, illumined by the red glare of the street lamps'.[87]

As Lecoq's fame spreads so he becomes more dependent on his talent for disguise.[88] This enables Gaboriau to set up fantastic set-pieces in which the criminals suddenly realize that Lecoq has discovered all. Like *L'Affaire Lerouge*, *Les Esclaves de Paris* revolves around the tragic consequences of the swopping of an aristocrat's legitimate and illegitimate children. The illegitimate son, Paul Violaine, escapes from the provincial orphanage in which he is placed and comes to Paris, hoping to work as a piano teacher. Ensconced in squalid rooms on the Rue de la Huchette, he joins forces with Mascarot, whose employment agency is the front for a massive blackmail ring. Mascarot has the guilty secrets of the entire city carefully recorded on little paper cards, and together he and Paul connive to destroy the true heir, André, a painter. Although Lecoq does not appear until page 187, he has been on the track of the blackmailers and establishes that a respectable banker, M. Martin-Rigal, the blackmailer Mascarot and Tantaine, a harmless old man who lives above Paul, are one and the same person.

Martin-Rigal/Mascarot/Tantaine is about to kill off his several false identities and escape with his ill-gotten gains when the final meeting of his gang at Martin-Rigal's well-appointed home is rudely interrupted by a banging noise outside. The evil mastermind goes to investigate, only to freeze, his arms outstretched.

> In the passage beyond stood a most respectable looking
> gentleman, wearing gold-rimmed spectacles, and behind
> him appeared a commissary of police, wearing his scarf of
> office, with half a dozen agents in the rear. The same name
> came to the lips of the three associates: 'Monsieur
> Lecoq!' And at the same time this terrible conviction
> entered their brains: 'We are lost!'

Lecoq advances, curious to inspect what lies before him. His expression is compared to that of a playwright watching the scene he has lovingly crafted performed on stage for the first time.[89] One of Mascarot's allies springs on another, accusing him of being an informant. A third quietly swallows a suicide pill. Mascarot is convicted and thrown in prison, where he loses his mind. André is restored to his dukedom and lives happily ever after.

Although there is still a fairy-tale element in Gaboriau's fiction, this remains in the background, with the the main focus being the detective and, to an extent, Paris itself. Gaboriau's city is a maelstrom into which the unfortunate disappear, apparently without trace, and where the evil come to assume new identities, the better to pursue their crimes.[90] As Dr Watson would later note of his own capital city, it was 'that great cesspool into which all the loungers and idlers of the Empire are irresistibly drained'.[91] Whereas Sherlock Holmes's cases are described from the perspective of this kindly veteran army doctor, however, Lecoq's are narrated by an anonymous third person. Gaboriau did not give his detective a sidekick to whom he could explain his methods – except once.

In June 1870, as rumours of war grew ever louder, a second series of posters appeared across Paris. These asked a certain M. J.-B. Casimir Godeuil to present himself at the offices of the *Petit Journal*. Who was this Godeuil? There was clearly something important at the heart of the mystery, because the posters kept going up all month. Finally, on 3 July the *Petit Journal* trumpeted that it 'had good news to impart to its readers. J.-B. CASIMIR GODEUIL IS FOUND!!' It was Millaud again, up to his old tricks, announcing the first instalment of the memoirs of a great detective. Though Gaboriau had abandoned Lecoq, Millaud had managed to persuade him to begin another detective series, starring the fictional detective Godeuil.[92]

The first instalment was serialized in the *Journal* between 8 and 19 July, the day on which France declared war on Prussia. Entitled 'Le Petit Vieux des Batignolles: un chapitre des memoires d'un detective' ('The little old man of Batignolles: a chapter from a detective's memoirs'), the story opens with Godeuil as a medical student aged twenty-three, living in the Rue Monsieur-le-Prince, near the École de Médecine. He becomes fascinated by Monsieur Méchinet, whose apartment is the other side of the hall. This being a Parisian apartment block, he has ample opportunity to note the odd hours at which his neighbour comes and goes, often in curious disguises. One night Méchinet knocks at Godeuil's door, asking him to dress a wound he has received. A kind of friendship begins. When

Méchinet is summoned by a mysterious message while he is playing a game of dominoes with Godeuil, the latter asks to accompany him, changing the course of his own life for ever.

The pair arrive at the scene of a murder, where Méchinet elbows his way through the surrounding crowd of gawpers. Inside a body lies on the floor in a pool of blood. The word 'MONIS' is scrawled in blood on one of the floorboards. The attending *commissaire* apologizes for calling Méchinet out, because he has already arrested the guilty man, the deceased's nephew, a man named Monistrol (identified by the victim's final scrawl, and by his own confession). When Méchinet refuses to take this cast-iron explanation as conclusive, the *commissaire* taunts him for his supposed obstreperousness.[93]

Of course, the scrawl is a red herring, the confession false and Méchinet is proven correct in the end. Thanks to Vizetelly's publication of an English translation in early 1886, Méchinet arrived on the scene just in time to help Arthur Conan Doyle, who wrote the manuscript of *A Study in Scarlet* in March of that year. As in *The Little Old Man of Batignolles*, Doyle has the murderer write a misleading word in his victim's blood. Once again the police officer gleefully points this out to the detective, who refuses to accept the latter's explanation of it. *A Study in Scarlet* may have borne Doyle's trademark, but there are signs implicating Gaboriau in this mystery. Though Gaboriau's death prevented him relating the further adventures of Méchinet, Doyle in a sense made that unnecessary, by assuming Gaboriau's mantle.

Born in Edinburgh in 1859, Arthur Ignatius Conan Doyle was one of nine children born to the artist Charles Doyle. The family's fortunes were in decline owing to the alcoholism of Arthur's father, who was reduced to drinking furniture polish or thieving from his own children in order to feed his habit. Thankfully Arthur's uncles provided the means for him to attend various boarding schools, notably the Jesuit academy Stonyhurst. In 1876 he entered medical school in Edinburgh, having briefly visited both London and Paris over the course of the preceding two years. Doyle subsequently jobbed in several general practices in Sheffield, Aston and Plymouth before moving to Bush Villas, Portsmouth, in 1882. He had been submitting short stories to *Chambers' Journal* and other periodicals for a few years, with mixed results.

With time on his hands in Portsmouth as he waited for clients to this, his first attempt at a general practice of his own, Doyle now had a stab at writing a novel. Confined to bed in early 1884 by a bladder infection, he set to reading best-sellers, with a view to working out what publishers wanted. By this point 'Gaboriau's Sensational Novels' [Fig. 32] had been selling

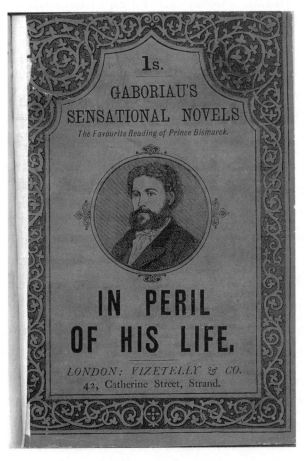

FIG. 32: Cover of the Vizetelly edition of Gaboriau, *In Peril of His Life, 1884.*

well for three years.[94] There was a precedent for translating Gaboriau into an English context, in the shape of James Hain Friswell, a journalist and essayist from the stable of G. A. Sala. In 1884, Vizetelly issued Friswell's rip-off of *L'Affaire Lerouge* in paperback, just in time for Doyle to read it.[95]

Confronted with a crime scene, both Gaboriau's Lecoq and Doyle's Holmes are eager to get the arrogant, bumbling Gévrol/Lestrade out of the way, in order to leave themselves a clear field in which to work. This work involves entering a quasi-trancelike state, albeit marked by feverish, bestial activity.[96] Their observations complete, both detectives snap out of this state as quickly as they entered it, declaring that they have solved the mystery. They do not, however, share the explanation with the police, with their companions, or with us.

Like Lecoq and Méchinet, Holmes regularly goes for long periods without food or sleep, damns the official police with faint praise and is able to disconnect his mind totally from a case when further cogitation is bootless. Lecoq, Méchinet and Holmes work for love of the art, rather than for money. They make occasional allusions to the great criminals they might have been, a fascinating counter-factual, which itself reflects a sense that they lack an overarching moral framework, that they remain indifferent to the broader repercussions of what they do.[97] Tabaret, Lecoq's elderly mentor, at one point moans that 'the race of great criminals is dying out', leaving 'a crowd of low offenders who are not worth the shoe-leather expended in pursuing them . . . It is enough to disgust a detective, upon my word.' Holmes would have said 'amen' to that.[98]

This is not to say that Doyle lifted material from Gaboriau in anything like the crude fashion Friswell had done.[99] Apart from the three longer stories the Holmes tales are remarkably compact, with short cuts that are almost crude taken at points to save words. Though written almost as quickly, Gaboriau's works were multi-volume novels, with extensive back stories of the kind Doyle tried only once, in *A Study in Scarlet,* where we suddenly find ourselves transported to the sinister Mormon theocracy of Utah.[100]

Lecoq has a romantic past and Méchinet is married, whereas Holmes is uninterested in love and leaves women, whom he finds inscrutable (with one exception), to Watson. Doyle borrowed from Poe's Dupin as well as from Gaboriau.[101]

Though Holmes owed a sizeable debt to Vidocq and Gaboriau, he could be somewhat ungrateful. In the opening pages of *A Study in Scarlet*, Watson, like the narrators of *L'Affaire Lerouge* and *The Little Old Man of Batignolles* before him, endeavours to work out what profession or activity might explain Holmes's curious habits. Watson has clearly read Vidocq and Gaboriau. However, when he tells Holmes of his conjecture that the latter is a detective *à la* Lecoq, Holmes takes it as an insult. Referring to *Monsieur Lecoq*, Holmes sneers that he could have solved the case much faster. 'I could have done it in twenty-four hours. Lecoq took six months or so. It might be made a text-book for detectives to teach them what to avoid.'[102]

Like Lecoq, Holmes has a showman's pleasure in the sudden 'reveal'. This narrative conceit is so common in twentieth-century detective fiction that it is unnecessary to cite individual examples from Hercule Poirot, Father Brown or Miss Marple. Even the irritation of characters summoned to observe such a scene has become part of the device ('Why have you called us all here, Poirot?'). Such moments were a gift to Doyle's illustrator, Sidney Paget, a textual *tableau vivant* similar to those exhibited at the Oxford and other West End music halls in the 1880s and 1890s. When the cabman carrying Holmes's luggage into his sitting room in *A Study in Scarlet* is identified by the detective as the murderer Jefferson Hope, the assembled company perform like a well-trained troupe of music-hall performers. 'For a second or two we might have been a group of statues,' Watson recalls. 'Then, with an inarticulate roar of fury, the prisoner wrenched himself free from Holmes's grasp and hurled himself through the window.'[103]

A key element that Doyle and his successors derived from Gaboriau was the tension between magic and reality. On the one hand the reader has a 'double-minded' desire to believe in an omniscient detective. We don't simply find our faith in the detective reassuring or comforting, we derive actual pleasure from it. In the traditional theological context, faith is something that is given or withheld by a divine power. It does not lie in the power of mortals. In this specific context, however, we consciously seek to subscribe to this willed belief in a being with 'miraculous' powers. We want to be in this state of nonage, even though we know there is, as Watson notes, 'a touch of charlatanism in it'.[104] Another part of us, however, wants to have the 'trick' explained, and hence demystified. Like Lerouge, Holmes can seem reluctant to offer such explanations, knowing full well that they can leave him looking like 'a very ordinary individual'.[105]

Though the connections that link a battered hat with a daring jewel heist are superficial, 'hidden in plain sight', they can be seen at a glance only fleetingly, even by a detective with second sight. As Dupin puts it, these facts are discerned most clearly out of the corner of one's eye, 'in a sidelong way', rather than full on.[106] 'The things that stare us in the face,' Méchinet observes, 'are frequently those that most easily escape our view.'[107] Detective fiction thus invests all aspects of daily life with a magic that can be glimpsed for a second, just in passing, the way a *flâneur* would see it. Even if the source of that excitement and that meaning are obscure, the mundane clutter of the modern city becomes exciting and deeply meaningful in the process.

The journey from Rétif's 'Spectator-Owl' to Doyle's Holmes did not merely span two cities, it spanned a century. Given the reputation held by the *mouchard* in late eighteenth-century Paris, it is striking that such a reassuring figure of just retribution should have emerged from the French capital, rather than the British, which – eventually – adopted the London bobby as a patriotic figure. For the Parisian police force, it was a remarkable story of redemption, from despised political spy of the *ancien régime* to protector of the honest bourgeoisie and keeper of the city's secrets.

In detective fiction the metropolis is a palimpsest. At first glance it is incomprehensible. If surveyed from a distance, it is impossible to understand except as a 'megacity', made up of several different cities, each with their own morals, etiquette, styles of architecture, dress and language. As one of Gaboriau's detectives notes, what is disgraceful in the Rue de Lécluse is quite proper in the Rue Vivienne.[108] Like our alter ego in the Holmes stories, Dr Watson, the middle-class reader is at home in just one of these cities. We are aware of the other cities' existence, but only dimly, at second hand. Part of us finds it difficult to imagine how life can go on so differently in places that, measured in miles, are not widely separated. As *Blackwood's Magazine* pointed out in 1825, addressing the slums around Lambeth's Webber Row, 'who can be the people – of what means, or order, that reside here? A fact, of which the dweller two miles off knows no more than the inhabitant of Kamschatka!'[109] The mutual indifference of strangers has, of course, always been part of urban life but it remains deeply unsettling, and becomes all the more so the bigger the city becomes.

We are fascinated by detectives because they decipher the metropolis, reading it as a coherent whole, locating the hidden connections that unite different neighbourhoods, ranks and professions. Though the web is one of violent crime, it is nonetheless reassuring to know that 'there's the scarlet thread of murder running through the colorless skein of life', precisely because as we unravel it we are bringing justice to bear on evil.[110] There is something comforting in understanding that the mundane trivia of our everyday lives have a meaning, that there is a signal in the white noise that forms the constant background to city life. Just as Baudelaire's *flâneur* 'distills the eternal from the transitory', so the detective points out 'the great issues that may hang from a boot-lace'.[111] As Holmes put it, 'My life is spent in one long effort to escape from the commonplaces of existence.'[112] Far from solving the mysteries of the city by means of scientific investigation, the detective re-enchants it for us. He creates mystery.

FIG. 33: Charles Heath after A. C. Pugin, 'General View of Paris',
from *Paris and its Environs*, 1830.

CHAPTER SIX

Dead and Buried

In 1863, Charles Dickens paid a visit to Kensal Green Cemetery, located a mile north-west of Paddington, between the Harrow Road and the Grand Union Canal. As he noted in his account in *All the Year Round*, the French believed that the English were driven by melancholy and spleen to make cemeteries their 'principal promenades'. For his part, Dickens agreed, confessing that he enjoyed wandering in churchyards. There the oppressor and the oppressed, the servant and the master, the great and the small lay together, united by death. 'Of the English Cemetery, however, I knew nothing, until, on a blazing July afternoon, I set out for Kensal Green.'[1]

Unlike graveyards, which surrounded a parish church in the heart of the city, cemeteries were located outside its confines, and were not necessarily associated with a single parish community. Though Kensal Green had opened as London's first cemetery in 1832, for Dickens the concept and even the word itself were still novel. Admittedly, Roman London had three cemeteries, all on the north side of the river, located next to main roads. The east cemetery was sited near today's Prescot Street in Tower Hamlets. After the fourth century, however, burial outside the city wall (extramural burial) had given way to the less sanitary Christian custom of burying the faithful near churches or shrines. Proximity to holy sites may have been intended to benefit the soul of the faithful departed, but in the long term this practice created a public health hazard.

As a result, by the early modern period, the very idea of creating special suburban enclaves for burial was unsettling, as was the concept of such experiments being organized as commercial enterprises. The architects Christopher Wren and Robert Hooke had urged the establishment of extramural burial grounds as part of their plans for rebuilding London after the Great Fire of 1666. A deadly cholera epidemic had struck the capital the previous summer, putting increasing pressure on the graveyards of its parish churches. Thanks to a third member of the Royal Society, John Evelyn, it had become possible to link such outbreaks with the problem of overcrowded graveyards in a new way. Epidemics were seen to be the cause of graveyard overcrowding, but graveyard overcrowding could also be seen as a cause of epidemics.

John Evelyn's *Fumifugium: or the inconveniencie of the aer and smoke of London dissipated* (1661) was among the earliest works to consider air circulation as an urban problem, and it explicitly linked graveyard smells with poor public health. Thanks to William Harvey's discovery of the circulation of the blood, standing air was now viewed as stagnant air and therefore unhealthy. But how could clean, wholesome air circulate within a city without also circulating the harmful effluvia produced by slaughterhouses, soapworks and decomposing bodies? Robert Hooke's solution was to move all these facilities outside the city walls. Cemeteries were as much a part of Wren's plan for post-fire London as straight avenues, wide piazzas and well-ventilated market places. Few of such plans were realized, however. The devastation was so extensive that City authorities feared reconstruction would be discouraged by land swops and legal squabbles over compensation for properties seized to create new streets. Nobody wanted a ghost town, however well planned. London let slip its last great opportunity to pause, survey its present shape and in turn shape its patterns of future development.

Kensal Green and the other garden cemeteries established in London in the 1830s and 1840s (often referred to as the Magnificent Seven) borrowed from the Parisian model of suburban burial grounds, developed under the Napoleonic regime, as well as being influenced by the catacombs in the south of Paris, which were opened to the public in 1815. Dickens introduces 'a Frenchman, with wife and family' into his description in *All the Year Round*, 'chattering' and 'eating bon-bons, and gazing round the cemetery with a critical air, as if comparing it with cemeteries of their own land'.

Although this association with Paris brought with it a hint of anticlerical sentiment, in all other respects the benefits of associating London's new cemeteries with Paris's Père Lachaise were overwhelmingly positive. Set in what had been the garden of Louis XIV's Jesuit confessor (François d'Aix de La Chaise), the cemetery had opened in 1804. A decade later it was firmly established as one of the sights of the city. Situated a mile and a half to the east of Notre Dame on Mont Louis, the 'Cemetery of the East' (as it was officially known) enjoyed excellent views over the metropolis. Long before the construction of the Sacré Coeur, before the Eiffel Tower, Père Lachaise was the place visitors and Parisians alike went to survey the capital as a whole.

Tour guides insisted on a visit, and images of Paris also drew attention to its charms. Charles Cole's *Imperial Paris Guide,* published to coincide with the 1867 Exhibition, hailed the view as unmissable.[2] The Japanese artist Yushio Markino included the view in his illustrations for *The Colour of Paris* (1914).[3] A key figure in establishing the cemetery as an outlook as well as a sight in itself was Augustus Charles Pugin. Of Swiss extraction, Pugin was born in the Parisian parish of St Sulpice. In the 1790s he moved to London, attending the Royal Academy schools and working in the studio of John Nash, the architect behind Regent Street and the new villas and terraces put up around Regent's Park in the 1820s. A talented draughtsman, Pugin went on to work for the city's premier print-seller, Rudolph Ackermann. Together they published *The Microcosm of London* in 1808, a series of images of public buildings accompanied by short descriptive texts.

With the end of the Napoleonic Wars in 1815, Pugin was able to re-establish contact with his French relations, and to return to his native city, now accompanied by his son, also named Augustus, who had been born in their home in Keppel Street, Bloomsbury, in 1812. Regular visits to Paris inspired the elder Pugin to produce a French equivalent to the highly successful *Microcosm*. In 1830, *Paris and its Environs* appeared, a two-volume work consisting of engravings after Pugin's sketches, with short explanatory texts by L. T. Ventouillac. Although the sites illustrated covered a surprisingly wide range, including the morgue and the Montmartre abattoir, ten of the 200 engravings were devoted to Père Lachaise. The second volume included a 'General View of Paris' [Fig. 33, p. 210], the by then classic view of the city: from Père Lachaise.

Indeed, such was the fame of the cemetery that Ventouillac felt the need to apologize for the book's fulsome praise of a place with which he assumed people would already be familiar. 'We fear being tedious to some of our readers on the subject of this cemetery,' he wrote, for 'What Englishman has not seen the cemetery of Père la Chaise?' He went on to quote an anonymous English traveller's account of his own response to the cemetery, which remarked on how the Parisians had taken death and 'strewed him o'er and o'er with sweets . . . they have made the grave a garden.'[4]

The elder Pugin's views focussed on particular groups of monuments, such as the tombs of generals Foy, Masséna and Lefebvre. Trees, surprisingly rough paths, ladies with parasols and praying Parisians of humbler station emphasized the site's informal charms. Visitors were expected to admire the way in which they could stumble upon a shady corner, or suddenly catch an unsuspected glimpse of Notre Dame or the Panthéon. Some images featured crude wooden crosses among the massive obelisks and columns, presenting the cemetery as a classless space in which rich and poor reposed cheek by jowl. In fact the poor were relegated to the largely unvisited north-western edge.

But *Paris and its Environs* was certainly correct in stating that the Parisians had 'made the grave a garden' and stripped it of the horrors associated with high-density intramural burial. The cemetery that so many Londoners revered and sought to translate to their own capital had its origins in a series of gardens laid out by French aristocrats in the 1770s and 1780s. The fact that these private pleasure grounds were themselves inspired by early eighteenth-century English gardens, such as Stowe, and by the verse of Thomas Gray and Edward Young, adds a further twist to this example of Anglo-French exchange. On this occasion, it required reflecting on an important issue of public health and establishing whose job it was to tackle it. As we shall see, the creation of cemeteries loosened the Church's traditional control of the dead. But could private enterprise be trusted to take up this responsibility? If not, was it to be shouldered by new central government bodies or the old parish system?

It also involved thinking about how to accommodate the dead decently and respectfully, close enough to the bereaved to be easily accessible, but not so close as to be a hazard to their health. Dickens seems to have found Kensal Green satisfactory enough. He admired the careful management of the General Cemetery Company (GCC) that operated it, as witnessed by the fat line of ledgers containing descriptions of every interment that had taken place there and by the security arrangements, which included an armed nightwatchman. But he clearly found some of the commercial arrangements ridiculous, commenting that the charge of one guinea a foot for memorial plaques in the cemetery's Monumental Chambers (above its main range of catacombs) 'reminded me strangely of advertisement charges, and of the bill-stickers' hoardings which deface our streets'. The wreaths of glass or porcelain flowers (called 'immortelles') available for sale in local shops put him in mind of 'so many wedding-rings from the fingers of departed Brobdingnagians'.[5]

215

Dickens, who had written satires of elaborate mourning rituals, heavily criticized the undertakers' exploitation of the bereaved in a series of articles he wrote for his other periodical, *Household Words*, in 1850–1. Undertakers used peer pressure to add pointless extras to the coffins, mourners, hearse and coaches they were paid to provide. In addition to being wasteful, meaningless mummeries in themselves, such rites had the equally harmful effect of causing London's poor to emulate them. This was something they could attempt only by going deeply into debt or by saving up through a Burial Club, which offered a simple form of burial insurance, paying fixed sums on the death of a family member. Club funds were often mismanaged, however, and supposedly led some of the poor to poison their own children in order to secure the pay-out: a shocking and unsubstantiated claim, which Dickens himself appears to have believed.

Dickens also savaged the trading in relics of Wellington, which rose to fever pitch around the time of his death in 1852. This extended to the renting of rooms overlooking the route along which the notoriously overloaded funeral car was to pass. The English way of death represented a scene of 'almost incredible degradation'.[6] At its heart lay a bourgeois desire to keep up with the Joneses, or rather, with 'Mrs Grundy'. As if fearful of challenging such sacred customs, Dickens wrote several of his articles as if they had issued from the beak of a raven, one of a number of speeches inviting humans to prove their superiority to other animals by abandoning irrational practices. Even as this raven notes the incontrovertible facts, he has to admit that it is hopeless to expect his listeners to change. Londoners will uphold these abusive customs 'because you WILL be gen-teel parties to the last'.[7] As we shall see, a similar combination of hard-nosed business acumen and unexamined instinct, of disgust and sentimentalism, lay behind the construction of these new suburbs for the dead in Paris and London.

Elegies and Elysiums

The Monceau estate (now the Parc Monceau, in the 8th arrondissement) of the Duc de Chartres is a good place to trace the emergence of the modern cemetery. While it imitated the English landscape garden style, the Parc Monceau also developed it, creating a new kind of garden that in turn served as a model for the cemeteries of Napoleonic Paris. Louis Carrogis laid out the Monceau gardens between 1773 and 1778. They featured a *bois des tombeaux* ('tomb wood'): a 'natural' forest planted with urns on pedestals and rustic pyramids. Though snaking paths do appear in Lesueur's engraving [Fig. 34] of the wood, the well-dressed promenaders shown admiring it are all off piste, accepting the unspoken invitation to drift among the scattered monuments as the fancy takes them. The formal French-style gardens of Versailles, designed by Le Nôtre in the seventeenth century, contained a wealth of allegorical detail that would be 'lost' if the visitor strayed from the preordained itinerary laid down by Louis XIV,

FIG. 34: Carmontelle, 'Bois des Tombeaux' from *Jardin de Monceaux*, 1779.

who wrote several guides to the gardens.[8] At the Parc Monceau, getting lost *was* the preordained itinerary, intended to create a mood of pleasant melancholy rather than relay coded messages about absolutist power.

The monuments dotted about the *bois des tombeaux* were intended to remind visitors of Egyptian tombs or, in the case of the urns, Roman monuments for the deposit of cremated remains. In reality there were no bodies or ashes interred in the grounds. This was in keeping with the English model developed in the 1720s and 1730s, at Alexander Pope's riverside garden and grotto in Twickenham, at William Shenstone's garden at The Leasowes and at aristocratic parks such as Stowe and Castle Howard. Pope's garden (which he rented from 1719; as a Roman Catholic he could not own property) featured an obelisk to the memory of his mother, who was buried in the parish church of St Mary's. Shenstone's garden was full of monuments alluding to loss of youth and life. It contained an urn dedicated to his deceased brother, who, again, was buried elsewhere. Stowe's Elysian Fields contained a more ambitious Temple of English Worthies designed by William Kent as well as detached monuments to William Congreve and, later, General Wolfe. Such gardens lent the 'natural' combinations of wood and greensward, associated with the English landscape style, an elegiac atmosphere, a surprisingly studied pose of informality.

There was a decided anti-Establishment feel to gardens such as Stowe, where a ruined Temple of Modern Virtue embodied a political sally against the venal regime of Robert Walpole, Britain's first prime minister. As Pope was a Roman Catholic with close ties to Jacobite rebels such as Francis Atterbury, his garden also represented a place of self-imposed exile in which to ponder what might have been. The heretical political views and paranoia of *philosophe* Jean-Jacques Rousseau, a Protestant in Roman Catholic France, led him to seek exile in Switzerland. When Rousseau died at the Ermenonville estate of the Marquis de Girardin in 1778, his body was buried in its own 'tomb forest' of poplars on a small island in a lake. This became a site of pilgrimage for his Enlightenment followers, so much so that the paths of the surrounding English-style garden (which contained monuments to William Penn, Isaac Newton, René Descartes and Voltaire), as well as the banks of the lake, were trampled bare. One English tourist found being separated from the actual tomb so unbearable that he swam across the lake so as to be able to weep, dripping, directly over the sarcophagus.

Although an earlier generation of poets including Pope and Shenstone had prepared the ground, it was Thomas Gray's *Elegy Written in a Country Church-yard* (1751) and Young's *The Complaint: or, Night Thoughts on Life, Death and Immortality* (1742) that did most to encourage this mood in France. Young's original poem was followed by *Night the Second. On Time, Death, Friendship* and then by *Night the Third. Narcissa*. Translated into French verse as *Les Nuits d'Young* in 1769 (there had been earlier prose translations), it was the 'Narcissa Episode' that had the greatest impact. It told of the hurried midnight burial of the beautiful bride Narcissa in a 'stolen grave' (i.e. one already occupied), the young consumptive having been denied proper burial in a churchyard on the grounds of her Protestant faith. The real-life Narcissa was Elizabeth Temple (Gray's stepdaughter), who died at Lyons aged just eighteen in 1736, shortly after her marriage to Henry Temple, and was buried at eleven at night in a hospital cemetery.

The refusal to grant Elizabeth/Narcissa a grave provoked Gray to rail against the pitiless bigotry of the Roman Catholic Church. 'While nature melted, superstition raved;' he wrote, 'That mourn'd the dead; and this denied a grave.' Enlightened thinkers, and other members of the fashionable aristocratic elite who wished to appear as such, were only too happy to join Gray in shaking their heads over 'the cursed ungodliness of zeal'. Narcissa joined the Calas family in being seen as a symbol of innocent virtue subjected to inhuman punishment by Roman Catholic superstition.

A *Caverne d'Young* or 'Young's Cave' was excavated in the grounds of a garden at Franconville-La-Garenne in the 1780s by its owner, Claude-Camille-François, Comte d'Albon, alongside a pyramid to the count's ancestors and a monument to William Tell. Maupertuis Park, designed by Alexandre-Théodore Brongniart for the Marquis de Montesquiou, featured a monument to another victim of Roman Catholic violence: Admiral Gaspard de Coligny, a Protestant war hero assassinated by Roman Catholics on St Bartholomew's Day in 1572. Fashionable French aristocrats were clearly willing to delve quite deep into their nation's past (as well as Britain's past) in search of historical figures for their guests to get worked up about.[9]

Gray's *Élégee écrite sur un Cimetière de Campagne* first appeared in French in the April 1765 issue of the *Gazette Littéraire de l'Europe*, in a verse translation by Jean-Baptiste Suard.[10] The *Elegy* viewed the modest gravestones and unsophisticated funerary inscriptions of the village dead as a homily on vanity. Though confined to a humble setting, 'The short and simple annals of the poor' had their own tales of ambition and heroism to tell, which seemed all the more poignant for being commemorated 'With uncouth rhimes and shapeless sculpture deck'd'.[11] Whilst its popularity strikes us as unmerited today, the *Elegy* encouraged the tendency to view graveyards as places to bemoan the unjust manner in which inscrutable Posterity granted fame to one individual and oblivion to another, without any apparent regard to their actual merits. Meanwhile other aspects, such as God, the soul, the promise of resurrection and the fear of perdition, were entirely ignored. 'God' may be the last word of the *Elegy*, but He is otherwise absent. The levelling effect of death is there, but the levelling is the result of our own sentimental efforts, not an effect of the overwhelming power of God.

The English-style gardens of Monceau and Ermenonville were a world away from the graveyards of eighteenth-century Paris. Here as in London the dead were squeezed into parish burial grounds. Unlike London, however, the majority were buried in mass graves. It was in 1186 that the Parisian burial ground of Les Innocents (near the present-day Les Halles) had first been walled in, and in 1765 no less than eighteen parishes were still using it. Every six months a new fifty-metre-long pit was opened up and the old one covered over – so that the dead lay for months with only a thin covering of lime over them. After sufficient time had passed, each mass grave would be opened once more; the skulls and bones would be removed and deposited in geometrical patterns in one of the charnel houses that surrounded the site, although these were little more than wooden sheds with doors designed to allow visitors to peer inside.

When part of the space available was lost to road widening under Louis XIV, accommodation became even more cramped, while the presence of markets just the other side of the wall raised concerns about the effects on public health of having so much fetid matter jammed into one place.[12] Mercier was one of those who spoke out against this. Among the urban improvements he prescribes for Paris in his *Parallèle* is the demand that Les Innocents be cleared as far west as St Eustache, its soil purified and a massive market place laid out on top.[13] The closure of Les Innocents had been ordered by the *parlement* of Paris in 1765, but nothing had been done. In November 1785, the *parlement* tried again, this time with success. Over fifteen months cartloads of remains were disinterred and taken to the Porte d'Enfer on the southern edge of the city, where they were deposited into a network of disused stone quarries. In 1787 the remains at St Eustache and St Étienne-des-Grès were also transferred there. Only after Père Lachaise had achieved its purpose would anyone think of transforming such places into a tourist attraction, as the catacombs of Paris are today.

The cult sentimental novelist Bernardin de Saint Pierre was the first to draw on the Monceau-style English tomb garden as a solution to graveyard overcrowding in his book *Études de la Nature* (1784), in which one chapter urged the creation of an 'Elysium' in Paris. Though he did not propose any specific site or design, his picture of this facility anticipates Père Lachaise, not least in its emphasis on attracting tourists. 'They already travel here in order to live,' he noted, 'they would certainly come here to die.' The 'Elysium' would also serve to maintain social cohesion, by refusing to acknowledge distinctions of class.[14]

Saint Pierre expressed regret at the manner in which 'public' gardens such as the Tuileries and the Arsenal were in fact inaccessible to many, shut out by the Swiss guards who patrolled their entrances. Anticipating criticism that the idea of universal access was utopian, that the masses would deface or destroy monuments, Saint Pierre insisted that once these masses were made to appreciate that the Elysium was 'theirs', they would behave properly. 'They will come to watch over their own behaviour, far more closely than Swiss guards ever could.'[15] As with the 'Wauxhalls', a new kind of public space would, it was suggested, inspire new, better forms of public behaviour founded on self-surveillance, rather than placing increased burdens on an absolutist regime.

This patriotic ideal foreshadows the stern pieties of the revolutionary authorities after 1789. It even demonstrates pretensions to make Paris's cemeteries into Europe's capital of virtue. The Roman togas, blushing maidens and pyres, choreographed as part of Robespierre's cult of the Supreme Being, lent the massive public festivities an air of being of a piece with this egalitarian Elysium. And yet the ideals of 1789 seem to have bypassed burial practices. The National Assembly and later the Directory ignored cemetery proposals such as that advanced by the architect Antoine-Laurent-Thomas Vaudoyer, who urged the transformation of the Champs Elysées into a *voie d'honneur*: an 'avenue of honour' modelled on the Via Appia, the trunk road lined with tombs leading out of ancient Rome.

In April 1791, Soufflot's church of St Geneviève on the Mont St Geneviève was redesignated the Panthéon, a sort of Valhalla for national heroes. Although its windows were blocked up to create a more funereal atmosphere, proposals put forward by Quatremère de Quincy and Maille Dussaussoy, to envelop it with a *bois des tombeaux*, were not implemented.[16] The Panthéon remained marooned on a bald patch of unlandscaped dirt. While traditional religious observance went underground or simply tailed off in the later 1790s, the dead continued to be carted off to mass graves in provisional burial grounds at Montparnasse, Montmartre, La Marguerite, the Charité hospital, Vaugirard, Clamart and an area next to the park at Monceau. There they were dumped in mass graves, each containing between 1,200 and 2,000 bodies. A few shovels of quicklime provided a sometimes ineffective repellent against feral dogs. Despite its republican ideals and the cult of its fallen leaders, the Revolution seems to have made burial conditions for most Parisians even more squalid than they already were.[17]

For some reason an exception seems to have been made for those killed in revolutionary riots. After the Réveillon riots (which actually pre-dated the attack on the Bastille by several months), the September Massacres (1792) and other large disturbances, the dead were taken to the catacombs, where they were first exhibited (so that relatives could identify the missing) and then walled up. Even if this hardly counted as 'burial', it was more of a resting place than another disused quarry, that of Montmartre (on today's Rue Coulaincourt), where the burial site was open to the sky and particularly gruesome. When architect Pierre-Louis Roederer made the novel suggestion that Paris build paired cemeteries, with an 'Elysium' for good citizens and a pit for condemned criminals, he presumably had Montmartre in mind for the latter. As the mayor of the 1st arrondissement noted, 'This is not a cemetery, it is an abyss.'[18]

Père Lachaise

Change came around 1799, when Napoleon overthrew the Directory and proclaimed himself First Consul, then 'First Consul for Life' and finally (in 1804) Emperor of the French. The hopes of 1789 had disintegrated into regicide, civil war, the Terror of 1793 and then European war. The population of Paris actually fell during these years. Not as a result of the September Massacres or the guillotine, bloody as they were; more likely because immigration stopped or went into reverse, with recent immigrants fleeing the hunger, fear and uncertainty that stalked the city's streets. In addition to bringing political stability, the concordat that Napoleon negotiated with the Pope in 1801 helped to ease tensions between church and state. Starting in Easter of that year, the Sabbath was restored. Unlike Robespierre, Napoleon had no pretensions to create his own religion.

In 1799 the Institut National des Sciences et des Arts announced that that year's architectural Grand Prix would be for the design of 'an Elysium or public cemetery'. Entries echoed the designs of Étienne-Louis Boullée in their stern, almost brutal classicism and in a certain sublime, inhuman scale. They nonetheless spurred into action the Prefect of Paris, Nicolas Frochot. Elected to the Estates General in 1789, Frochot was imprisoned during the Terror, being released on the fall of Robespierre. He was elected again to the National Assembly, but resigned upon being appointed the first Prefect of the Seine and of Paris by Napoleon in 1800. He served the Consulate and the Empire in this capacity until 1812, by which time the disgusting and confused state of the city's burial grounds had largely been addressed.

By an edict of 12 March 1801, Frochot ordered the creation of three cemeteries: to the north, south and east of Paris. He also proposed to the Interior Minister, Chaptal, that the park at Monceau (confiscated by the revolutionary authorities in 1793) be appropriated as a real *bois des tombeaux*. Though this plan was not realized, the regional government for the *département* of the Seine designated Montmartre and the Charité (i.e. the burial ground of the hospital of the same name) as public cemeteries in December 1802 and March 1803 respectively. In March 1804, Frochot acquired the Mont Louis site and set about transforming it, although the dilapidated seventeenth-century home of La Chaise himself remained standing until 1819 and a chapel was not erected until 1825. A small western cemetery was opened at Passy in 1820, while the much larger 'Cemetery of the South' (i.e. Montparnasse) opened in 1825. However, there was never any doubt that, of them all, Père Lachaise was the most distinguished. The Imperial Decree on Burials of 12 June 1804 consolidated these advances, banning burial within cities as well as mass graves.

The site of Père Lachaise rises a total of twenty-seven metres, from the level of the Boulevard de Ménilmontant to the crest of Mont Louis. Though its western side ascends gently and levels out at the top, it is in all other respects a challenging mix of small ridges and declivities. The layout was entrusted to Alexandre-Théodore Brongniart, then sixty-five, who had designed the English-style park at Maupertuis, mentioned above, and who later designed the Paris Bourse (stock exchange). Brongniart's designs for a grand entrance and a pyramidal chapel were deemed prohibitively expensive, and were only partly executed after his death in 1813. In terms of landscaping, Brongniart retained fountains and other features of the original planting by the Jesuits, fashioning secluded corners then known as the Bosquet Clary and the Bosquet du Dragon. Although he did create some straight avenues and formal *rond-points* or circuses, he resisted the urge to impose on the site a vast grid, of the kind the great Étienne-Louis Boullée had advocated in his unpublished *Essai sur l'art*.[19] Fittingly, both Brongniart and Frochot (who died in 1828) would be buried in Père Lachaise.

With the western and rear sections largely given over to unmarked paupers' graves (individual graves, rather than mass ones), the way was clear for the city to sell plots in the rest of the cemetery to Napoleonic notables, to leading military, literary and artistic figures, as well as to prominent businessmen. Many of the former were raised by public subscription, in a patriotic spirit that Saint Pierre would have approved of. These monuments consisted of Egyptian obelisks and Roman sarcophagi, carefully arranged in loose groupings so as to create a sense of distinct *quartiers* or neighbourhoods where kindred spirits could commune for ever. The obelisk to Marshal Masséna dominated one promontory. As other military leaders eventually came to rest near by, this area became known as the Rendez-Vous des Braves ('the meeting place of the brave'). The tomb of poet Jacques Delille formed the focus of a group of leading literary figures. In 1817, Molière and La Fontaine were transferred there and placed side by side.

The biggest draw, however, was a rare Gothic exception to this overwhelmingly Antique complex: the tomb reuniting the theologian Peter Abelard and the nun-scholar Heloïse, the star-crossed lovers of the twelfth century whose travails provided a subject for much medievalizing mawkishness in early nineteenth-century France. Cobbled together by Alexandre Lenoir out of fragments of the abbey of the Paraclète, which had been demolished during the Revolution, the monument is currently under restoration. Though some people are still exercised by speculation as to whether the unhappy pair are in fact reunited there, the monument is more interesting as a relic of Lenoir's groundbreaking Musée des Monuments Français.

Commandeering an abandoned Paris convent in 1794, Lenoir collected medieval monuments and statuary that would otherwise have been destroyed and put them on show to the public. He began with an 'Elysée' in the convent's garden, creating a medieval equivalent to the Parc Monceau's *bois des tombeaux*.[20] Arranged in a series of rooms that allowed visitors to take a sentimental journey back in time, the Musée taught Parisians to appreciate medieval art and architecture previously reviled as barbaric. Though curators would balk at Lenoir's willingness to fashion new 'originals' out of fragments from various different sources, the Gothic Revival, later championed by A. W. N. Pugin in England and, slightly later, by Viollet-le-Duc in France, emerged from the nostalgic romanticism of the sort Lenoir brought to Père Lachaise.

Meanwhile south of the river, Frochot and the Inspector-General of Quarries, Louis-Étienne-François Héricart-Ferrand, Viscount de Thury, had been busy since 1810, directing the transformation of the catacombs into an equally sentimental necropolis. In 1815, Thury published a *Description des Catacombes de Paris*, which documented their history and design, starting with the clearing of Les Innocents in 1785–6. Skulls and other bones were carefully arranged in stern, vaguely Neoclassical patterns, access was improved and an itinerary formed. The catacombs in Rome were an obvious precedent, one closely linked to the early history of the Christian Church. Though they had originally been consecrated in April 1786 and contained a chapel, in every other respect the Paris Catacombs put Young-style sentiment before dogma. Appropriate classical tags and extracts from poetry were added.[21]

In the half-century separating the laying out of the Duc de Chartres's Monceau estate in 1773 and the opening of the last of the four suburban cemeteries at Montparnasse in 1825, Paris had come up with a solution to the aesthetic, social, sanitary and sectarian challenges posed by the disposal of the dead in a metropolis. This problem had been permitted to fester for centuries, and the city would probably have continued using mass graves had it not been for the aristocratic parks of Monceau, Ermenonville and Gennevilliers. These informal gardens were based on English exemplars such as Stowe, as well as on English primers on landscape design by Horace Walpole and Thomas Whately. As such they formed part of the same Anglomania that inspired the 'Wauxhalls' of the 1770s and the arcades of the Palais Royal.

In the 1780s such gardens moved beyond the somewhat feeble sentimentalism of Gray and the melancholic posturing of Young to produce something more concrete. Unlike the Elysian Fields of Stowe, Saint Pierre's Elysium was not about disillusioned retreat from an irredeemably corrupt Establishment. It was idealistic, looking to the state to establish public cemeteries as schools of civic virtue, where true merit and service would be honoured above accidents of birth. The French Revolution soon dashed Enlightenment aristocrats' hopes of replacing their parchment patents of nobility with more substantial claims to elite status. For several years the garden cemetery ideal was lost from sight in the chaos of the Revolution, only to be revived as a Napoleonic Valhalla by Frochot and other imperial functionaries.

A Railway to the Other World

It was private enterprise rather than central government that brought a new urban space to London. Kensal Green was established by the GCC, a joint-stock company, which still runs the cemetery. The GCC was the brainchild of a barrister, George Frederick Carden. Fellow directors included the MP and printer Andrew Spottiswoode, Viscount Milton and the banker Sir John Dean Paul, as well as Augustus Charles Pugin. Carden had visited Père Lachaise cemetery in Paris in 1821, and was inspired to create something similar in London. After several false starts a company prospectus was printed in May 1830. With the encouragement of leading politicians such as the Whig 3rd Marquis of Lansdowne, shares worth £25 each were sold, land purchased and an architectural competition was announced, soliciting designs for the gates, lodges and chapels.

Graveyard overcrowding was rapidly getting worse. The population of London grew by half between 1801 and 1821, while the space available to accommodate its dead hardly grew at all. Church vaults were full. Churchyards were so packed that the ground within them was raised several feet above the surrounding pavements. Yet Carden's earlier attempts to get the ball rolling in 1825 had met with amused incredulity. In that year he had set up a General Burial-Grounds Association and published a prospectus, planning to raise £300,000 in £50 shares and use it to create a Parisian-style cemetery on Primrose Hill.

The financing target and the individual share price would prove overambitious in the long term, and seemed downright foolhardy in the bearish mood fostered by the 1825 banking crisis. But the failure of these early attempts was also due to a feeling that trading in death was distasteful, a case of the City's stock-jobbing spirit trespassing into a sensitive area. The 1825 crisis had seen the rapid deflation of a speculative bubble, marked by belated scepticism about the high-flown prose characteristic of company prospectuses earlier in the decade. Fittingly, perhaps, the future novelist and Conservative prime minister Benjamin Disraeli cut his teeth writing such prospectuses.

Carden's first attempt was satirized by another prospectus for a rival 'Life, Death, Burial and Resurrection Company'. Couched in rhyming couplets and attributed to 'Bernard Blackmantle',[22] the prospectus sought investors for 1 million shares of £1 each in an enterprise that would, it promised, replace disgustingly fetid graveyards with an appealing, even homely idyll:

> We've a scheme that shall mingle the 'grave with the gay,'
> And make it quite pleasant to die, when you may.
> First, then, we propose with the graces of art,
> Like our Parisian friends, to make ev'ry tomb smart.

The prospectus promised to replace the funeral sermon with glee singers, to erect a sumptuous hotel in which mourners could enjoy fine food (washed down with *vin de grave*) and dance twice a week to a band performing waltzes and quadrilles. It ended with a preposterous claim that the company also intended to bring the long dead back to life, 'That is, if the shares in our company rise,/If not 'tis a bubble, like others, of lies.'[23] The implication of this final couplet was obvious. The idea of harnessing commercial interests to provide a decent, sanitary alternative to inner-city burial grounds was offensive and mercenary, an unholy alliance of the English obsession with profit-seeking with a French *douceur de vivre*, neither of which had any place among the dead.

Pugin's son, the great designer and architect (also named Augustus), agreed and lampooned cemetery enterprise in his *Apology for the Revival of Christian Architecture* (1843). Along with his work *Contrasts* (1836), the *Apology* was a manifesto for Gothic Revival, seen as much as a moral as an aesthetic project. Pugin Senior had published views of Gothic architecture in the 1820s, drawing attention to a period and a style often associated with barbarism or dull antiquarianism. He was appealing to established picturesque taste. The younger Pugin's publications were anti-classical polemics that presented the recovery of English Gothic, not as a fashionable, picturesque folly, but as the salvaging of the nation's soul from centuries of 'pagan' worship of foreign idols, of Greece, Rome and Mammon.

Plate IV of the *Apology* [Fig. 35] features the Egyptian-style entrance to a 'New General Cemetery for All Denominations', a parody of William Hosking's entrance to Abney Park Cemetery, completed in 1840. Egyptian obelisks and Roman urns sprout around the central chapel. This cheery eclecticism was indeed typical of the monuments erected in the city's privately run cemeteries, the so-called Magnificent Seven (Abney Park, Brompton, Highgate, Kensal Green, Norwood, Nunhead and Tower Hamlets). This mingling of different styles continued for much of the century, although Egyptian and Greek-style monuments became less

FIG. 35: A.W.N. Pugin, 'New General Cemetery for All Denominations', *Apology for the Revival of Christian Architecture*, 1843.

common after the 1880s, when Celtic-style crosses began to appear. It is this variety that gives these cemeteries their charm – at least to us. To a Gothic crusader such as Pugin, it smacked of promiscuousness. Like the palace-fronted terraces of Nash's Regent's Park, Pugin's 'General Cemetery' is brick stuccoed to look like stone. It therefore lacks that truth to materials that Pugin and, later, John Ruskin associated with Gothic architecture.

With its aggressive invitation to 'Observe the Prices!' and a newly patented Shillibeer (a combined hearse and mourner's coach) pulled up outside, the 'General Cemetery' is ecumenical in more ways than one. 'All denominations' and all styles of monument are admitted. This tolerance is, Pugin seems to be suggesting, the product of a base commercial spirit, evinced by the reminder on one of the walls that this cemetery has 'no connection with the company over the way'. Rather than reflecting shared values, beliefs and history, the 'General Cemetery' has made death a matter of consumer choice.

There are many options available, at good prices, but ultimately they are value-free, interchangeable and insubstantial. In 1848 an anonymous pamphlet linked the cemetery company to the latest stock-market bubble by dubbing it 'A railway company to th' other world'.[24] It linked the riot of competing styles of monument to Parisian vanity, which made Père Lachaise a 'monumental chaos'.[25] As the nineteenth century progressed the Evangelical focus on spiritual rebirth and salvation, common in the 1810s and 1820s, waned. Heaven evolved from a semi-abstract vision of blissful union with Jesus into a more domestic place of family reunion.[26] In the first half of the nineteenth century, however, Londoners were not yet prepared to see either the cemetery or the hereafter furnished as if it were (in Blackmantle's phrase) 'a gay drawing room'.

Nor were architects ready to design them. Although Sir John Soane, Sir Jeffry Wyattville and others were alive to the romantic potential of medieval and Egyptian funerary architecture, this did not translate into a willingness to cooperate with the GCC or enter their design competition, which does not seem to have attracted any distinguished entrants.[27] Wyattville refused an invitation from Dean Paul to act as consultant to Kensal Green, adding that he thought 'very few architects would like to interfere in the manner proposed'.[28] Cemeteries may have represented a new type of commission, but they also had a whiff of anticlericalism. In part this stemmed from their association with Paris, the city of free-thinking atheists and blood-soaked revolutionaries.

But it also reflected a concern that removing the dead from the purlieus of a parish church, to a cheery setting designed to (in Carden's words) 'render imperceptible . . . decay in Nature', would cut the ties linking living Londoners with their predecessors. Passing burial grounds or graves on the way to and from church or in the course of one's daily business not only reminded the living of their mortality (and hence their need to look to the state of their souls), but also fostered a sense of the neighbourhood community. It was pleasant to imagine that community as one that transcended generations, even if constant immigration made that sense of continuity seem somewhat fragile.

Parish clergy relied on burial fees for a significant proportion of their income, as much as 40 per cent in the case of one Marylebone parish. Cemeteries represented a serious threat to this. Yet companies like the GCC needed the support of the Anglican and other churches if they were to secure custom and in particular if they were to get the local bishop to consecrate the Anglican section of their grounds. A schedule of fees was negotiated with the Bishop of London as well as with the incumbents of specific parishes. The rector of St Marylebone turned from being an opponent to a supporter of the Kensal Green scheme, but only after negotiating an extra two shillings and sixpence per burial service on top of the fees agreed by his bishop.[29]

Today it is hard to appreciate just how much weight was placed on sectarian divides among Protestants: between Anglicans, who buried their dead in consecrated ground, and Dissenters, who did not, and who resented paying tithes to support their parish's (Anglican) clergy. It was in the interests of a company such as the GCC to cater to both communities, if it could. Originally the Company seems to have concluded that two separate cemeteries were required, and they considered a number of sites south of the river upon which to build a Dissenting cemetery. In fact, a group of leading Congregationalists would establish their own Dissenting cemetery in 1840, north of the river at Stoke Newington. Abney Park Cemetery was formed on a site with a rich Puritan heritage, having formerly been the estate of a leading Puritan, Charles Fleetwood, Cromwell's son-in-law.[30]

Jealousies and rivalries had been exacerbated by a struggle for control of the Company between Carden and the architect John Griffith of Finsbury. Carden and Griffith disagreed on whether the cemetery should be built in a Gothic or a Greek Revival style. In March 1832, Carden, Paul, Pugin and other directors had awarded first and second prizes in their architectural competition to Henry Edward Kendall, a little-known architect who had produced a romantic if rather expensive-looking design in Gothic Revival. This included a water gate on the canal that would have allowed Venetian-style funerals by barge. When Griffiths began pushing his own alternative design in a more affordable Greek Revival style, Carden fought back, spreading rumours about the Anglican clergy's long list of demands, raising fears that Dissenters would be entirely excluded.

Instead a second plot of land was acquired at Kensal Green, formerly the site of the Plough Inn. Contiguous Dissenting and Anglican sections were separated by a metal fence, and there were separate entrances as well as separate chapels. In the 1830s some Anglican bishops refused to accept shared chapels, or even the idea of having separate chapels as part of a linked structure. Thus the chapels at the Cemetery of St James at Highgate designed by Stephen Geary, which extend either side of a gatehouse-cum-office, were a daring step on the part of the London Cemetery Company that opened it in 1839. Equally daring was the GCC's willingness to enter into discussions with the Abbé de la Porte of Portman Square, with a view to selling his Roman Catholic flock a plot for £600.

There were significant financial and religious obstacles that the GCC had to negotiate before it could take the major step of securing an Act of Parliament in June 1832. This incorporated the Company and empowered it to raise £200,000 in £20 shares. In January 1833 the Anglican section was consecrated by Charles Blomfield, Bishop of London. The first burial came on 31 January. Take-up of GCC shares was initially slow, necessitating piecemeal construction. Blomfield had to officiate in a temporary Anglican chapel made of wood. The modest Dissenters chapel was completed in 1834, the more ornate Anglican one in June 1837. Both sat on top of ranges of catacombs, supplemented by a third line of catacombs running along part of the cemetery's north wall. Meanwhile the shareholders had received their first divided in 1835, by which point their shares had increased in value by 12 per cent.

Resurrection Men

This encouraging if slow turn in the fortunes of this newfangled cemetery was helped by the success of two burial grounds in Liverpool and Glasgow, which opened in 1825 and 1832 respectively. Both advertised themselves under the name 'necropolis' (city of the dead), which was presumably felt to be more easily understood than the word 'cemetery'. More important, however, was the role played by the scandal unleashed in Edinburgh, which added yet another unfamiliar word to the lexicon of death: 'burking'. In 1828–9, William Hare and William Burke were accused of having killed a number of guests staying in their guest house and selling the bodies to the city's medical schools for dissection. The resulting trial and conviction, which attracted considerable attention, revealed that the pair had 'burked' sixteen individuals, most of them elderly, handicapped or homeless. Under an Act of Parliament in 1752, medical schools had secured a legal supply of corpses: judges were able to sentence convicted murderers to undergo posthumous dissection rather than the gibbet. In practice the surgeons were often cheated of their due. Dissection was popularly held to deny the deceased a chance of resurrection, and so those bereaved at the scaffold would go to almost any lengths to preserve the fresh body from the authorities, abducting it by force, if necessary.

Allocated an annual six cadavers under the 1752 Act, in 1828 London medical schools were dissecting 592 each year.[31] Demand was far outrunning supply. A black market sprang up in corpses exhumed from parish graveyards under the cover of darkness by gangs of so-called 'resurrection men'. Burke and Hare dispensed with the nocturnal digging and coffin-breaking by creating their own corpses. Although Hare turned King's Evidence, Burke was convicted and hanged in 1829. His remains were handed over to the surgeons, and between 30,000 and 40,000 people filed past during a special public viewing of his partly dissected body.

Resurrection men had been plying their grisly trade for over a century, creating a market for new inventions such as metal coffins as well as burial vaults, which provided the better-off with relative security. Although the writer Laurence Sterne was recognized on a Cambridge dissection slab in 1768 (and reinterred intact), for the most part resurrection men targeted the anonymous poor. In 1795 a riot broke out in a Lambeth churchyard after a series of particularly conspicuous instances of body-snatching. In this situation, as at Greenwich in 1832, crowds alerted to recent activity marched to their parish graveyard and began digging up their loved ones' coffins, only to find them empty.[32] The Burke–Hare murders gave such fears a new twist, highlighting the complicity (to say no worse) of otherwise highly respectable medical men. Soon London had its own Burke and Hare in a certain Mr Bishop and his associate Williams, who racked up sixty-one recorded body-snatchings and 'burked' three vagrants before being run to ground. Meanwhile Joshua Naples and Ben Crouch continued body-snatching, with the support and encouragement of the staff of St Thomas's and Guy's hospitals respectively.[33]

By focussing the public's attention on the horrors to which those buried in parish graveyards were subject, these scandals added greatly to the appeal of the Magnificent Seven. All cemetery companies made a show of security, with thick, high walls and nightwatchmen. At Kensal Green the nightwatchman was armed with a blunderbuss and a 'tell tale' clock-powered mechanism was installed. The watchman 'punched in' at regular intervals and fired off his blunderbuss each night at exactly midnight to reassure those within earshot that he was on the prowl against resurrectionists.[34] The tell-tale mechanism was proudly pointed out to Charles Dickens when he came to report on the cemetery for *All the Year Round*.

Catacombs provided even more reassurance and were also fashionably Parisian. Such was their popularity that considerable sums were invested by all of the Magnificent Seven. Even at Abney Park, where the Dissenting board initially balked at such showy luxuries, a small catacomb was built in 1840. By ordering that unclaimed bodies of paupers from workhouses and hospitals were to be used for dissection, the Anatomy Act of 1832 removed much of the fear of body-snatching, at least among the upper classes. For the poor, it added a new source of shame to the workhouse and lent a new dread to hospitals, too. As a group of petitioners from Lambeth noted, the Anatomy Act introduced 'a new and refined species of Burking'.[35]

Without sustained demand for catacombs among richer clients, several cemetery companies had cause to regret their initial enthusiasm in building them. The West of London and Westminster Cemetery Company at Brompton had its architect Benjamin Baud design three long ranges of catacombs, one of them following the course of the western wall, which ran alongside Kensington Canal (now the District Line tube). The cost proved unsustainable and Baud was dismissed while still being owed money. At Highgate the catacombs at the end of the famed Egyptian Avenue did not sell out and were adapted much later for use as a columbarium (i.e. a repository for cremated remains).

Those at Kensal Green were a runaway success. Demand for places in the catacombs under the Anglican chapel was boosted in 1843, when the coffin of HRH Augustus Frederick, Duke of Sussex rested there for a few weeks while his burial site on the central walk was being made ready. As in Paris, celebrity patronage was much sought after as a marketing tool, and where a famous individual's body could not be secured (the GCC had hoped to get the actor Edmund Kean) companies toyed with monuments to famous hymn writers, poets or other historical figures, perhaps hoping that the public would fail to notice that these individuals were in fact buried elsewhere.[36]

After a shaky start several cemetery companies' stock rose and they began paying out healthy dividends, although their promoters did not have a long-term business plan. In his important pamphlet *On the Laying Out, Planting, and Managing of Cemeteries* (1843), the garden designer John Claudius Loudon had critiqued the adoption of a picturesque, park-like planting such as that adopted at Norwood, seeing it as just one aspect of an inappropriate commercial model that was unsustainable in the long term. Loudon believed that rather than being allowed to become neglected ruins, cemeteries should in time be cleared of monuments and turned into public parks, as befitted a space intended to benefit the public at large.[37]

The doctor and campaigner George Alfred Walker did more than anyone else to draw attention to the repulsive goings-on at London's inner-city burial grounds in the 1840s. The worst excesses were, he found, in those small, privately run vaults under Enon Chapel and other Dissenting chapels, which processed unbelievably large numbers of bodies in a manner too gruesome to describe here.[38] Although some claimed that he was in the pay of the cemetery companies, in fact Walker believed that cemeteries 'ought *not* to be in the hands of joint-stock companies. They ought to be NATIONAL INSTITUTIONS.'[39] He urged the nationalization of cemetery companies and the adoption of a system of fixed-price funerals, with a view to ending what he saw as the exploitation of the bereaved by grasping undertakers.

Rather than representing a distinct profession in Victorian London, most undertakers worked as such only as a sideline to their main business as cabinet-makers or upholsterers. A given 'job' was often passed along a line of contractors and subcontractors, with all the hefty mark-ups that implied. There were healthy kickbacks, too, for those (including doctors) who drew the undertaker's attention to a nearby death. Pricing was far from transparent and clients faced steady pressure to include expensive 'optional extras' in the name of giving their loved one a 'decent' funeral. Walker's solution would have replaced this confusing system with something along the lines of the national system of *pompes funèbres* found in Paris and across France: a straightforward system that provided decent funerals at affordable, fixed prices.

While no such steps were taken to curtail what Dickens attacked as 'trading in death' by undertakers, criticism of private enterprise in cemeteries was more effective.[40] Here Walker's efforts as a publicist were aided by the investigative energies of Edwin Chadwick, whom we met in Chapter 1. In 1843 Chadwick published a report on urban burial grounds in which he advocated the nationalization of the Magnificent Seven and the establishment of fixed-price funerals. His report showed the pitiful lengths to which working-class Londoners were willing to go for a 'decent' funeral. Bodies were kept for days, putrefying in already cramped and poorly ventilated hovels, while funds were scraped together to pay the undertaker. All this effort and anxiety was spent to stage what Chadwick's research found was in fact a garbled parody of a baronial funeral.[41] Unfortunately other developments such as Chartist agitation and the repeal of the Corn Laws in 1846 prevented the government from paying sufficient attention to his findings. Chadwick's lack of political savvy did not help.

Only with the return of cholera to the city in the later 1840s and the creation of a General Board of Health in 1848 was there the public support and government infrastructure necessary to act. Under the Metropolitan Interments Act of 1850, the Board of Health was empowered to close inner-city burial grounds to new interments. Though this did not close all such sites as had the Imperial Decree of 1804 in Paris, it was a significant step. It also created a London-wide Metropolitan Burial District with the power to buy out and expand cemeteries established by companies like the GCC and to create its own new ones. A fee of six shillings and tuppence would be paid to the minister (Anglican or Dissenting) officiating at a burial in these cemeteries. Though the government did buy out Brompton Cemetery's shareholders, Treasury parsimony prevented the Board (whose long-term status was itself uncertain) from doing much else.

In 1852 a new Act abolished the Metropolitan Burial District. Parish vestries were now given the power to establish their own Burial Boards, able to purchase land and create parish cemeteries funded by the rates. Making up for lost time, parishes such as St Pancras and St Marylebone managed to buy land, build chapels and open new cemeteries as early as 1854. In 1856 the City of London opened a particularly splendid cemetery for the Square Mile, on Wanstead Flats in Essex. Though generally less theatrical than the likes of Highgate, these cemeteries were far from mundane. Thanks to the impact of Pugin and other 'Goths', their lodges, gates and chapels were all in the Gothic style, though the monuments erected by the better-off remained as eclectic as ever. Ratepayer support has ensured that these monuments were spared the shocking vandalism meted out to monuments in the Magnificent Seven over the course of the twentieth century.

London may have appropriated the Parisian cemetery, but it did not do so in an uncritical manner. Doubts remained surrounding overly showy burials and monuments. There is a clear sense of ambivalence in *Paris and its Environs*, of the cemetery as a place in which to debate Anglo-French attitudes to life and death. The first-time English visitor to the cemetery is described as initially charmed by the surprisingly cheery atmosphere, free of the gloomy yew trees, carved skulls and skeletons he associates with English burial grounds. 'To meet sad thoughts and overpower or allay them by other lofty and tender ones is right,' he writes, 'but to shun them altogether, to affect mirth in the midst of sighing, and divert the pangs of inward misfortune by something to catch the eye and tickle the sense, is what the English do not sympathize with.' At this point another voice interrupts, parenthetically, noting that 'a shrewd Frenchman perhaps may ask, how then do they so often consult their wine cellars in their grief?' Then we return to the 'English traveller's' account, which concludes, somewhat oddly, by stating that 'mirth' in the face of death is preferable. 'It is an advantage the French have over us.' [42] The Londoner here is in two minds about whether a Parisian response is entirely appropriate.

The First Garden Suburbs

For London the shift towards extramural burial anticipated later, more familiar trends. Parisians and Londoners had travelled to pretty villages such as Auteuil and Twickenham to build fashionable *bijou* retreats in the early eighteenth century, in some cases a good deal earlier. The suburbs were also known for their market gardens and for highwaymen. The suburb as a middle-class way of life associated with a particular system of daily commuting did not exist until the late nineteenth century. Marketed as an escape from the city, the suburb was nonetheless part of it, radically altering how people experienced London and Paris. Extramural cemeteries played an important role in this process, providing models for the layout and design of housing for the living.

When Père Lachaise, Kensal Green and their imitators first appeared, they were partly surrounded by fields. Within three or four decades the city overwhelmed them. Even in their current state they nonetheless afford a remarkable opportunity to experience an ideal city, a city that nineteenth-century city-dwellers managed to create only for the dead. In these necropolises, curving paths snake among trees, subtly demarcating areas assigned to different classes of wealth. Each family has its proud plot, at once intimate and showy, located as close to the 'desirable' central paths as the family can afford to be. Gothic, Egyptian, Celtic and Greek-style monuments sit cheek by jowl in cheerful eclecticism. Meanwhile the poor are largely invisible, relegated to unmarked paupers' graves on the cemetery's periphery.

Such huge complexes required large undeveloped sites of a kind that could be found only at some distance from the city. Kensal Green's managers arranged for an omnibus operator to lay on a service and toyed with the idea of a canal-based funeral service. The railroad boom of the 1840s afforded a more promising solution to the transport problem. Railroad companies were slow to realize the potential afforded by commuters, and in the early years their trains bypassed the suburbs. Only with the Cheap Trains Act of 1883 did the state force companies to cater to the lower classes. Railroad-focussed 'bedroom communities' for the dead therefore were created before those for the living, in the shape of the London Necropolis, Brookwood (1854), and, twenty years later, Haussmann's plan for Méry-sur-Oise.

Brookwood was established after the London Necropolis and National Mausoleum Company purchased from Lord Onslow 2,000 acres of Woking Common. The intent was to produce a cemetery so vast that it would satisfy London's burial needs for ever. Even if only 500 acres were landscaped, it was the world's largest cemetery when it opened in 1854 and it still remains an impressive complex. The London and South Western Railway line cut across the site, ensuring easy and cheap access to London. A branch line was run off, which led to two stations, one in the Anglican, consecrated half of the cemetery, and the other in the unconsecrated half, serving everyone else. Meanwhile a special funeral terminus was built on

York (now Leake) Street, next to Waterloo station. Special funeral trains carried coffins and mourners there and back once a day. The train service continued to operate until World War Two.[43]

Many London parishes used Brookwood as an overspill, or as a place to relocate remains disturbed as a result of road widening, new bridges or tunnelling for the Underground. Special spacious square plots enabled them to maintain their separate identity even at some distance from the city itself. Today the disposition of Brookwood's 234,000 dead reflects in counterpoint the story of the capital's expansion, the gradual erosion of traditional parochial ties and the development of its transport infrastructure. Whereas some parts are organized by parish, others are divided up according to profession. London's bakers and actors have their own dedicated areas. Within each subsection plots are clearly ranked according to their positioning relative to major paths, junctions and other features. Unlike the better-known cemeteries of London itself, there was also room for paupers at Brookwood, in the less favoured, unlandscaped southern section.

In Paris, Haussmann clearly recognized the importance of finding space for the dead in the well-planned city and he followed the example set by Brookwood. Although additions had been made during the early nineteenth century to the three cemeteries of the east (Père Lachaise), north (Montmartre) and south (Montparnasse) discussed earlier in this chapter, a third of the total area had been placed beyond use by the selling of permanent concessions (which gave one family sole rights to a certain plot). It had been possible to satisfy Paris's need for burial space only by continuing the practice of dumping the poor in a common grave. This continued even after Napoleon III insisted in 1850 that the practice be stopped, that even the indigent be given a plot of their own for at least five years. Had this policy been followed to the letter, Haussmann calculated, all available space would have been used up within five years.

In 1860 the municipalities surrounding Paris were incorporated within the city, increasing its population from 1.1 million to 1.6 million overnight.

Yet none of the annexed villages and towns had more than an acre or two of spare burial capacity. Having calculated that Paris needed an area of 850 hectares in order to grant every Parisian a thirty-year concession, in 1864 Haussmann appointed a commission to find suitable sites for two massive cemeteries, one to be sited to the north, one to the south. The only site deemed to have the right soil and sufficient room was at Méry-sur-Oise, eight miles to the north-west of Paris.

By 1867 his engineers had worked out the route and construction costs of a special railway that would link the new cemetery with dedicated funerary stations located next to the existing cemeteries at Montmartre, Montparnasse and Père Lachaise. Parisians would be less upset by the novelty, Haussmann reasoned, if the final journey of their loved ones initially followed the familiar route to one of these cemeteries. Those who wished to could then say their farewells at the station, with only close relatives and friends accompanying the body on the subsequent twenty-minute ride to Méry. Concerned that land prices in the area would spike once rumours of the plan leaked, Haussmann worked quietly with the mayor of Méry to buy up plots. The whole scheme would, he calculated, cost 15 million francs, including the railroad and stations.

Haussmann's plan came in for criticism in the Senate, with complaints that the site was too remote, making it impossible for the poor to visit their loved ones' graves on All Souls and All Saints day, as was traditional. The pre-emptive purchase of land at Méry also fuelled a mood of rising impatience with Haussmann's costly improvement schemes. In 1870, Haussmann was dismissed by Napoleon III, whose own rule ended shortly afterwards in the disaster of the Franco-Prussian War. The scheme was not reconsidered until 1874. It was then decided that it was inappropriate to let a municipality run a railroad, even one as short as the planned Méry funeral service. Instead it was proposed that the Chemin de Fer du Nord be contracted to build and operate a service branching off their line, which ran along the opposite bank of the Oise from Méry. The company refused, however. Meanwhile extensions of the cemeteries at Ivry-Gentilly and Saint-Ouen rendered the crisis less urgent. Although a modified version of the scheme was formally adopted in 1881, it was never implemented.[44] Today the wooded estate of La Garenne de Maubuisson, by far the largest plot purchased for the scheme, is owned by the municipality of Méry. This public green space is all that remains of Haussmann's scheme for a necropolis that would have served the needs of Paris's dead for all time.

But what of suburbs for the living? The development of the Eyre Estate in St John's Wood in the years between 1804 and 1856 would seem to be the first example of a landowner adopting and then implementing an overall scheme for a villa suburb. This was closely followed by John Nash's scheme for an elite suburb in neighbouring Regent's Park. Now lost, the 'Alpha Cottages' erected between 1804 and 1811 along Alpha Road were the beginning of Walpole Eyre II's plans for a residential quarter from which most trades, any places of public entertainment and any Dissenting house of worship (Roman Catholic ones were acceptable) were excluded. Declining family fortunes, however, and the construction of a new railway terminus at Marylebone at the close of the century prevented Eyre's scheme from being fully carried out. The early twentieth century saw the estate encourage the erection of decidedly unsuburban mansion blocks.

To see St John's Wood as the first 'garden suburb' is a stretch of the imagination.[45] Garden cemeteries faced the same challenges at roughly the same time, including those dictated by denominational divides and transport. How could the same space serve as 'home' to Anglicans and Dissenters? How could it achieve accessibility without losing that sense of being a quarter apart, at a certain remove from the hubbub of the city? Not only did garden cemeteries meet these challenges more successfully, but coverage by Dickens and others ensured that they were seen to do so. In John Claudius Loudon, the suburban cemetery and the villa found one and the same architect, an architect whose manuals of villa and cemetery design were widely copied, including in the United States, where the earliest 'garden cities' (so-called) appeared.[46]

The garden cemetery anticipated the garden city in layout as well as in social make-up. Promoters of garden cemeteries and garden suburbs alike initially vowed to be socially inclusive, accommodating the middle class as well as the working man. Indeed, several of the Model Dwelling Companies described in Chapter 1 experimented with working-class housing estates in the countryside, instead of apartment blocks in the city centre.[47] Shaftesbury Park in Battersea (1872) is one example, anticipating by thirty years the LCC's own 'cottage estates' at White Hart Lane in Tottenham and the nearest Parisian equivalent by much longer. However, the MDC estates were eventually taken over by the lower middle class, the same stratum of society that was filling the endless terraced houses ('villas' in name only) of West Ham, Leyton and Walthamstow, with their postage-stamp front gardens.[48]

By the time architects Raymond Unwin and Barry Parker wrote *Town Planning and Modern Architecture* (1909) in praise of their Hampstead Garden Suburb, it was clear that the principle of inclusion had fallen by the wayside and that this new enclave was an escape from the city, rather than a model city in itself. Indeed, it was open season on the lower middle class. In a mixture of snobbery and a Ruskinian eye for 'craft', the book looked forward to 'an alien Power' destroying all the 'Acacia Villas' of the lower middle class. It began by assuming an 'average family with one or more servants' that was very far from being 'average'.[49] The resulting estate has at least maintained a distinct identity, even as it has become surrounded by developments for a lower class. Though garden cemeteries did manage to accommodate a wider range of people, in all other respects Bernard Blackmantle's satire of 1825 is eerily prescient in its vision of a landscape of 'alcoves, and bowers, and fish-ponds, and shrubs,/Select, as in life, from intrusion of scrubs.' As a garden cemetery for the living, Hampstead Garden Suburb is both 'select' and free from 'scrubs'.[50]

State provision of housing of the kind found in the LCC's estates was unknown in the nineteenth century, apart from the workhouse. Debates over cemeteries nonetheless foreshadowed twentieth-century discussions surrounding state welfare policies and free enterprise. Even those who acknowledged the need to do something about overcrowded inner-city graveyards feared that new cemeteries might shift the balance between state intervention and private enterprise, resulting in a more 'Continental' emphasis on central planning and the use of compulsory purchase to push through 'improvements'. In the 1840s there was a concern that public health experts like Chadwick might yoke together sanitary issues with more familiar ones concerning the supposed inferiority of London's public buildings in order to build a case for the nationalization of the undertaking and cemetery business.

In fact, it fell to a Conservative Home Secretary, James Graham, to implement Chadwick's recommendations. The funds allocated were limited, and only one cemetery company was nationalized. Undertaking was not nationalized into a monopoly like the French 'pompes funèbres'.[51] Although the kind of funeral flummery abhorred by Dickens survived longer among the poor of the East End (and was very much present at the funeral of the gangster 'Reggie' Kray in October 2000), by the 1880s it was in decline among the middle class. By that point most London parishes had established their own cemeteries (far beyond the parish boundary), funded by the rates. Though the city's authorities are again faced with a crisis that they are refusing to address, Victorian London faced and solved its burial crisis.[52]

Viewed from the heights of London's Nunhead or Paris's Père Lachaise, the Great Wen is tamed: a city of aquatint, a pretty keepsake in a foliage frame. Even today, in their overgrown and vandalized state, cemeteries allow us to glimpse the ideal city of the nineteenth century, in which the conflicting needs of commemoration, sanitation, transportation, business, fashion and social distinction are held in balance. Cemeteries modelled an artificial, picturesque 'nature' that had very little to do with the real countryside. It was its fashionable Englishness as much as its 'naturalness' that explains this landscape's appeal to a late eighteenth-century French elite. Spirituality in contrast had scarcely a role. The caesura of the revolutionary cult of reason as well as Napoleon's nationalization of burial ensured that London could reimport this model as the garden cemetery without having to worry too much about associations with either Jacobin atheism or Roman Catholic superstition. The Church of England would play surprisingly little part in the reform of burial habits, adopting an uncoordinated if largely passive attitude to the new cemeteries and, later in the century, to the rise of cremation.

Today the thirty-two London boroughs contain more than 130 cemeteries, more than half of which were established by 1890. Though largely ignored, together they cover a sizeable percentage of London's 607 square miles. They accommodate the vast majority of Londoners, a community predicted to grow by 50,000 a year until 2030.[53] In 1860, Charles Dickens made a point of visiting the city's cemeteries on his 'night walks':

> It was a solemn consideration what enormous hosts of dead
> belong to one old great city, and how, if they were raised
> while the living slept, there would not be the space of a
> pin's point in all the streets and ways for the living to come
> out into. Not only that, but the vast armies of dead would
> overflow the hills and valleys beyond the city, and would
> stretch away all round it, God knows how far: seemingly, to
> the confines of the earth.[54]

As Lewis Mumford noted in his landmark work *The City in History*, 'urban life spans the historic space between the earliest burial ground and the final cemetery, the Necropolis, in which one civilization after another has met its end.'[55] It is fitting, therefore, that our journey to Mercier's 'other Paris', which began in the jolting darkness of the diligence, should end here, on the heights of Nunhead Cemetery, looking out over the city below.

Notes

Introduction: Rough Crossings

1 Information on route, stops, timings, etc., is taken from the anonymous 1786 manuscript, 'Petites notes d'un voyage à <u>Londres</u> en Partant de <u>Paris</u>', tipped into a copy of Jean Mazzinghy, *The New and Universal Guide through the Cities of London and Westminster* (London: C. Dilly, 1785). Lewis Walpole Library (hereafter referred to as LWL), 646 75 M45.

2 James Rutlidge (ed.), *Le Babillard*, 95 numbers, 4 vols (January 1778–April 1779), vol. 1, pp. 1–4, 29–30. Extracts are available in a modern edition, edited by Raymonde Monnier, *Paris et Londres en miroir: extraits du Babillard de Jean-Jacques Rutlidge* (Saint-Étienne: Université de Saint-Étienne, 2010). See also Ralph A. Naplow, *The Addisonian Tradition in France: Passion and Objectivity in Social Observation* (Rutherford, NJ: Farleigh Dickinson University Press, 1990).

3 Rutlidge (ed.), *Le Babillard*, 16 (20 March 1778), vol. 1, p. 258.

4 Ibid., 25 (5 May 1778), vol. 2, p. 9.

5 Ibid., 28 (20 May 1778), vol. 2, pp. 51–7.

6 I am grateful to Simon Macdonald for this information. See Macdonald, 'British communities in late eighteenth-century Paris' (unpublished PhD thesis, University of Cambridge, 2011), ch. 5.

7 John Wilkes to William Fitzherbert, 10 September 1764. Matlock, Derbyshire County Record Office (Fitzherbert Papers), F8244.

8 De Boissy, *Le François à Londres, comédie* (The Hague: Jean Neaulme, 1747).

9 Samuel Foote, *The Englishman in Paris, a Comedy, in two acts* (London, 1753), p. 24.

10 Maxine Berg, *Luxury and Pleasure in Eighteenth-century Britain* (Oxford: OUP, 2005).

11 Samuel Foote, *The Englishman Return'd from Paris. A farce in two acts* (London, 1756), Prologue.

12 Stephen Mennell, *All Manners of Food: Eating and Taste in England and France from the Middle Ages to the Present,* 2nd edn (Chicago: University of Illinois Press, 1996), p. 129.

13 Léon Béclard, *Sébastien Mercier, sa vie, son œuvre, son temps* (Zurich and New York: Georg Olms Verlag, 1982; originally published 1903), p. 4.

14 Louis-Sébastien Mercier, *Tableau de Paris*, 12 vols (Amsterdam, 1782–8). Sadly, the *Tableau* is available in English only in an abridged form. Helen Simpson (ed.), *The Waiting City: Paris, 1782–88, being an abridgement of Louis-Sébastien Mercier's 'Le tableau de Paris'* (Philadelphia: J.B. Lippincott, 1933). Jeremy D. Popkin (ed.), *Panorama of Paris, Selections from 'Tableau de Paris'* (Philadelphia: Pennsylvania State University Press, 1999). Extracts from the *Tableau* were translated and published by Joseph Parkyn Macmahon, as *Paris in miniature: taken from the French picture at full length, entitled Tableau de Paris: interspersed with remarks and anecdotes: together with a preface and a postface by the English Limner* (London: printed for G. Kearsly, 1782).

15 Claude Bruneteau and Bernard Cottret (eds), *Louis-Sébastien Mercier. Parallèle de Paris et de Londres* (Paris: Didier Erudition, 1982: hereafter cited as Mercier, *Parallèle*), p. 53.

16 P. Grosley, *Londres* (Lausanne, 1770), p. 83.

17 Henri Decremps, *Un Parisien à Londres*, 2 vols (Amsterdam: [n.p.], 1789), vol. 1, p. 115.

18 Mercier, *Parallèle*, p. 61.

19 Again, this practical information is from the anonymous 1786 'Petites notes' in the LWL. See note 1.

20 As such it was closely related to the utopia Mercier presented in his *L'An deux mille quatre cent quarante* (1771). Yet the *Parallèle* is overlooked in Anthony Vidler's wide-ranging discussion of Mercier as an urbanist. Anthony Vidler, 'Mercier as Urbanist: the utopia of the real', in Vidler, *The Scenes of the Street and Other Essays* (New York: Monacelli, 2011), pp. 170–82.

21 Mercier, *Parallèle*, pp. 182–3.

22 For a discussion of the concept, see Paolo Napoli, *Naissance de la police moderne: pouvoir, normes société* (Paris: Éditions de la Découverte, 2003), ch. 1.

23 *The World*, 189 (12 August 1756), p. 1133.

24 In 1766, Adam Smith noted that 'police' was a word 'which properly signified the policey [*sic*] of civil government, but now it only means the regulation of the inferiour [*sic*] parts of government, viz. cleanliness, security, and cheapness or plenty'. Adam Smith, *Lectures on Jurisprudence*, R. L. Meek, D. D. Raphael and P. G. Stein (eds) (Oxford: OUP, 1978), p. 486.

25 Laurent Turcot, 'L'émergence d'un espace plurifonctionnel: les boulevards parisiens au XVIIIe siècle', *Histoire urbaine*, 12 (April 2005), pp. 89–115.

26 Richard Sennett, *The Conscience of the Eye: The Design and Social Life of Cities* (New York: Random House, 1990).

27 BL Maps Crace XVII/3. Peter Whitfield, *London: A Life in Maps* (London: British Library, 2006), p. 66; Kathryn A. Morrison, *English Shops and Shopping: An Architectural History* (New Haven: Yale University Press, 2003), pp. 16–18.

28 Mercier, *Parallèle*, p. 116.

29 For a discussion see Jonathan Conlin, 'Wilkes, the Chevalier d'Eon and the "dregs of liberty": an Anglo-French perspective on ministerial despotism', *English Historical Review*, 120 (November 2005), pp. 1–38.

30 Mercier, *Parallèle*, p. 166.

31 Ibid., pp. 127–8. For a discussion of charitable institutions in London see Donna T. Andrew, *Philanthropy and Police: London Charity in the Eighteenth Century* (Princeton, NJ: Princeton University Press, 1990).

32 Mercier, *Parallèle*, pp. 138, 166.

33 Ibid., p. 117.

34 Ibid., ch. 36.

35 Ibid., ch 27.

36 Ibid., p. 79.

37 Leonard Schwarz, 'London, 1700–1840', in Peter Clark (ed.), *The Cambridge Urban History of Britain,* 3 vols (Cambridge: Cambridge University Press, 2000), vol. 2, p. 652.

38 Here I draw on James Donald, *Imagining the Modern City* (London: Athlone, 1999), ch. 2.

39 For an excellent survey of this literature see Claire Hancock, *Paris et Londres au XIXe siècle: représentations dans les guides et récits de voyage* (Paris: Editions du CNRS, 2003).

40 Linda Colley, *Britons: Forging the Nation, 1707–1837* (New Haven: Yale, 1992); Jeremy Black, *Natural and Necessary Enemies: Anglo-French Relations in the Eighteenth Century* (London: Duckworth, 1986).

41 For the seventeenth century, however, see Karen Newman, *Cultural Capitals: Early Modern London and Paris* (Princeton: Princeton University Press, 2007), and for the nineteenth, Donald J. Olsen, *The City as a Work of Art: London, Paris, Vienna* (New Haven: Yale University Press, 1986).

42 As Werner and Zimmermann note, in *histoire croisée*, 'entities and objects of research are not merely considered in relation to one another but also *through* one another, in terms of relationships, interactions, and circulation'. Michael Werner and Bénédicte Zimmermann, 'Beyond comparison: *histoire croisée* and the challenge of reflexivity', *History and Theory*, 45: 1 (2006), pp. 30–50 (38).

43 'Intelligence of Marybone Gardens', newspaper clipping, 1776. Westminster Archive (WA), Ashbridge Collection (AC), 710/779.

44 Ibid.

45 Mercier, *Parallèle,* p. 73.

46 Ibid., p. 70.

Chapter One: The Restless House

1 Henri Decremps, *Un Parisien à Londres*, 2 vols (Amsterdam: [n.p.], 1789), vol. 2, pp. 131–2.

2 Jean-François Cabestan, *La Conquête du plain-pied: l'immeuble à Paris au XVIIIe siècle* (Paris: Picard, 2004), pp. 42–3.

3 Ibid., pp. 280–1.

4 Ibid., p. 256.

5 Ibid., p. 215.

6 Marc-Antoine Laugier, *Essai sur l'Architecture* (new edn, Paris: Duchesne, 1755), p. 228.

7 Pierre Pinon, 'La formation du IXe arrondissement: de la Chaussée-d'Antin au faubourg Poissonière', in Jacques Lucan (ed.), *Paris des Faubourgs: Formation, Transformation* (Paris: Picard, 1996), pp. 21–33 (23).

8 Rutlidge, *Le Babillard*, 1: 178 (20 February 1778), p. 11.

9 Dan Cruickshank and Neil Burton, *Life in the Georgian City* (London: Viking, 1990), pp. 99, 101.

10 Ibid., p. 125.

11 Mercier, *Parallèle,* p. 141; Cesar de Saussure, cited in Cruickshank and Burton, *Life in the Georgian City*, p. 52.

12 Cruickshank and Burton, *Life in the Georgian City*, p. 60.

13 Susannah Morris, 'Market solutions for social problems: working-class housing in nineteenth-century London', *Economic History Review,* new series, 54: 3 (August 2001), pp. 525–45 (536). See also Anthony S. Wohl, *The Eternal Slum: Housing and Social Policy in Victorian London* (London: Transaction, 2002), ch. 6.

14 Morris, 'Market solutions for social problems', p. 530. The Peabody's ability to undercut the MDCs led to charges that they were 'unfair traders'. Wohl, *The Eternal Slum*, p. 158.

15 'Falling houses and model dwellings', *The Builder*, 40 (3 December 1853), p. 721. Returns of 7, 8 or even 10 per cent were mooted. Wohl, *The Eternal Slum*, p. 142.

252

16 Indeed, it has been suggested that it was the MDCs' clamour for larger sites that influenced the approach taken in the Artisans' and Labourers' Dwellings Improvement Act, while the MBW had little input. J. A. Yelling, *Slums and Slum Clearance in Victorian London* (London: Allen and Unwin, 1986), pp. 16–7, 24.

17 'New Buildings, Farringdon Road', *The Builder*, 32 (5 December 1874), p. 1003.

18 Francis Butler to the Editor, *The Builder*, 32 (19 December 1874), p. 1056.

19 Ann-Louise Shapiro, *Housing the Poor of Paris, 1850–1902* (Madison: University of Wisconsin Press, 1985), p. 32.

20 The Revd Wyatt Edgell, cited in Charles Gatliff, 'On improved dwellings and their beneficial effect on health and morals', *Journal of the Statistical Society of London*, 38: 1 (March 1875), pp. 33–63 (57). For the claim that MDCs simply served those who could have afforded to live somewhere else, see Wohl, *The Eternal Slum*, pp. 147, 150, 163–4, 170.

21 See Arthur Newsholme, 'The vital statistics of Peabody Buildings and other artisans' and labourers' block dwellings', *Journal of the Statistical Society of London*, 51: 4 (March 1891), pp. 70–111.

22 Gatliff, 'On improved dwellings', p. 43.

23 Stanley's *Through the Dark Continent* was published in 1878. For another example of this analogy in the context of Jack London's *People of the Abyss* (1903), see Lawrence Phillips, 'Jack London and the East End: socialism, imperialism and the bourgeois ethnographer', in Lawrence Phillips (ed.), *A Mighty Mass of Brick and Smoke: Victorian and Edwardian Representations of London* (Amsterdam: Rodopi, 2008), pp. 213–34.

24 'A Lady Resident', 'Sketch of Life in Buildings', in Ellen Ross (ed.), *Slum Travelers: Ladies and London Poverty, 1860–1920* (London: University of California Press, 2007), pp. 41–4 (44).

25 James Hole in *International Health Exhibition* (1884), p. 51.

26 LCC and borough architects borrowed plans from MDCs as a guide to their own projects. Wohl, *The Eternal Slum*, p. 175; Yelling, *Slums*, p. 42.

27 Shapiro, *Housing the Poor of Paris*, p. 51; Pierre Lavedan, *Histoire de l'Urbanisme à Paris* (Paris: Hachette, 1975), p. 341.

28 Note in particular the abridgement of the scene in which the cook Adèle gives birth and the heavily edited account of Octave Mouret's rape of Marie Pichon. Émile Zola, *Piping Hot! (Pot-Bouille): A Realistic Novel* (London: Vizetelly, 1885), pp. 368, 82.

29 Anthony Cummins, 'Émile Zola's cheap English dress: the Vizetelly translations, late-Victorian print culture, and the crisis of literary value', *Review of English Studies*, 60 (2009), pp. 108–32 (112). Henry was helped by his son, Ernest Alfred,

who checked the proofs of his Zola translations. For the younger Vizetelly's recollections of his father's trial, see his *Émile Zola, Novelist and Reformer: An Account of His Life and Work* (London: John Lane, 1904), pp. 252–81.

30 Andrew Lycett, *Conan Doyle: the Man Who Created Sherlock Holmes* (London: Weidenfeld and Nicolson, 2007), p. 174.

31 But Pinkerton's translation did live on, reprinted three times in the 1950s, as well as in 1986. Émile Zola, *Restless House*, trans. Percy Pinkerton (London: Grafton, 1986).

32 Louis Chevalier, *Labouring Classes and Dangerous Classes in Paris during the First Half of the Nineteenth Century*, trans. Frank Jellinek (London: Routledge and Kegan Paul, 1973), pp. 198–9; Shapiro, *Housing the Poor of Paris*, pp. 36, 43, 45.

33 Émile Zola, *Pot Luck,* trans Brian Nelson (Oxford: Oxford University Press, 1999) p. 286.

34 Ibid., p. 105.

35 Ibid., p. 243.

36 'French Flats', *Building News*, 3 (20 February 1857), p. 181.

37 'Living on Flats', *Saturday Review* (23 October 1875), p. 516.

38 'Houses in Flats for London', *The Builder*, 34 (8 January 1876), p. 25.

39 W. H. White to the Editor, *The Builder*, 34 (25 March 1876), p. 291.

40 'My concierge', in Blanchard Jerrold, *At Home in Paris: At Peace and at War,* 2 vols (London: William Allen, 1871), vol. 1, pp. 41–62; Bayle St John, *Purple Tints of Paris: Character and Manners in the New Empire,* 2 vols (London: Chapman and Hall, 1854), vol. 1, p. 42 (quote), pp. 43–47.

41 Hancock, *Paris et Londres*, p. 131.

42 'Flats for the Middle Classes', *Building News*, 15 (15 May 1868), p. 323.

43 'Falling houses and model dwellings', *The Builder*, pp. 721–2.

44 'Flats for the Middle Classes', p. 323.

45 '"Buildings," – "Mansions," – "Flats," – "Residences," – "Dwellings"', *The Builder*, 36 (12 January 1878), p. 31.

46 *Transactions of the Institute of British Architects* (1877), p. 63. White responded in 'Middle-class houses in Paris and central London', *The Builder*, 36 (12 January 1878), p. 42.

47 J. N. Tarn, 'French flats for the English in nineteenth-century London', in Anthony Sutcliffe (ed.), *Multi-Storey Living: The British Working-Class Experience* (London: Croom Helm, 1974), pp. 19–40 (quote, p. 35).

48 '"Buildings," – "Mansions,"', p. 32.

49 'Houses in Flats for London', p. 27.

50 '"Buildings," – "Mansions,"', p. 32; 'Houses in Flats for London', p. 26; Eales, 'Dwellings in Flats', *Building News*, 46 (7 March 1884), p. 362.

51 'Houses in Flats for London', p. 25.

52 'Living on Flats', p. 516.

53 'Houses in Flats for London', p. 26.

54 Quoted in *The Builder*, 34 (22 January 1876), p. 82.

55 'Dwellings in Flats', p. 363.

56 Jerrold, *At Home in Paris,* pp. 60, 48.

57 Ibid., p. 59.

58 'Dwellings in flats', p. 363.

59 'Architectural Association', *The Builder*, 46 (15 March 1884), p. 386.

60 '"Buildings," - "Mansions,"', p. 31.

61 'Palatinate Buildings, New Kent Road', *The Builder*, 34 (1 January 1876), p. 8.

Chapter Two: The Street

1 Symons to James Dykes Campbell, 6 October 1889. Karl Beckson and John M. Munro (eds), *Arthur Symons: Selected Letters, 1880–1935* (Basingstoke: Macmillan, 1989), p. 53.

2 Charles Baudelaire, 'The Painter of Modern Life' [originally published in *Le Figaro*, 26 and 28 November, 3 December 1863], in Charles Baudelaire, *The Painter of Modern Life and Other Essays*, trans. Jonathan Mayne (London: Phaidon, 1964), pp. 1–40 (9).

3 Baudelaire, 'Painter of Modern Life', p. 12. See also 'The Salon of 1846', in Baudelaire, *Art in Paris, 1845–1862*, trans. Jonathan Mayne (Oxford: Phaidon, 1965), p. 117.

4 Charles Baudelaire, 'Les foules', *Le Spleen de Paris* [1869], in Baudelaire, *Oeuvres Complètes,* 2 vols (Paris: Gallimard, 1975-6), vol. 1, p. 291.

5 For one example, taken from Rétif de la Bretonne, see Laurent Turcot, *Le Promeneur à Paris* (Paris: Gallimard, 2007), p. 407.

6 T. J. Clark, *The Painter of Modern Life* (New York: Thames and Hudson, 1985). For Guys in London, where he worked as a tutor of French and drawing to the children of Thomas Calvert Girton, see Margaret Rose, *Flaneurs and Idlers* (Bielefeld: Aisthesis, 2007), p. 24.

7 Walter Benjamin, *Das Passagen-werk*, ed. Rolf Tiedem, 2 vols (Frankfurt: Suhrkamp, 1983), vol. 1, p. 525. See Eric Hazan, 'Les Flâneurs', in Hazan, *L'Invention de Paris: il n'y a pas des pas perdus* (Paris: Seuil, 2002), pp. 393–423. There are odd indications in the *Passagen-werk* that Benjamin recognized that

London might have been more of an influence. He suspected, for example, that Poe's and Baudelaire's images of Paris as coloured by the anxieties of industrialization may in fact have reflected London more than the French capital. See *Passagen-werk,* vol. 1, p. 566.

8   Newman has argued that *flâneurs* existed in seventeenth-century London and Paris, but the individuals she cites (e.g. John Donne) did not describe solitary walks, and hence cannot be considered as *flâneurs*. Karen Newman, *Cultural Capitals: Early Modern London and Paris* (Princeton: Princeton University Press, 2007), ch. 3.

9   Henri Decremps, *Un Parisien à Londres,* 2 vols (Amsterdam: [n.p.], 1789), vol. 1, p. 89.

10   Mercier, *Parallèle,* p. 95.

11   Daniel Cruickshank and Neil Burton, *Life in the Georgian City* (London: Viking, 1990), pp. 13–18; Donald Olsen, *Town Planning in London: the Eighteenth and Nineteenth Centuries* (New Haven: Yale University Press, 1964), pp. 39–42.

12   Mercier, *Parallèle*, p. 60.

13   I am grateful to Laurent Turcot for providing this information.

14   Fayçal El Ghoul, *La Police Parisienne dans la seconde moitié du XVIIIe siècle (1760-1785),* 2 vols (Tunis: Université de Tunis I, 1995), vol. 1, pp. 190–206. Chevalier, *Labouring Classes and Dangerous Classes*, pp. 464–5, note 5.

15   Turcot, *Le Promeneur à Paris,* p. 34.

16   [Rétif de la Bretonne], *Les Nuits de Paris, ou le Spectateur Nocturne*, 14 vols (London: [n.p.], 1788–9), vol. 10, p. 2365. See also [Caraccioli], *Dictionnaire critique, pittoresque et sentencieux, propre à faire connoître les usages du siècle, ainsi que ses bizarreries*, 2 vols (Lyon: Benoît Duplain, 1768), vol. 1, p. 33.

17   Turcot, *Le Promeneur à Paris,* p. 72.

18   Ibid., p. 185.

19   Clare Brant and Susan E. Whyman (eds), *Walking the Streets of Eighteenth-Century London: John Gay's Trivia* (Oxford: Oxford University Press, 2009).

20   Decremps, *Un Parisien à Londres*, vol. 1, pp. 92–3.

21   Ibid., vol. 1, p. 99.

22   Ibid., vol. 1, p. 103.

23   Ibid., vol. 1, p. 114.

24   Ibid., vol. 1, pp. 118–20.

25   Gabriel Bonno, *La constitution britannique devant l'opinion français de Montesquieu à Bonaparte* (Paris: H. Champion, 1931).

26   Edmond Dziembowski, *Un nouveau patriotisme français, 1750–70* (Oxford: Voltaire Foundation, 1998); Edmond Dziembowski, 'The English political model in eighteenth-century France', *Historical Research*, 74 (2001), pp. 151–71.

27　Choiseul to Chatelet, 23 May 1768. Archives de Ministère des Affaires Etrangères, Paris. Correspondance Politique Angleterre 478, f.328.

28　Anon., *Lettre sur l'émeute arrivée à Londres le 2 Juin 1780, et sur les anglais* ([n.p.] 1780), p. 4.

29　Key figures here were the French diplomat and transvestite the Chevalier d'Eon and the playwright Caron de Beaumarchais. See Jonathan Conlin, '"Faire le Wilkes": the Chevalier d'Eon and the Wilkites', in Simon Burrows et al., *The Chevalier d'Eon and his Worlds: Gender, Politics and Espionage in the Eighteenth Century* (London: Continuum, 2010).

30　Mercier, *Parallèle*, p. 89.

31　Ibid., p. 109.

32　Ibid., p. 108.

33　For a different view of these much-discussed areas, see Daniel Vaillancourt, *Les Urbanités Parisiennes au XVIIe siècle: le livre du trottoir* (Quebec: Presses de l'Université Laval, 2009).

34　Anon., *La Réflexion faite un peu tard, ou le voyageur Babillard* (London: [n.p.], 1788), p. 8.

35　Colin Jones, *Paris: Biography of a City* (London: Penguin, 1994), p. 327.

36　See Jonathan Conlin, 'Vauxhall on the Boulevard: pleasure gardens in Paris and London, 1759–89', *Urban History*, 35: 1 (May 2008), pp. 24–47.

37　Colin Bailey, Kim de Beaumont et al., *Gabriel de Saint-Aubin, 1725–1780* (Paris: Louvre, 2008), cats 51, 52a, 52b. A similar layout showing a hat-makers is illustrated, p. 214, Fig. 1.

38　Cited in Morrison, *English Shops and Shopping*, p. 33.

39　Ibid., p. 35.

40　Ibid., pp. 43, 50.

41　Edward Planta, *A New Picture of Paris*, 16th edn (1831), cited in Claire Hancock, *Paris et Londres au XIXe siècle: representations dans les guides et récits de voyage* (Paris: Editions du CNRS, 2003), p. 193.

42　By limiting the number of streets leading off its eastern edge it also served as 'a boundary and complete separation between the Streets and Squares occupied by the Nobility and Gentry, and the narrow Streets and meaner Houses occupied by mechanics and the trading part of the community'. *Select Committee on the Office of Works* (1828), p. 74.

43　Jonathan Conlin, 'Le Musée de Marchandises: the origins of the Musée Cognacq-Jay', *Journal of the History of Collections*, 12: 2 (2000).

44　In her study of city guides and travelogues, Hancock has noted a contrast between scholarly obsession with *passages* (a response to Benjamin's *Passagen-werk*) and the views of contemporaries, who did not see them as all that significant. Hancock, *Paris et Londres au XIXe siècle*, pp. 195–6.

45 As Richard Sennett notes, in ceasing to haggle over prices city-dwellers no longer needed to learn how to act shocked or pretend to walk away. This was just one way, he argues, in which the nineteenth-century bourgeoisie of Paris and London squandered the precious public realm they had inherited. Richard Sennett, *The Fall of Public Man* (London: Penguin, 2002), p. 142. Albert Smith noted that the 'lounger' just did not have the means to buy anything, even if he did pass most of his day looking at shops. Albert Smith, *Natural History of the Idler upon Town* (London: D. Bogue, 1848), p. 29.

46 Morrison, *Shops and Shopping*, p. 39.

47 Mercier, *Parallèle*, p. 144.

48 Laurence Sterne, 'The Pulse. Paris.', 'The Husband. Paris.', *A Sentimental Journey Through France and Germany* (Oxford: Oxford University Press, 1968), pp. 69–73.

49 The New Exchange (1667), Middle Exchange (1672) and Exeter Change (1676) featured stalls on one or more floors, staffed by attractive women selling gloves, hose, silks and themselves (according to some observers). Morrison, *Shops and Shopping*, p. 34. See also Anon. [John Dunton], *The Night-Walker: or, evening rambles in search after lewd women*, 2 vols (London: James Orme, 1697), vol. 1, pp. 11–12.

50 This is one reason why the scholarly search for a *flâneuse* seems slightly beside the point. Janet Wolff offers a refreshing break from this earnest endeavour in 'Gender and the haunting of cities (or, the retirement of the flâneur)', in Aruna D'Souza and Tom McDonough (eds), *The Invisible Flâneuse? Gender, Public Space, and Visual Culture in Nineteenth-Century Paris* (Manchester: Manchester University Press, 2006), pp. 18–31 (24).

51 When scholars have mentioned the *flâneur* in an eighteenth-century or early nineteenth-century context, they have fought shy of relating it directly to the *promeneur* in Paris or the 'rambler', even when their descriptions of the latter figures closely resemble the classic Baudelairean definition of a *flâneur*. Eric Hazan notes that 'Les prodromes de ce phénomène initiateur de la modernité . . . s'égrènent tout au long du XVIIIe siècle finissant,' but he does not explore these seeds in any depth. Hazan, *L'Invention du Paris*, p. 395. Turcot describes his 'Parisian *promeneur*' as 'someone who, by viewing the city from a certain remove, determines the conditions by which the urban subject is individualised. His movement through the city is unique and personal', *Le Promeneur à Paris*, p. 13. Karen Newman has admittedly suggested that there were *flâneurs* in seventeenth-century Paris and London. This is an anachronism, however, as the accounts she quotes are of social

walking (not solitary *flânerie*). London or Paris print culture was not yet developed enough to make possible the type of journalism practised by Addison and Steele. Karen Newman, *Cultural Capitals: Early Modern London and Paris* (Princeton: Princeton University Press, 2007), pp. 62–3.

52 Anon., *Le Flâneur au Salon* (Paris: Aubry, 1809), p. 7.

53 Ibid., p. 11.

54 Henry and Jules, *Le Flâneur, comédie-vaudeville en un acte* (Paris: Lacourière, 1825); Dumersan, Brazier and Gabriel, *La Journée d'un Flâneur, comédie en quatre actes* (Paris: J.-N. Barba, 1827).

55 Henry and Jules, *Le Flâneur,* p. 3.

56 Ibid., p. 22.

57 Cited in Rose, *Flaneurs and Idlers,* p. 2.

58 The earliest example of this is an 1819 field guide to cafés, pocket-sized, with entries on no less than sixty establishments, apparently penned by Étienne-François Bazot. 'Un Flâneur patenté', *Les Cafés de Paris, ou revue politique, critique et littéraire des moeurs du siècle* (Paris: Lécrivain, 1819).

59 This is demonstrated by the tendency for signs to remain when shopkeepers moved, something that was partly responsible for some of the odd combinations of trade and sign that emerged over time. The sign was first and foremost a geographic marker, and that function trumped all others.

60 August Philippe Herlaut, 'L'éclairage des rues de Paris à la fin du XVIIe siècle et au XVIIIe siècle', *Mémoires de la Société de l'histoire de Paris*, 43: pp. 130–240 (177); Jean-Paul Willesme, *Histoires des Enseignes du Musée Carnavalet* (Paris: Paris-Musées, 1996), p. 14; Edouard Fournier, *Histoires des Enseignes de Paris* (Paris: E. Dentu, 1884), pp. 21–5; Mercier, *Tableau de Paris*, vol. 2, p. 204.

61 Jonathan Conlin, '"At the expense of the public": the 1762 Signpainters' Exhibition and the public sphere', *Eighteenth-Century Studies*, 36: 1 (2002).

62 Molière, *Les Fâcheux* (Paris: Libraire des Bibliophiles, 1874), p. 66 (III, ii). See also *Tatler*, 18 (21 May 1709). Donald Fredric Bond (ed.), *The Tatler*, 3 vols (Oxford: Clarendon, 1987), vol. 1, pp. 144–7.

63 *The Spectator*, 28 (2 April 1711).

64 Roche, *Le Peuple de Paris*, pp. 229–32; Julie Ann Plax, *Watteau and the Cultural Politics of Eighteenth-Century France* (Cambridge: Cambridge University Press, 2000), p. 163. See also Richard Wrigley, 'Between the street and the salon: Parisian shop signs and the spaces of professionalisation in the eighteenth and early nineteenth centuries', *Oxford Art Journal*, 21: 1 (1998), pp. 43–67.

65 Mercier, 'L'Orthographe publique', in *Tableau de Paris,* vol. 1, pp. 107–10 (107–8).

66 Mercier, 'Enseignes', in *Tableau de Paris*, vol. 1, pp. 215–16.

67 Ibid., vol. 1, p. 108.

68 Jennifer Uglow, *Hogarth: A Life and a World* (London: Faber, 1997), p. 518.

69 Mercier, *Tableau de Paris*, vol. 5, pp. 123–6 (123).

70 Ibid., vol. 5, pp. 123–6 (125).

71 The card game seems to have been played with a board, the cards determining whether a particular player's piece moved forward a certain number of squares or fell back. Fournier, *Enseignes*, pp. 313–16. For a long time the *Petite Dictionnaire critique et anecdotique des enseignes de Paris* was thought to be by Honoré de Balzac. It has since been attributed to G.-L. Brismontier, with Balzac serving only as editor. See also Édouard Wattier, *Musée en plein air, ou choix des enseignes les plus remarquables de Paris* (Paris: G. Engelmann, 1824).

72 Willesme, *Enseignes*, p. 9.

73 George Dodd, *The Food of London* (London: Longmans, Brown, Green, 1856), pp. 474–5. Ten years later came the first historical study of English signboards, by Jacob Larwood and John Camden Hotten.

74 *Spectator*, 4 (5 March 1711).

75 *Spectator*, 1 (1 March 1711).

76 Lawrence E. Klein, 'The polite town: shifting possibilities of urbanness, 1660–1715', in Tim Hitchcock and Heather Shore (eds), *The Streets of London: From the Great Fire to the Great Stink* (London: Rivers Oram, 2003), pp. 27–39.

77 Julie Ann Plax, *Watteau and the Cultural Politics of Eighteenth-Century France* (Cambridge: Cambridge University Press, 2000), ch. 3. For a different view, see Turcot, *Le Promeneur*, pp. 32–4.

78 Edgar Allan Poe, 'Man of the Crowd' [1840], in Poe, *Tales of Mystery and Imagination* (Oxford: Avenel, 1985), pp. 339–48; Dickens's short-lived periodical *Old Humphrey's Clock* [1840–1] described the solitary nocturnal wanderings of Old Humphrey in a series of tales; and the character also figured in *The Old Curiosity Shop*, which was originally serialized in *Old Humphrey's Clock*.

79 Louis Huart, *Physiologie du flâneur* (Paris: Lavigne, 1841), p. 1.

80 Rose, *Flaneurs and Idlers*, p. 17.

81 Albert Smith published five 'Social Zoologies', all available at one shilling. In his *Idler upon Town*, Smith was less discriminating than Huart, encompassing 'loitering *flâneurs*' as well as 'the simple pavement-beater of Regent Street; the listless bachelor of small independence ... the dangler about the *coulisses* of the theatres ... the quiet 'mooners' about the streets ... the mere sight-seer from the country' and even 'the street boy'. *Natural History of the Idler upon Town* (London: D. Bogue, 1848), pp. 6–7, 110.

82 Huart, *Physiologie*, p. 10.

83   Ibid., p. 16.

84   To take Gay's *Trivia* at first hand, as evidence that 'flanerie is not even presented as an option', as Alison O'Byrne does in a recent essay, therefore risks missing the dry Augustan satire for which this author is justly known. O'Byrne, 'The art of walking in London: representing urban pedestrianism in the early nineteenth century', *Romanticism*, 14.2 (2007), pp. 94–107 (97).

85   Vic Gatrell, *City of Laughter: Sex and Satire in Eighteenth-Century London* (London: Atlantic, 2006), p. 45. For a different view see O'Byrne, 'Art of walking', p. 101. As noted below, similar accidental encounters feature in Huart's *Physiologie du flâneur*.

86   Huart, *Physiologie*, p. 12.

87   See Anon., 'L'Homme Affiche', in Musée Carnavalet, Cabinet des Arts Graphiques, dossier I (Moeurs-Enseignes). This print has been dated 1823 by an unknown hand, which also notes that it was a 'nouvelle invention de cette époque'.

88   George Scharf, BM 1862.0614.1171 (column and Egyptian temple), BM 1862.0614.1136 (coffee mill).

89   BM 1862.0614.1090.

90   Musée Carnavalet, Cabinet des Arts Graphiques, dossier I (Moeurs-Enseignes). For Chéret, see Camille Mauclair, *Jules Chéret* (Paris: Maurice Le Gatrec, 1930).

91   Huart, *Physiologie*, p. 16. See also Benjamin, *Das Passagen-werk*, vol. 1, p. 565.

92   For a rare acknowledgment that those who wrote about him were 'also using him as a source of humour, rather than as a symbol of the urban "alienation"', see Rose, *Flaneurs and Idlers*, p. 42.

93   I am grateful to Brian Cowan for drawing my attention to this. See his 'The curious Mr Spectator: virtuoso culture and the man of taste in the works of Addison and Steele', *Media History*, 14: 3 (2008), pp. 275–92.

94   Michel de Certeau, looking down at the city from the top of the World Trade Center in New York, describes his urban walker as 'an Icarus', whose 'elevation transfigures him into a voyeur'. 'The exaltation of a scopic and gnostic drive: the fiction of knowledge is related to his lust to be a viewpoint and nothing more.' The *flâneur* thus combines knowledge and self-effacement: the vanishing point of the urban panorama. Michel de Certeau, 'Walking in the city', in Certeau, *The Practice of Everyday Life*, trans. Steven Rendall (Berkeley: University of California Press, 1984), pp. 91–110 (92).

95   As Richard Dennis notes, the *flâneur* is 'an identity in crisis'. Richard Dennis, *Cities in Modernity: Representations and Productions of Metropolitan Space, 1840–1930* (Cambridge: Cambridge University Press, 2008), p. 151. To quote Wolff again, it

will be no great loss 'to ask the *flâneur* to cede his position in the center of the stage, and to take up, instead, a place on the margins, as just one of the city's inhabitants.' Wolff, 'Gender and the haunting of cities', p. 24. I am aware of the irony of coming to this conclusion at the end of a long chapter about this very subject. Mercier, *Tableau de Paris*, vol. 5, p. 251.

Chapter Three: The Restaurant

1 Joris-Karl Huysmans, *Against Nature [À Rebours]*, trans. Margaret Mauldon (Oxford: Oxford University Press, 1998), p. 171.

2 Mercier, *Nouveau tableau de Paris,* in Rebecca Spang, 'Aux origines du restaurant parisien' in Alberto Capatti et al., *À Table au XIXe siècle* (Paris: Flammarion, 2001), pp. 172–181 (172).

3 Eric Hobsbawm, *The Age of Revolution, 1789–1848* (New York: Vintage, 1996), p. 184. See also Jean-Paul Aron, *The Art of Eating in France: Manners and Menus in the Nineteenth Century* (London: Peter Owen, 1975), p. 18. For more recent examples of the myth of a post-1789 flood of unemployed chefs, see Alan Borg, *A History of the Worshipful Company of Cooks of London* (London: privately printed, 2011), pp. 114, 141; Edwina Ehrman et al., *London Eats Out: 500 Years of Capital Dining* (London: Museum of London, 1999), p. 76.

4 Huysmans, *Against Nature*, p. 144.

5 Rebecca Spang, *The Invention of the Restaurant: Paris and Modern Gastronomic Culture* (Cambridge, Mass.: Harvard University Press, 2000), p. 35. The Rue de Poulies no longer exists, but its course ran between the Rue Saint-Honoré and what is now the Rue de Rivoli, just east of today's Rue du Louvre.

6 Mercier, *Parallèle*, p. 74.

7 Louis, Chevalier de Jaucourt, in Jean Le Rond d'Alembert and Denis Diderot (eds), *Encyclopédie ou dictionnaire raisonnée des sciences . . .*, 17 vols (Paris: Briasson, 1751–65), vol. 4, pp. 537–8 (art. 'Cuisine').

8 For an excellent discussion see Spang, *The Invention of the Restaurant*; Paul Metzner, *Crescendo of the Virtuoso: Spectacle, Skill, and Self-Promotion in Paris during the Age of Revolution* (Berkeley: University of California Press, 1998), pp. 55–7.

9 Jean-Jacques Rousseau, *Émile, or on Education,* trans. Allan Bloom and Christopher Kelly (Lebanon, NH: Dartmouth College Press, 2010), p. 295.

10 See Blagdon's description of Beauvilliers in 1801, which he describes as characteristic in its set-up. Francis Blagdon, *Paris as It Was and as It Is*, 2 vols (London: C. and R. Baldwin, 1803), vol. 1, p. 441.

11 Mathurin Roze de Chantoiseau, *L'Ami de tout le monde, ou Précis d'un plan de banque générale de crédit public* (Bibliothèque de l'Arsenal, 12357, ff. 204–9). For the debate on the French fisc see Jonathan Riley, *The Seven Years War and the Old Regime in France: The Economic and Financial Toll* (Princeton: Princeton University Press, 1986).

12 Spang, *The Invention of the Restaurant*, pp. 20–24. For the earlier Fielding scheme see Miles Ogborn, *Spaces of Modernity: London's Geographies, 1680–1780* (London: Guilford Press, 1998), ch. 6. Several such offices opened in seventeenth- and eighteenth-century Paris. David Garrioch, *The Making of Revolutionary Paris* (Berkeley: University of California Press, 2002), p. 241.

13 [Roze de Chantoiseau], *Essai sur l'Almanach général d'indication d'adresse personnelle et domicile fixe, des Six Corps, Arts et Métiers* (Paris: Duchesne, 1769), [n.p.].

14 The word did not have the same meaning in the eighteenth century that it does today; instead of describing the violent, epochal overthrow of a whole regime, the term was then commonly used to refer to periodic changes in fortune whose ultimate cause was mysterious.

15 Mercier, *Tableau de Paris*, ch. 97, vol. 2, pp. 173–7 (174).

16 [François-Marie Mayeur de Saint Paul], *Tableau du nouveau Palais Royal*, 2 vols (London: Maradan, 1788), 1: 65–6.

17 Spang, *The Invention of the Restaurant*, p. 65.

18 Barbara K. Wheaton, 'Les Menus', in Alberto Capatti et al., *À table au XIXe siècle* (Paris: Flammarion, 2001), p. 99. For a full transcript of the menu at Beauvilliers's restaurant in the Palais Royal in 1801, see Francis Blagdon, *Paris as It was and as It is,* 2 vols (London: C & R Baldwin, 1803), pp. 444–52. For a later menu (1814), also including prices, see Aron, *Art of Eating*, pp. 35–6.

19 [Rétif de la Bretonne], 'La Belle Restauratrice', in *Les Contemporaines, ou Avantures des plus jolies Femmes de l'âge présent*, 22 vols (Leipzig: Büschel, 1780), vol. 20, pp. 467–503 (467–8).

20 [de Saint Paul], *Tableau*, 1: 64.

21 Blagdon, *Paris as It was and as It is*, vol. 1, p. 444. See also Wheaton, 'Le menu dans le Paris du XIXe siècle', pp. 90–101.

22 [Rétif de la Bretonne], *Les Contemporaines*, vol. 20, p. 467.

23 Thomas Brennan, *Public Drinking and Popular Culture in Eighteenth-Century Paris* (Princeton: Princeton University Press, 1988), pp. 122–3. Caraccioli in 1768 does

note that people of all ranks, including 'élégantes', ate at modest prices in *gargotes*, which he defines as a 'sorte de petit cabaret qu'on trouve dans tous les coins de Paris, et ou l'on donne à manger au plus juste prix'. However, the term *gargote* was often used to refer to low 'dives', and here once again the historian is confronted with a dearth of evidence. [Caraccioli], *Dictionnaire critique, pittoresque et sentencieux*, 2 vols (Lyons: Benoît Duplain, 1768), vol. 1, p. 242.

24 Brennan, *Public Drinking*, p. 115.

25 Roger Dion, *Histoire de la vigne et du vin en France des origines au XIXe siècle* (Paris: privately printed, 1959), p. 515. Anon., *The gates of Paris, or Brandy-rumps detected* (1786). LWL, 786.05.31.02.

26 [A. C. Cailleau], *Le Waux-hall populaire, ou, les, fêtes de la guinguette* (Paris [1769]).

27 Daniel Roche discusses this approach with regard to Mercier and Rétif in *Le Peuple de Paris*, p. 47.

28 Mercier, *Parallèle*, p. 125. See also André-Charles Cailleau, *Le Waux-hall populaire; ou, les fêtes de la guinguette* (Paris: [n.p.], 1769).

29 Brennan, *Public Drinking*, pp. 145, 155, 158, 176n. See also Louis Charles Fougeret de Monbron, *Le Cosmopolite, ou le citoyen du monde* [1750–9] (Paris: Ducros, 1970), pp. 160–65. On the emergence of discrete elite and plebeian resorts see Garrioch, *Revolutionary Paris*, p. 263; Robert M. Isherwood, *Farce and Fantasy: Popular Entertainment in Eighteenth-Century Paris* (Oxford: Oxford University Press, 1986), ch. 6.

30 Arthur Young, *Travels in France during the years 1787, 1788, and 1789*, ed. Constantia Maxwell (Cambridge: Cambridge University Press, 1929), pp. 45, 98 (quote). The establishment shown in Thomas Rowlandson, *A table d'hote, or French ordinary* (1810), BM 1872.1012.4956, seems much grander.

31 Samuel Pepys's diary, entry for 12 May 1667.

32 Ehrman et al., *London Eats Out*, p. 39.

33 [Ralph Rylance], *The Epicure's Almanack* [1815], ed. Janet Ing Freeman (London: British Library, 2012), p. 104.

34 The Sun Tavern was in Fish Hill Street. Pepys diary, entry for 1 August 1660.

35 According to the anonymous 'Petites notes', f. 113. See note 1, p. 249.

36 Ehrman at al., *London Eats Out*, p. 40; Mennell, *All Manners of Food*, p. 136. For an engraving of a Pottage Island cookshop see I. Smith's *Fable V: The Beau and the Beggar* (1747).

37 *The London Spy*, 10 (1699), cited in *The London Spy*, ed. Paul Hyland (East Lansing, MI: Colleagues Press, 1993), p. 188.

38 See Tobias Smollett, *The Life and Adventures of Roderick Random* [1748],

ed. O. M. Brack (Athens, GA: University of Georgia Press, 2012), p. 70.

39   Anon., *Low-life, or one half of the world knows not how the other half lives* (London, 1764), p. 56.

40   [Rylance], *The Epicure's Almanack*, pp. 7, 76, 123.

41   It is also possible that the name derives from the insistence on paying cash, that is, on the absence of credit. Few London eateries offered credit, however, so this is not a convincing explanation. See F. G. Stephens and M. Dorothy George, *Catalogue of Political and Personal Satires Preserved in the Department of Prints and Drawings in the British Museum*, 12 vols (London: British Museum,1870–1954), vol. 9, cat. 12655.

42   For a print of Johnson and Boswell dining in such an establishment, see Henry William Bunbury, *A Chop-House* (1781). BM Satires 5922.

43   Brennan, *Public Drinking*, p. 129.

44   Anon., 'Petites notes', f. 114.

45   [Rylance], *The Epicure's Almanack*, p. 16.

46   For a discussion see Janet Ing Freeman's introduction to [Rylance], *The Epicure's Almanack*, p. xliv.

47   For a 1910 photograph of the exterior, see Borg, *A History of the Worshipful Company of Cooks*, p. 140. It was then known as Birch and Birch, and the window is labelled 'Birch's Soup Rooms'. See also [Rylance], *The Epicure's Almanack*, p. 17.

48   By 1815 a 'Monsieur Barron' had taken over this establishment (the Nassau Coffee House). The quotes are from Rylance's *Almanack* of 1815; Barron's is the only one of the 650 establishments surveyed to be described as being run by a 'restaurateur'. [Rylance], *The Epicure's Almanack*, p. 132.

49   *Affiches, annonces, avis divers*, 82 (19 October 1769), pp. 918–19.

50   Pierre Jean-Baptiste Le Grand d'Aussy, *Histoire de la vie privée des françois* [1782], 2nd edn, 3 vols (Paris: Laurent-Beaupré, 1815), vol. 2, p. 256. For the 'Wauxhall' fad see Jonathan Conlin, 'Vauxhall on the Boulevard: pleasure gardens in London and Paris, 1759–1789', *Urban History*, 35: 1 (May 2008).

51   Beauvilliers's establishment was thought for some time to be the first restaurant. Jean-Anthelme Brillat-Savarin, *The Philosopher in the Kitchen [La Physiologie du Goût]*, trans. Anne Drayton (Harmondsworth: Penguin, 1970), p. 273.

52   *Affiches, annonces, avis divers*, 82 (19 October 1769), pp. 918-19.

53   Mennell, *All Manners of Food*, p. 138. For a similar argument by a Victorian food writer, see Abraham Hayward, *The Art of Dining* (London: John Murray, 1853), p. 23.

54   Borg, *A History of the Worshipful Company of Cooks of London*, p. 86.

55   'An Injured Freeman' to the Master, reproduced in Borg, *A History of the Worshipful Company of Cooks*, app. 10.

56 Rebecca Spang has challenged this account, pointing out that it is both frequently cited and unsubstantiated, and arguing that depicting *ancien régime* guilds as hidebound and unyielding is simplistic. But, it must be said, researching the history of restaurants often involves qualified acceptance of evidence that is softer than one might wish. See Spang, *The Invention of the Restaurant*, pp. 9–10, 250–1. Compare Mennell, *All Manners of Food,* p. 138; Metzner, *Crescendo of the Virtuoso*, p. 65.

57 Spang, *The Invention of the Restaurant*, p. 24.

58 Ibid., pp. 74–5.

59 Mercier, *Le Nouveau Paris*, 6 vols (Paris: Fuchs, 1798), vol. 3, p. 174.

60 For a discussion of the Festival of Federation (14 July 1790) see Spang, *The Invention of the Restaurant*, ch. 4.

61 See the comments on 'The Chevaliers and the Abbés', in Brillat-Savarin, *The Philosopher in the Kitchen* [*La Physiologie du Goût*], pp. 151–2, 352–3.

62 Paul Vermond, 'Les Restaurants de Paris', *Revue de Paris* 17 (1835), pp. 109–121 (110).

63 Grimod de la Reynière, *Almanach des Gourmands*, 2 (1805), pp. 69–71.

64 Vermond, 'Les Restaurants de Paris', p. 111.

65 Gerrit Houckgeest painted King Charles I, Queen Henrietta Maria and Charles, Prince of Wales, dining in public in 1635. Borg, *A History of the Worshipful Company of Cooks*, p. 83, Fig. 33.

66 [Rylance], *The Epicure's Almanack*.

67 Grimod de la Reynière, *L'Almanach des Gourmands*, 2 (1805), p. 233.

68 See 'J'ay bien de la peine à gouverner mon Empire', a satire on Louis XV's experimenting with doing his own cooking in his palaces at La Muette and Choisy, with the Prince de Dombes. Charles-Germain de Saint Aubin et al., *Livre des caricatures tant bonnes que mauvaises*. Waddesdon Manor, 675.1–388 (165).

69 Brillat-Savarin, *The Philosopher in the Kitchen,* p. 295. See also Mennell, *All Manners of Food*, p. 115.

70 James Grant, *Paris and its People*, 2 vols (London: Saunders and Ottley, 1844), vol. 1, p. 180.

71 Henry Matthews, *Diary of an Invalid*, 2nd edn (London: John Murray, 1820), p. 480.

72 Félix-Auguste Duvert and Boniface Xavier, *Les Cabinets Particuliers; folie-vaudeville en un acte* (1840); Eugène Labiche, *Un Garcon de chez Véry; comédie en un acte* (1850) and *La Cagnotte; comédie-vaudeville en cinq actes* (with Alfred Delacour, 1864).

73 Paul Gavarni [Sulpice Guillaume Chevalier], *Un Cabinet Particulier*, lithograph (1837).

74 Jean Louis Forain, *Scène de cabinet particulier* (c.1880s/1890s). BM 1949,0411.3235.

75 *Affiches, annonces, avis divers*, 82 (19 October 1769), p. 919.

76 Louis Véron, *Mémoires d'un bourgeois de Paris,* 6 vols (Paris: G. de Gonet, 1853–5), vol. 2, p. 2.

77 Bruno Girveau, 'Le restaurant pour tous', in Capatti et al., *À Table au XIXe siècle*, pp. 82–196 (183–5); Rachel Rich, *Bourgeois Consumption: Food, Space and Identity in London and Paris, 1850–1914* (Manchester: Manchester University Press, 2011), pp. 154–5; Aron, *Art of Eating*, pp. 71, 185.

78 Vermond, 'Les Restaurants', p. 120. For Catcomb, an establishment on the Rue Neuve-des-Petits-Champs, admired for its roast beef *prix fixe* of twenty-one sous and its notoriously rude English staff, see Aron, *Art of Eating*, pp. 54–55, 185.

79 John Townshend, *Universal Cooke* (1773). See also John Farley, *London Art of Cookery* (1783); Richard Briggs, *English Art of Cookery* (1788); Francis Collingwood and John Woollams, *Universal Cook and city and country housekeeper* (1792). Farley worked at the London Tavern, Bishopsgate Street; Briggs at the White-Hart, Holborn; and Collingwood and Woollams at the Crown & Anchor, Strand.

80 Alexis Soyer, *The Gastronomic Regenerator* (London: Simpkin and Marshall, 1846), pp. 294–5.

81 Metzner, *Crescendo of the Virtuoso*, pp. 70–72.

82 George Augustus Sala and Alexis Soyer, *The Book of the Symposium, or, Soyer at Gore House* (London: J. K. Chapman, 1851), cited in Ruth Cowen, *Relish: the Extraordinary Life of Alexis Soyer* (London: Phoenix, 2007), p. 154.

83 Lambeth Borough Archives, Minet Library. Vauxhall Scrapbooks v.13, ff. 133, 135, 170, 173.

84 Cowen, *Relish*, p. 227.

85 As Hayward noted, Soyer was 'more likely to earn his immortality by his soup-kitchen, than by his soup'. Hayward, *Art of Dining,* p. 77.

86 Sala noted that some of these 'roast and boiled' establishments in Cheapside experimented with the 'restaurant' moniker in the 1850s, without much success. George Augustus Sala, *Twice Round the Clock; or the hours of the day and night in London* (London: Houlston and Wright, 1859), p. 142. See also Anon., *London at Dinner: or, Where to Dine* (London: Robert Hardwick, 1858), pp. 9–10.

87 Blanchard Jerrold, *The Epicure's Year Book, and Table Companion* (London: Bradbury and Evans, 1868), pp. 110, 113.

88 As Rich notes, there was no obvious French equivalent for 'dinner party', apart from *diner prier* or the ungainly *diner avec cérémonie*. In London, she argues, there was a greater emphasis on getting the company rather than the food right. In Paris it was common to invite friends to arrive after dinner, joining guests who

had arrived earlier and dined, a practice unthinkable in London. Rich, *Bourgeois Consumption*, p. 99.

89 Felicity Kinross, *Coffee and Ices: The Story of Carlo Gatti in London* ([n.p.]: privately printed, 1991).

90 Gregory Houston Bowden, *British Gastronomy: The Rise of Great Restaurants* (London: Chatto & Windus, 1975), p. 31.

91 Aron, *Art of Eating*, pp. 31–3, 44–6, 56, 58, 80; Jerrold, *The Epicure's Year Book*, pp. 114–17 (116), 212. D'Orsay cited in Hayward, *Art of Dining*, pp. 37–9.

92 Charles Elmé Francatelli, *The Modern Cook* [1845], ed. C. Herman Senn (London: Macmillan, 1911). The recipe for lark pie, calling for one dozen larks, is on p. 214.

93 Jerrold, *Epicure's Year Book*, p. 80.

94 Soyer, *Gastronomic Regenerator*, pp. 561–2 (and illustration bound in before index). Although it is unclear whether he invented it, Soyer also gives a recipe for a *Bombe demi glacé à la Mogador*, which featured a ball of vanilla ice cream in a lake of brandy, which was set alight shortly before serving. Ibid., p. 560.

95 Derek Taylor, *Fortune, Fame and Folly: British Hotels and Catering from 1878 to 1978* (London: IPC Business Press, 1977), p. 4.

96 Donald Bassett, 'Victorian cakes and architecture', *British Art Journal*, 11: 2 (2010), pp. 76–9.

97 Auguste Escoffier, *Souvenirs Inédits* (Marseille: Jeanne Laffitte, 1985), p. 107.

98 Brennan cites an example in which a woman was accosted as a prostitute even though she was in a mixed party that included her husband. Brennan, *Public Drinking*, pp. 147–8.

99 Anon., *London at Dinner; or, Where to Dine* (London: Robert Hardwick, 1858), p. 11.

100 Rich, *Bourgeois Consumption,* p. 161.

101 *The Lady,* (27 September 1888), cited in Rich, *Bourgeois Consumption*, p. 143 (see also p. 157).

102 Rich, *Bourgeois Consumption,* p. 138.

103 Erika Rappaport, *Shopping for Pleasure: Women in the Making of London's West End* (Princeton: Princeton University Press, 2000), pp. 102–3.

104 Ibid., pp. 34–6.

105 Brillat-Savarin, *The Philosopher in the Kitchen*, p. 13.

106 For a searching discussion of the relationship between British and French cuisine see Mennell, *All Manners of Food*, ch. 5.

107 Ehrman et al., *London Eats Out*, p. 26.

108 Anon., *The English Alderman in Paris, taking measure for a suit à la mode!* (1772). BM 2010.7081.353. The most famous example is of course Hogarth's *The Invasion,*

Plate 1 (1756), in which would-be French invaders roast frogs outside an inn named 'Soup meagre [sic] à la Sabot Royal' ['thin soup at the royal clog']. An anonymous coloured etching of c.1815 shows English officers dining in a Parisian restaurant; the fatter has just farted, and dismisses his companion's warning that the French party in the next room might think the worse of the English for it. *Les Français ils vont dire que vou être pas poli, My lord! Pah! les Français? vous s'havez bien qu'ils n'entendent pas le anglais.* BM 1989,1104.62. See also the series of satirical prints published by Plancher in Paris entitled *Suprême bon ton* (1815), such as BM 1861,1012.392 and BM 1861,1012.399.

109 Finkelstein has argued that dining out represents a 'simulacrum of enjoyment'; a set of behaviours, practised naively that nonetheless remain disingenuous and artificial. 'The incivility of dining out occurs where sociality is without engagement, that is, when the individual does not examine the purposes of his/her actions but acts from habit or in response to the anonymous edicts of conventions.' Joanne Finkelstein, *Dining Out: A Sociology of Modern Manners* (New York: NYU Press, 1989), p. 12.

110 Mennell, *All Manners of Food*, p. 135.

111 Brillat-Savarin, *The Philosopher in the Kitchen*, p. 379 ('Privations').

112 Huysmans, *Against Nature*, p. 114.

Chapter Four: The Dance

1 [Louis Huart], *Mémoires de Rigolboche*, 2nd edn (Paris: [n.p.], 1860), p. 6.

2 Ibid., p. 186.

3 Ibid., pp. 8–9.

4 Ibid., p. 69.

5 Ibid., pp. 73–4.

6 Symons to James Dykes Campbell, 6 October 1889. Karl Beckson and John M. Munro (eds), *Arthur Symons: Selected Letters, 1880–1935* (Basingstoke: Macmillan, 1989), p. 53.

7 Eugène François Vidocq, *Mémoires de Vidocq, chef de la police de sûreté, jusqu'en 1827*, 4 vols (Paris: Tenon, 1829), vol. 3, pp. 77–85.

8 Alan Borg and David Coke, *Vauxhall Gardens* (New Haven: Yale University Press, 2012), p. 340.

9 The name is sometimes found as 'Tinkson', sometimes as 'Tickson'. Gilles-Antoine Langlois, *Folies, Tivolis et Attractions: les premiers parcs de loisirs parisiens* (Paris: Action Artistique de la Ville de Paris, 1991), pp. 166–7.

10 Mercier, *Parallèle*, p. 125. See also André-Charles Cailleau, *Le Waux-hall populaire; ou, les fêtes de la guinguette* (Paris: [n.p.], 1769).

11 For the opéra *bals* see Anne Martin-Fugier, *La vie élégante ou la formation du Tout-Paris, 1815–48* (Paris: Fayard, 1990), pp. 130–4.

12 The figure is Gasnault's estimate of the number that would have been operating at any one time in this period, and he does not appear to be distinguishing between *bals* and *guinguettes*. François Gasnault, *Guinguettes et Lorettes: bals publics et danse social à Paris entre 1830 et 1870* (Paris: Aubier, 1986), p. 34.

13 'Elle n'accepte pas vraiment le tout-vénant, ne favorise pas l'anonymat,' Gasnault notes. 'On y prolonge les solidarités d'atelier, on y renoue avec une origine commune.' Gasnault, *Guinguettes*, p. 41.

14 In 1848, however, Alfred Delvau's *Hardeur et décadence des grisettes* was already proclaiming the passing of the *grisette*. Jerrold Seigel, *Bohemian Paris: Culture, Politics, and the Boundaries of Bourgeois Life, 1830–1930* (Baltimore: Johns Hopkins University Press, 1986), p. 42.

15 Cited in François Brunet, *Théophile Gautier et la danse* (Paris: Honoré Champion, 2010), p. 26.

16 Gasnault, *Guinguettes*, p. 155.

17 "Folies d'Asnières", from the series *Paris et ses environs. Fêtes des environs de Paris.* Cabinet des Art Graphiques, Musée Carnavalet. Dossier 78/1 (Moeurs – Bals Publics).

18 Gasnault, *Guinguettes*, pp. 25–7, 47–54 (quote, 49).

19 Pierre Véron, *Paris s'amuse* (Paris: E. Dentu, 1861), p. 63.

20 Bibliothèque Nationale de France, Arts du Spectacle, Receuil Bal Mabille, Ro.12953.

21 Langlois, *Folies, Tivolis et Attractions*, pp. 52–3.

22 Gasnault, *Guinguettes*, p. 232.

23 Anon. [Paul Mahalin], *Mémoires du Bal Mabille* (Paris: [n.p.], 1864), pp. 99–100.

24 Mogador's marriage proved short, however, and her husband's family refused to support her after his death, denying her the fairy-tale ending.

25 Anon., *Mémoires du Bal Mabille*, p. 35.

26 'Finette', *Mémoires de Finette* (Paris: E. Pache, 1867), p. 36.

27 Cited in Anthony Bennett, 'Music in the halls', in J. S. Bratton (ed.), *Music Hall: Performance and Style* (Milton Keynes: Open University, 1986), p. 11.

28 *La-di-da, or the city toff.* BL, H.2522.b.1(1).

29 'Champagne Charlie', British Library, H1650e (9).

30 Today's champagne producers have been less eager to accept such endorsements, however, and in some cases (such as Kristal) have accused performers of bringing

their product into ill-repute by referring to it in their songs. Their nineteenth-century forebears were not so foolish.

31 Brian Harrison, *Drink and the Victorians: The Temperance Question in England, 1815–1872* (London: Faber & Faber, 1971), pp. 248–51.

32 André L. Simon, *A History of the Champagne Trade in England* (London: Wyman and Sons, 1905), pp. 107–44.

33 Programme in Victoria and Albert Museum, Theatre Collection, file 'Alhambra 1868'.

34 *The Censor* (20 June 1868), p. 43.

35 Advertisement in *The Era* (2 October 1870).

36 *The Era* (16 October 1870).

37 *The Era* (23 October 1870).

38 Finette insisted that it had not been inspired by Daniel Auber's *La Muette de Portici* (1828), a popular opera set among Neapolitan fishermen. 'Finette', *Mémoires*, p. 34.

39 Cited in W. Macqueen-Pope, *Gaiety Theatre of Entertainment* (London: W. H. Allen, 1949), p. 23.

40 This skirt had been shortened in the 1840s, apparently to increase ballet's appeal to male audiences. Clare Parfitt, 'Capturing the cancan: body politics from Enlightenment to Postmodernity' (PhD diss., University of Surrey, 2008), p. 68.

41 Bayle St John, *Purple Tints of Paris: Character and Manners in the New Empire*, 2 vols (London: Chapman and Hall, 1854), vol. 2, p. 275.

42 'Do the Clodoches dance?', *The Era* (28 April 1872).

43 Derek B. Scott, *Sounds of the Metropolis: The Nineteenth-Century Popular Music Revolution in London, New York, Paris and Vienna* (Oxford: Oxford University Press, 2008), ch. 6.

44 Macqueen-Pope, *Gaiety Theatre of Entertainment*, pp. 177–81, 237, 254.

45 Rupert Christiansen, *The Visitors: Culture Shock In Nineteenth-Century Britain* (London: Chatto and Windus, 2000), p. 216. For skirt dancing, see J. E. Crawford Flitch, *Modern Dancing and Dancers* (London: Grant Richards, 1912), ch. 5.

46 Musée Carnavalet, Cabinet des Photographies, CARPH002740, CARPH002741, CARPH002742. Compare these images of between 1880 and 1890 with the earlier (1870?) carte de visite of Rigolboche seated with her head resting on her palm, one of the many undigitised images in her performer's dossier at the Carnavalet.

47 BNF Arts du Spectacle, Recueil Eldorado, Ro15714. See also Philippe Luez, *Yvette Guilbert: sa vie ses chansons* (Paris: Fortin, 1994).

48 In 1892, Oller went on to build another iron music hall, the Olympia, on the

Boulevard des Capucines. For 'exotic dancing' at the Moulin Rouge see Anne Décoret-Ahiha, *Les danses exotiques en France, 1880–1940* (Pantin: Centre National de la Danse, 2004), p. 124.

49　'The Folies Bergère is an unsuccessful attempt to imitate an English music hall,' Symons noted, 'and a successful attempt to attract the English public.' Arthur Symons, *Colour Studies in Paris* (London: Chapman and Hall, 1918), p. 34.

50　J.-K. Huysmans, *Parisian Sketches,* trans. Brendan King (Sawtry: Dedalus, 2004), pp. 42–3.

51　In 1888, M. R. Mythe published a Scottish-themed 'fairy ballet' entitled *Le Chateau de Mac-Arrott* (Paris: Tresse et Stock, 1888), which also featured happy clan members dancing in kilts.

52　'Rodrigues' [Eugène Rodrigues-Henriques], 'Les excentricités de la danse', *Gil Blas*, suppl. 10 May 1891. Reproduced in Claudine Brécourt-Villars and Jean-Paul Morel (eds), *Jean Avril: Mes Mémoires* (Paris: Phébus, 2005), pp. 146–7.

53　'Intermède par Grille d'Egout', reprinted in Brécourt-Villars and Morel (eds), *Jane Avril,* pp. 153–5.

54　'Gay Paree', British Library, H3980.2 (56).

55　'We All Had One', British Library, H3627 (65).

56　'Gay Paree', British Library, H3980.2 (56).

57　'Four Englishmen in Paree,' British Library, H3980.2 (80). See also 'I've Been to Gay Paree,' H3627 (32).

58　Alhambra programme for week of 5 November 1890. Westminster Archives, III/7J/2, Portfolio 17.

59　'Music Hall Matters', *St Paul's* (15 February 1896), p. 330.

60　Symons, *Colour Studies in Paris*, p. 95.

61　For this relatively unresearched art form, see Barry J. Faulk, *Music Hall and Modernity: The Late-Victorian Discovery of Popular Culture* (Athens: Ohio University Press, 2004), ch. 5.

62　For the *caf'concs*, see Thérésa, *Mémoires de Thérésa, écrites par elle-même* (Paris: Dentu, 1865), pp. 230f.; François Caradec and Alain Weill, *Le Café Concert, 1848–1914* (Paris: Arhème Fayard, 2007).

63　*Le Calino* (13 February 1869).

64　See Bernard Gendron, *Between Montmartre and the Mudd Club: Popular Music and the Avant-Garde* (Chicago: University of Chicago Press, 2002), p. 62. As Scott notes, this too could become fodder for tourists. Scott, *Sounds of the Metropolis*, p. 215.

65　Scott, *Sounds of the Metropolis*, pp. 43–50.

66   For a discussion see Parfitt, 'Cancan', ch. 3; Rae Beth Gordon, *Why the French Love Jerry Lewis: From Cabaret to Early Cinema* (Stanford: Stanford University Press, 2001).

67   'The training of dancing troupes: a talk with Mr. John Tiller', *The Sketch* (19 September 1895), pp. 435–6.

68   Bowles was speaking at another cancan indecency trial at the Court of Common Pleas. *The Era* (13 December 1874).

69   For 'old Montmartre', see Seigel, *Bohemian Paris*, ch. 12.

Chapter Five: The Underworld

1   'Advertisement' in Adolphe Belot, *The Drama of the Rue de la Paix* (London: Vizetelly, 1880), p. i.

2   Ibid., p. 34.

3   Ibid., p. 37.

4   Ibid., p. 38.

5   Vizetelly cites this on the flyleaf to Émile Gaboriau, *The Little Old Man of Batignolles and other stories* (London: Vizetelly, 1886).

6   Martin A. Kayman, *From Bow Street to Baker Street: Mystery, Detection and Narrative* (New York: St Martin's Press, 1992), p. 131. It is curious that, despite Gaboriau's name being mentioned in this context, the author otherwise ignores him. For a fuller discussion of Gaboriau see R. F. Stewart, . . . *And Always a Detective: Chapters on the History of Detective Fiction* (London: David & Charles, 1980), ch. 12.

7   As Michael Saler has noted, Holmes was the first fictional character to benefit from such 'double-mindedness'. Saler, '"Clap if you believe in Sherlock Holmes": mass culture and the re-enchantment of modernity, *c.* 1890–*c.* 1940', *Historical Journal*, 46: 3 (September, 2003), pp. 599–622.

8   Arthur Conan Doyle, 'A scandal in Bohemia', in Doyle, *Sherlock Holmes: The Complete Novels and Stories,* 2 vols (New York: Bantam Dell, 1986), vol. 1, pp. 239–63 (239).

9   Clive Emsley, 'From ex-con to expert: the police detective in nineteenth-century France', in Clive Emsley and Haia Shpayer-Makov, *Police Detectives in History, 1750–1950* (Aldershot: Ashgate, 2006), pp. 61–77 (61).

10   Hence he has been ignored by those writing the history of the genre. Voltaire's *Zadig* (1747) and a number of other pre-1788 texts have been described as

detective stories. Binyon's dismissal of them is convincing. Although his claim that Poe marks the birth of the genre could be disputed, for the reasons given here, otherwise his account agrees with that given here, in emphasizing the importance of Gaboriau. T. J. Binyon, *Murder Will Out: The Detective in Fiction* (Oxford: Oxford University Press, 1989), pp. 2–5.

11   Rétif de la Bretonne, *La Semaine Nocturne: Sept Nuits de Paris,* 2 vols (Paris: Guillot, 1790).

12   See for example Anon., *L'Esprit d'Addisson* [sic] *ou les beautés du Spectateur, du Babillard et du Gardien* (Yverdon: Soc. Littéraire et Typographique, 1777). Ralph A. Naplow, *The Addisonian Tradition in France: Passion and Objectivity in Social Observation* (Rutherford, NJ: Farleigh Dickinson University Press, 1990).

13   The place of publication indicated on the title page is London, but it should be noted that at this period works published in France were often disguised as London publications, to hide the fact that the work in question had not been subjected to the usual censorship. [Rétif de la Bretonne], *Les Nuits de Paris, ou le Spectateur Nocturne*, 14 vols (London: [n.p.], 1788–9).

14   Holmes derives great pleasure from having these labels thrown at him by an enraged Dr Grimesby Roylott in 'The Speckled Band', in Doyle, *Sherlock Holmes*, vol. 2, p. 109. See also Rutlidge, *Le Babillard*, 4.1 (15 January 1778), *p. 69*.

15   Cited in Karlheinz Stierle, *Der Mythos von Paris: Zeichen und Bewußtsein der Stadt* (Munich: DTV, 1998), p. 110.

16   [Rétif de la Bretonne], *Les Nuits de Paris*, vol. 6, pp. 1266–7.

17   Ibid., vol. 14, pp. 3357–8.

18   Mercier, *Parallèle*, p. 80. Louis-Sébastien Mercier, 'Spies', in *Panorama of Paris: Selections from 'Tableau de Paris',* trans. Jeremy D. Popkin (Philadelphia: Pennsylvania State University Press, 1999), p. 36.

19   For the elusive, mercurial Meusnier, see Robert Muchembled, *Les Ripoux des Lumières: corruption policière et Révolution* (Paris: Seuil, 2011).

20   Simon Burrows, 'Despotism without bounds: the French secret police and the silencing of dissent in London, 1760–1790', *History*, 89 (2004), pp. 525–48; Jonathan Conlin, 'Wilkes, the Chevalier D'Eon and the dregs of liberty: an Anglo-French perspective on ministerial despotism, 1762–1771', *English Historical Review*, 120 (2005).

21   Simon Burrows, 'The innocence of Jacques-Pierre Brissot', *Historical Journal*, 46: 4 (2003), pp. 843–71 (864).

22   'Plan', in [Rétif de la Bretonne], *Les Nuits de Paris,* vol. 1, pp. 3–4. Contrast this with the *réverbères* in Mercier's utopian city, which are described as being fixed to the wall, and leaving no shadows at all: Louis-Sébastien Mercier, *L'An deux mille*

quatre cent quarante (Paris: Ducros, 1971), p. 233.

23 Alain Cabantous, *Histoire de la nuit: XVIIe–XVIIIe siècle* (Paris: Fayard, 2009), pp. 262–8; Michael R. Lynn, 'Sparks for sale: the culture and commerce of fireworks in early Modern France', *Eighteenth-Century Life*, 30: 2 (Spring 2006), pp. 74–97.

24 This blaze and its damage was captured in depictions by Hubert Robert, Gabriel de Saint-Aubin, Jean-Baptiste Raguenet and others. Bailey et al., *Gabriel de Saint-Aubin*, pp. 60–63, cat. 29; Cabantous, *Histoire de la nuit*, pp. 50–52.

25 Here and in what follows I draw on a pioneering work, Craig Koslofsky, *Evening's Empire: A History of the Night in Early Modern Europe* (Cambridge: Cambridge University Press, 2011) as well as Cabantous, *Histoire de la nuit*.

26 Jonathan Swift complained of the added expense of his taking sedan chairs, for fear of being attacked if he walked home alone. *Correspondence of Jonathan Swift*, ed. Harold Williams, 5 vols (Oxford. Clarendon, 1963–5), vol. 2, pp. 524–5. For the growing gulf between natural and polite rhythms, see Richard Steele, *The Tatler*, 263 (14 December 1710); Bond (ed.), *The Tatler*, vol. 3, pp. 330–34 (331).

27 *Spectator*, 454 (11 August 1712).

28 Hogarth's idea was quickly copied by the painter Nicolas Lancret and also by Jean Mondon II, who produced a series of paintings entitled *The Four Times of Day* (National Gallery) and a series of four engravings after Mondon II by Antoine Aveline, entitled *Les Heures*. But neither depicted the city streets, only town-house interiors and gardens. See Sean Shesgreen, *Hogarth and the Times-of-the-Day Tradition* (Ithaca: Cornell University Press, 1982).

29 August Philippe Herlaut, 'L'éclairage des rues de Paris à la fin du XVIIe siècle et au XVIIIe siècle', *Mémoires de la Société de l'histoire de Paris*, 43: 130–240 (131).

30 In the City of London, the 9 p.m. curfew was confirmed by mayoral proclamation in 1383, and the duty to put out lanterns was confirmed by Acts of Common Council in 1599 and 1646. A 1662 Act set a penalty of one shilling for default, but it is not clear whether this was collected. E. S. de Beer, 'The early history of London street-lighting', *History* 25 (1941), pp. 311–24 (313–15); John Beattie, *Policing and Punishment in London, 1660–1750: Urban Crime and the Limits of Terror* (Oxford: Oxford University Press, 2001), p. 208. The frequency with which Londoners and Parisians were reminded of their duty to hang out lights suggests that it was not universally carried out.

31 Koslofsky, *Evening's Empire*, p. 159.

32 Murray Melbin, *Night as frontier: colonizing the world after dark* (London: Collier Macmillan, 1987), pp. 38–40.

33 Herlaut, 'L'éclairage', 133; Cabantous, *Histoire de la nuit*, pp. 364–5 (n. 61). Paul Griffiths, 'Meanings of nightwalking in early modern England', *The Seventeenth*

Century, 13: 2 (Autumn 1998), pp. 212–38. See also Laura Gowing, '"The freedom of the streets": women and social space, 1560–1640', in Paul Griffiths and Mark S. R. Jenner (eds), *Londinopolis: Essays in the Cultural and Social History of Early Modern London* (Manchester: Manchester University Press, 2000), pp. 130–51.

34 After its 1771 merger with the *garde*, the latter disappeared in 1783. El Ghoul, *La Police Parisienne*, vol. 1, pp. 126–9. Jean Chagniot, 'Le Guet et la Garde de Paris à la fin de l'Ancien régime', *Revue d'Histoire Moderne et Contemporaine*, 20 (1973), pp. 58–71.

35 By the second quarter of the century these had been replaced with a wooden staff. Beattie, *Policing and Punishment*, p. 181.

36 As John Beattie notes, 'The idea behind the curfew – the 9pm closing down of the City – was not so much abolished as overwhelmed.' *Policing and Punishment*, p. 172.

37 Cabantous, *Histoire de la nuit*, pp. 235–6.

38 London's nightwatchmen were supposed to patrol from 9 p.m. to 7 a.m. in winter and from 10 p.m. to 5 a.m. in summer. The Paris patrols began earlier, at 5.30 p.m. (*guet*) and 7 p.m. (*garde*), and ended earlier, at 11 p.m., suggesting that there was little for them to do after that hour. But the hours shifted back later in the century: 9 p.m. to 1 a.m. in 1760 and 10 p.m. to 3 or 4 a.m. in 1770. Cabantous, *Histoire de la nuit*, p. 239; Beattie, *Policing and Punishment*, pp. 173–90 (190).

39 Beattie, *Policing and Punishment*, p. 180.

40 El Ghoul, *La Police Parisienne*., vol. 1, pp. 270–1; Koslofsky, *Evening's Empire*, p. 136.

41 El Ghoul, *La Police Parisienne*, vol. 1, p. 275. The boulevards were lit from the Porte Saint Antoine to the Porte du Temple, using the proceeds from licensing those entrepreneurs who rented out chairs to the fashionable Parisians who promenaded there. Cabantous, *Histoire de la nuit*, pp. 253, 258–9.

42 The Act (9 Geo. II, c. 20) confirmed the requirements imposed by the City's Common Council in 1735, namely that lamps be twenty-five yards apart in main streets, and be lit from sunset until sunrise between 10 August and 10 April, with no more 'dark nights' (i.e. exemptions when the moon was full). Beattie, *Policing and Punishment*, pp. 216–22.

43 It is not mentioned in Colin Jones, *Paris: Biography of a City* (London: Penguin, 1994) nor in Jean-Louis Harouel, *L'Embellissement des Villes: l'urbanisme français au XVIIIe siècle* (Paris: Picard, 1993).

44 There were complaints that the *réverbères* blinded coachmen and that their oil reservoirs were insufficiently filled, causing them to extinguish by 9 or 10 p.m. Louis-Sébastien Mercier, 'Réverberes', *Tableau de Paris*, new edn (Amsterdam:

1782), 65, t. I, pp. 212–14; Pierre Patte, *De la manière la plus avantageuse d'éclairer les rues d'une ville, pendant la nuit* (Amsterdam: [n.p.], 1766), p. 16; Wolfgang Schivelbusch, *Disenchanted Night: The Industrialization of Light in the Nineteenth Century* (Berkeley: University of California Press, 1988), p. 95. Those at junctions had four, at T-junctions three, while all other streets had two. The tripe oil did not burn cleanly, requiring regular cleaning. Colza oil was substituted in 1788. El Ghoul, *La Police Parisienne*, vol. 1, pp. 271–3, 275–6, 353 (n. 66).

45 Simone Delattre, *Les douze heures noires: la nuit à Paris au XIXe siècle* (Paris: Albin Michel, 2000), p. 583 (note 21).

46 In 1662 the Italian *abbé* Laudati de Caraffa secured a contract to operate a network of stations where Parisians could find *falots*, who were all numbered. Link-boys in London were freelance, though both were suspected of consorting with criminal elements. Fournier, *Enseignes,* p. 24; Herault, 'L'éclairage', pp. 133–4; Delattre, *Les douzes heures noires*, pp. 82–3, 85–6; Malcolm Falkus, 'Lighting in the dark ages of English economic history: town streets before the Industrial Revolution', in D. C. Coleman and A. H. John, (eds.), *Trade, Government and Economy in Pre-Industrial England: Essays Presented to F. J. Fischer* (London: Weidenfeld & Nicholson, 1976), pp. 248–73 (267); Schivelbusch, *Disenchanted Night*, p. 96 (n. 34). For depictions of link-boys see William Hogarth, *Times of Day: Night* (1743), BM 1880,1113.2803; Carington Bowles, *An Evenings Invitation; With a Wink from a Bagnio* (1773), BM 1935,0522.1.186; Thomas Rowlandson, *The Inn Door*, Yale Center for British Art, 1975B.3.112. El Ghoul, *La Police Parisienne*, vol. 1, pp. 278, 356 (n. 102).

47 Cruikshank, 'A Peep at the Gas Lights in Pall Mall'. LWL, 809.12.23.01.1.

48 Schivelbusch, *Disenchanted Night*, pp. 7–26 (26); Delattre, *Les douzes heures noires*, pp. 86–8; M. Falkus, 'The early development of the British gas industry, 1790–1815', *Economic History Review*, 2nd series, 35 (1982).

49 Gérard de Nerval, 'Les Nuits d'Octobre', in *La Bohème Galante* (Paris: Michel Lévy, 1861), pp. 191–231 (188).

50 There is no scholarly biography of Vidocq, although there is a useful discussion in Chapter 3 of Metzner, *Crescendo of the Virtuoso*. Jean Savant, *Le Vrai Vidocq* (Paris: Hachette, 2001) and James Morton, *The First Detective: The Life and Revolutionary Times of Eugène-François Vidocq, Criminal, Spy and Private Eye* (London: Ebury, 2004) cite a list of archives consulted, but Morton provides only a handful of references, and Savant none at all. Therefore both authors' claims – that Vidocq's ghosted memoirs are largely accurate – cannot be independently verified. These works, as well as Marie-Hélène Parinaud, *Vidocq: 'Le Napoléon de la Police'* (Paris: Tallandier, 2001), afford little more than a *rechauffée* of the *Mémoires*. The latter

are available in a modern English translation: François-Eugène Vidocq, *Memoirs of Vidocq: Master of Crime* (Edinburgh: AK Press, 2003).

51   Charles-Maurice Descombres has also been put forward as the author of the early volumes. See Régis Messac, *Le 'Detective Novel' et l'influence de la pensée scientifique* (Paris: Bibliothèque de la Révue de littérature comparé, 1929), pp. 277–9.

52   Smollett, *The Adventures of Roderick Random* (1748). See Alexandre Stroev, *Les Avanturiers des Lumières* (Paris: PUF, 1997).

53   He tried to cash in further on the success of his ghosted memoirs with a somewhat less flattering *Supplément* to the *Mémoires*. [L'Héritier], *Supplément aux Mémoires de Vidocq, ou dernières révélations sans réticence,* 2 vols, 2nd edn (Paris: Chez les marchands de nouveautés, 1831).

54   See Clive Emsley, 'Policing the streets of early nineteenth-century Paris', *French History,* 1 (1987), pp. 257–82; Howard G. Brown, 'Tops, traps and tropes: catching thieves in post-revolutionary Paris', in Clive Emsley and Haia Shpayer-Makov, *Police Detectives in History, 1750–1950* (Aldershot: Ashgate, 2006), pp. 33–60.

55   Eugène-François Vidocq, *Mémoires de Vidocq, chef de la police de sûreté, jusqu'en 1827,* 4 vols (Paris: Tenon, 1829), vol. 2, pp. 331–2.

56   François-Eugène Vidocq, *Les Voleurs, physiologie de leurs moeurs et de leur langage,* 2 vols (Paris: [n.p.], 1837). See also Anon., *Nouveau dictionnaire d'argot par un ex-chef de brigade sous M. Vidocq* (Paris: Chez les marchands des nouveautés, 1829).

57   Vidocq, *Mémoires de Vidocq,* vol. 3, pp. 137–8.

58   Émile Gaboriau, *The Little Old Man of Batignolles and other stories* (Gaboriau's Sensational Novels, London: Vizetelly, 1886), p. 23. Even Poe refers to 'the prejudice which always exists in Paris against the police' in 'The Mystery of Marie Rogêt', Edgar Allan Poe, *Tales of Mystery and Imagination* (Oxford: Avenel, 1985), p. 127.

59   Vidocq, *Mémoires de Vidocq,* vol. 3, pp. 332–3.

60   Ibid., vol. 3, pp. 165–6.

61   Ibid., vol. 4, pp. 27–8. Several dossiers from this Bureau are preserved in the Bibliothèque Historique de la Ville de Paris, MS2429, showing cases varying from chasing unpaid bills and tracing lost property to following wives suspected of infidelities. See also Dominique Kalifa, *Naissance de la Police Privé: détective et agences de recherches en France 1832–1942* (Paris: Plon, 2000), pp. 21–55.

62   Maginn went on to found the highly successful *Fraser's Magazine* in 1830, as an English answer to the famed *Blackwood's Magazine,* for which he had earlier worked in Edinburgh.

63   The dream was entered as evidence during the trial. Judith Flanders, *The Invention of Murder* (London: Harper, 2011), pp. 45–52.

64 J. M. Beattie, 'Early detection: the Bow Street Runners in late eighteenth-century London', in Emsley and Shpayer-Makov, *Police Detectives*, pp. 15–32 (23); John Styles, 'Sir John Fielding and the problem of criminal investigation in eighteenth-century England', *Transactions of the Royal Historical Society*, 5th series, 33 (1983), pp. 127–49; David J. Cox, *A Certain Share of Low Cunning: A History of the Bow Street Runners, 1792–1839* (Cullumpton: Willan, 2010), p. 30.

65 R. M. Morris, '"Crime does not pay": thinking again about detectives in the first century of the Metropolitan Police', and Haia Shpayer-Makov, 'Explaining the rise and success of detective memoirs in Britain', in Emsley and Shpayer-Makov, *Police Detectives*, pp. 79–102 (81) and 103–33 (109).

66 Anon. [Douglas Williams Jerrold], *Vidocq! The French Police Spy! A melodrama, in two acts* (London: J. Duncombe [n.d.]). See also Charles Dickens, 'Vidocq, French Detective', *All the Year Round* (14 and 21 July 1860), pp. 331–6, 355–60.

67 Dickens, 'Vidocq, French Detective', *All the Year Round* (21 July 1860), p. 359. Metzner, *Crescendo of the Virtuoso*, p. 107.

68 Nerval, 'Les Nuits d'Octobre', p. 181.

69 Georges Cuvier, *Discours sur les révolutions de la surface du globe*, 3rd edn (Paris: G. Dufour and Ed. Ocagne, 1825), pp. 95–6.

70 For criticism of the BM's natural history collections, see *Report of the Select Committee on the British Museum* (Parliamentary Papers, 1836, 10); Adrian Desmond, *The Politics of Evolution: Morphology, Medecine and Reform in Radical London* (Chicago: University of Chicago Press, 1989), ch. 6.

71 Vidocq, *Mémoires de Vidocq*, vol. 4, pp. 10–11.

72 Gaboriau himself makes the parallel between Lecoq's method and 'one of those naturalists who, on inspecting two or three bones, are able to reconstruct the creature to which they belonged' in *Monsieur Lecoq*. Cited in Messac, *Le 'Detective Novel'*, p. 505.

73 Arthur Conan Doyle, 'The Five Orange Pips', in Doyle, *Sherlock Holmes: The Complete Novels and Stories*, vol. 1, pp. 331–50 (343).

74 'I have a theory that the individual represents in his development the whole procession of his ancestors, and that such a sudden turn to good or evil stands for some strong influence which came into the line of his pedigree. The person becomes, as it were, the epitome of the history of his own family.' Doyle, 'The Adventure of the Empty House', in Doyle, *Sherlock Holmes*, vol. 1, pp. 759–80 (778).

75 Georges Cuvier, *Recherches sur les ossemens fossiles*, 10 vols, 4th edn (Paris: [n.p.], 1834–6), vol. 1, pp. 184–5.

76 For the scientific connections between London and Paris see Desmond, *The Politics of Evolution*, ch. 2. For the science of detection see Messac, *Le 'Detective Novel'*.

Anglophone scholars have overlooked these connections and Kayman ignores palaeontology entirely in his *From Bow Street to Baker Street*.

77 Edgar Allan Poe, *Tales of Mystery and Imagination* (Oxford World Classics, Oxford: Avenel, 1985), p. 88.

78 Poe, *Tales,* p. 100.

79 Paul Féval, *Les Mystères de Londres* (Paris: Phébus, 1998). On the influence of Fenimore Cooper on French crime fiction in the 1840s see Messac, *Le 'Detective Novel',* pp. 238–44.

80 See Richard Maxwell, *The Mysteries of Paris and London* (Charlottesville: University of Virginia Press, 1992), ch. 8.

81 See the excellent discussion in Stierle, *Der Mythos von Paris*, pp. 545–60.

82 Dickens and Wilkie Collins both created detectives such as Inspector Bucket (in *Bleak House*, 1852–3) and Sergeant Cuff (in *The Moonstone*, 1868) who seem more interesting and fully rounded than many of the supporting characters. Neither is allowed more than a bit part, however, on the fringes of the investigations under way in both novels. Though Dickens did write a number of short pieces of journalism on the police in the 1850s, he cannot be seen as playing a role in the emergence of a detective genre. For opposing accounts of his influence see the introduction to Peter Haining (ed.), *Hunted Down: The Detective Stories of Charles Dickens* (London: Peter Owen, 1996) and Kayman, *From Bow Street to Baker Street*, pp. 105–6.

83 Roger Bonniot, *Émile Gaboriau ou la Naissance du Roman policier* (Paris: J. Vrin, 1985), pp. 148–50. For earlier examples of 'scies' see H. Gourdan de Genouillac, *Les Refrains de la Rue de 1830 à 1870* (Paris: Dentu, 1879), pp. 52, 57, 70.

84 Paul Féval's *Les Habits Noirs* (1863) featured a character named Lecoq who operated a Vidocq-style *bureau des renseignements*. Gaboriau may have taken the name from him, although otherwise his police detective is quite different. See Messac, *Le 'Detective Novel'*, pp. 500–501.

85 Bonniot, *Émile Gaboriau.*

86 Gaboriau, *Monsieur Lecoq* (London: Downey and Co., 1901), p. 38.

87 Ibid., p. 190.

88 Gaboriau, *The Mystery of Orcival* (New York: Scribner and Sons, 1901), p. 53.

89 Gaboriau, *The Slaves of Paris* (London: Vizetelly, 1884), p. 204.

90 Gaboriau, *The Gilded Clique* (London: Vizetelly, 1886), p. 17.

91 Doyle, *A Study in Scarlet,* in Doyle, *Sherlock Holmes*, vol. 1, p. 4.

92 Bonniot, *Émile Gaboriau,* p. 274.

93 Gaboriau, *The Little Old Man of Batignolles,* p. 21.

94 Arthur Conan Doyle, *Sir Arthur Conan Doyle: Memories and Adventures* (Ware:

Wordsworth, 2007), pp. 62–3. Though it is unclear whether Doyle read Gaboriau in the original or in Vizetelly's translation, he certainly could read French. Messac, *Le 'Detective Novel'*, p. 588.

95 Friswell's daughter defended her father from the charge that he simply lifted the plot from Gaboriau (whom she referred to as 'Gobineau', confusing the crime author with the racial theorist Arthur de Gobineau). Laura Hain Friswell, *James Hain Friswell: A Memoir* (London: G. Redway, 1898), pp. 248–9.

96 Gaboriau, *Monsieur Lecoq*, p. 38. Compare Doyle, *A Study in Scarlet,* in Doyle, *Sherlock Holmes*, vol. 1, p. 29.

97 Gaboriau, *Monsieur Lecoq*, pp. 18–19; Doyle, 'The Adventure of Charles Augustus Milverton', in Doyle, *Sherlock Holmes*, vol. 1, pp. 906–23 (914).

98 Gaboriau, *Monsieur Lecoq,* p. 345. For Holmes's similar remark see Doyle, *A Study in Scarlet*, in Doyle, *Sherlock Holmes*, vol. 1, p. 19.

99 For the relationship between Gaboriau and Doyle's fiction see Messac, *Le 'Detective Novel'*, pp. 588–96; Stewart, . . . *And Always a Detective*, pp. 256ff. My assessment of the extent of Doyle's borrowing from Gaboriau is similar to Messac's, though I place more emphasis on *Le Petit Vieux des Batignolles*.

100 The American part of *A Study in Scarlet* drew, not on Gaboriau, but on Robert Louis Stevenson, whose novel *The Dynamiters* was clearly a strong influence. Lycett, *Doyle,* p. 118.

101 Poe, *Tales*, pp. 89–91. Elements of Poe's 'The Purloined Letter' are reproduced in Doyle's 'A Scandal in Bohemia', 'The Illustrious Client' and 'The Priory School'. For Doyle's acknowledgment of his debt to Gaboriau, see his autobiographical *Memories and Adventures* (Boston: Little, Brown, 1924), p. 74.

102 Doyle, *A Study in Scarlet*, in Doyle, *Sherlock Holmes*, vol. 1, p. 19.

103 Doyle, *A Study in Scarlet,* in ibid., vol. 1, p. 62. For another example, see Doyle, 'The Adventure of the Six Napoleons', in Doyle, *Sherlock Holmes*, vol. 1, pp. 924–45 (943).

104 Doyle, *The Sign of Four,* in ibid., vol. 1, p. 129.

105 Doyle, *A Study in Scarlet*, in ibid., vol. 1, p. 33.

106 Poe, *Tales,* p. 100.

107 Gaboriau, *The Little Old Man of Batignolles*, p. 14.

108 Ibid., p. 35.

109 The anonymous author begins his essay by quoting Mercier's *Tableau de Paris*. Anon., 'Thoughts upon thoroughfares', *Blackwood's Magazine*, 19: 97 (February 1825), pp. 155–66 (159).

110 Doyle, *A Study in Scarlet*, in Doyle, *Sherlock Holmes*, vol. 1, p. 37.

111 Doyle, 'A Case of Identity', in ibid., pp. 287–306 (297). For the link between

flâneur and detective see Benjamin, *Das Passagen-werk,* vol. 1, pp. 551 and 554.

112 Doyle, 'The Red-Headed League', in Doyle, *Sherlock Holmes,* vol. 1, pp. 263–87 (287).

Chapter Six: Dead and Buried

1 Charles Dickens, 'Cemetery, Kensal Green', *All the Year Round* 93 (19 September 1863).

2 Charles Cole, *Imperial Paris Guide* (London: J. C. Hotten, 1867), p. 17.

3 Lucien Descaves/Académie Goncourt, *The Colour of Paris: Historic, Personal and Local* (London: Chatto and Windus, 1914), after p. 50.

4 A.C. Pugin and Charles Heath, *Paris and its Environs,* 2 vols (London: Jennings and Chaplin, 1830), vol. 2, p. 130v.

5 Dickens, 'Cemetery, Kensal Green'.

6 'Trading in death' [*Household Words*, 27 November 1852] in Charles Dickens, *Complete Works Centennial Edition,* 36 vols (London: Heron, 1970), vol. 21, 'Miscellaneous Papers 1', pp. 374–84 (375).

7 Charles Dickens, 'From the Raven in the Happy Family II' [*Household Words*, 8 June 1850], in ibid., pp. 207–11 (209).

8 Robert W. Berger and Thomas F. Hedin, *Diplomatic Tours in the Gardens of Versailles under Louis XIV* (Philadelphia: University of Pennsylvania Press, 2008).

9 James Stevens Curl, 'Young's *Night Thoughts* and the origins of the garden cemetery', *Journal of Garden History*, 14: 2 (Summer 1994), pp. 92–118; James Stevens Curl, *Death and Architecture* (Stroud: Sutton, 2002).

10 'Élégee écrite sur un Cimetière de Campagne', *Gazette Littéraire de l'Europe*, 10: 5 (28 April 1765), pp. 217–24; '2nd Night', ibid., 21: 2 (4 July 1764), pp. 101–15.

11 Thomas Gray, *Elegy written in a country church-yard*, line 79.

12 M. de Horne, *Mémoire sur quelques objets qui intéressent plus particulièrement la salubrité de la ville de Paris* (Paris: J. Ch. Desaint, 1788), pp. 4–5. For a detailed discussion see El Ghoul, *La Police Parisienne*, vol. 1, pp. 226–35.

13 Mercier, *Parallèle,* p. 100.

14 Jacques-Henri Bernardin de Saint Pierre, *Études de la Nature*, 3 vols (Paris: Monsieur, 1784), 'D'Un Elysée', vol. 3, pp. 357–93 (388).

15 De Saint Pierre, *Études,* vol. 3, p. 390.

16 Richard A. Etlin, *The Architecture of Death: The Transformation of the Cemetery in Eighteenth-Century Paris* (Cambridge, Mass.: MIT, 1984), p. 245. See also

Joseph Clarke, *Commemorating the Dead in Revolutionary France: Revolution and Remembrance, 1789–1799* (Cambridge: Cambridge University Press, 2007), chs 3–4.

17 Clarke, *Commemorating the Dead*, p. 288.

18 Etlin, *The Architecture of Death*, p. 251.

19 Étienne-Louis Boullée, *Architecture: Essai sur l'art* (Paris: Hermann, 1968), pp. 132–7.

20 His immediate source of inspiration was probably the monument to the revolutionary martyr Marat, a popular place of pilgrimage erected in the garden of another former monastery, that of the Cordeliers. Francis Haskell, *History and its Images: Art and the Interpretation of the Past* (New Haven: Yale, 1993), ch. 9.

21 J. M. Bart, 'Une pensée sur les Catacombes de Paris', in L. Héricart de Thury, *Description des Catacombes de Paris* (Paris: Bossange et Masson, 1815), pp. 322–4 (323).

22 'Bernard Blackmantle' is identified as Charles Molloy Westmacott in the British Library catalogue. See Jane Rendell, *The Pursuit of Pleasure: Gender, Space and Architecture in Regency London* (London: Athlone, 2002), pp. 32ff., p. 153, n. 12.

23 'Bernard Blackmantle', 'The Life, Death, Burial and Resurrection Company', in 'Blackmantle', *The English Spy*, 2 vols (London: Sherwood, Gilbert and Piper, 1826), vol. 2, pp. 115–17.

24 Anon., *The Cemetery. A brief appeal to the feelings of society in behalf of extra-mural burial* (London: William Pickering, 1848), p. 20.

25 Ibid., pp. 24–5.

26 John Morley, *Death, Heaven and the Victorians* (London: Studio Vista, 1971).

27 Giles Waterfield (ed.), *Soane and Death* (London: Dulwich Picture Gallery, 1996).

28 James Stevens Curl (ed.), *Kensal Green Cemetery: The Origins and Development of the General Cemetery of All Souls, Kensal Green, London, 1824–2001* (Chichester: Phillimore, 2001), p. 77.

29 Ibid., p. 70.

30 Paul Joyce, *A Guide to Abney Park Cemetery* (Hackney: Save Abney Park Publications, 1984).

31 Ruth Richardson, *Death, Dissection and the Destitute* (London: Routledge and Kegan Paul, 1987), p. 54.

32 Ibid., p. 78 (Lambeth), p. 87 (Greenwich), pp. 224, 263.

33 Ibid., p. 62 (Naples), pp. 132ff. (Burke and Hare), pp. 191ff. (Bishop and Williams).

34 Curl (ed.), *Kensal Green Cemetery*, p. 87.

35 Richardson, *Death, Dissection and the Destitute*, p. 202.

36 Curl (ed.), *Kensal Green Cemetery*, p. 95.

37 John Claudius Loudon, *On the Laying Out, Planting, and Managing of Cemeteries* (London: Longman, 1843).

38 Peter C. Jupp, 'Enon Chapel: no way for the dead', in Peter C. Jupp and Glennys Howarth (eds), *The Changing Face of Death: Historical Accounts of Death and Disposal* (Basingstoke: Macmillan, 1997).

39 George Alfred Walker, *Practical suggestions for the establishment of national cemeteries* (London: Longman, 1849), p. 6.

40 Charles Dickens, 'From the Raven in the Happy Family 2' (originally published in *Household Words*, 8 June 1850); 'Trading in death' (*Household Words,* 27 November 1852) in *Complete Works Centennial Edition, Miscellaneous Papers I*, pp. 207–11, 374–84 (374–5).

41 Edwin Chadwick, *A Supplementary Report on the results of a special enquiry into the practice of interment in towns* (London: HMSO, 1843).

42 Pugin and Heath, *Paris and its Environs,* vol. 2, p. 130.

43 John M. Clarke, *The Brookwood Necropolis Railway* (Oxford: Oakwood, 1983).

44 *Mémoires du Baron Haussmann*, 3 vols (Paris: Victor-Hard, 1893), vol. 3, chs 12–13; E. Huet, *Chemin de Fer et Cimetière Parisien de Méry-Sur-Oise. Rapport de l'Ingénieur en Chef* (Paris: A. Chaix, 1876). See Frédéric Bertrand, 'Cimetières, jardins et colonies', in Simon Texier (ed.), *Les Parcs et Jardins dans l'urbanisme Parisien: XIXe–XXe siècles* (Paris: Action Artistique de la Ville de Paris, 2001), pp. 125–30.

45 Mireille Galinou, *Cottage and Villas: The Birth of the Garden Suburb* (New Haven, Yale University Press, 2010).

46 Alexander T. Stewart's Garden City was begun eighteen miles from New York in 1869. For this and other American suburbs see Robert A. M. Stern, *The Anglo-American Suburb* (New York: Architectural Design, 1981).

47 Wohl, *The Eternal Slum,* p. 147.

48 S. Martin Gaskell, 'Housing and the lower middle class, 1870–1914', in Gregory Crossick (ed.), *The Lower Middle Class in Britain, 1870–1914* (London: Croom Helm, 1977), pp. 159–83 (172, 179).

49 Raymond Unwin et al., *Town Planning and Modern Architecture at the Hampstead Garden Suburb* (London: T. Fisher Unwin, 1909), pp. 13–14.

50 See note 24.

51 A monopoly that lasted until 1993, when it was ended after formal complaints from Brussels.

52 Julie Rugg and Nicolas Pleace, *An Audit of London Burial Provision* (London: Greater London Authority, 2011).

53 ONS figures quoted in Rugg and Pleace, *An Audit*, Fig. 2.1.

54 Charles Dickens, 'The Uncommercial Traveller', *All the Year Round* (21 July 1860), pp. 348–352 (351).

55 Lewis Mumford, *The City in History: Its Origins, its Transformations, and its Prospects* (London: Secker and Warburg, 1961), p. 7.

Select Bibliography

General Works

Histories or 'biographies' of Paris and London in isolation are legion, and it would be foolish to make recommendations. However, the books listed below are worth noting, either because they offer a comparative perspective or because they provide exciting and engaging models for writing about urban space and identities.

Italo Calvino, *Invisible Cities* (New York: Harcourt, Brace,1972).

Richard Dennis, *Cities in Modernity: Representations and Productions of Metropolitan Space, 1840–1930* (Cambridge: Cambridge University Press, 2008).

James Donald, *Imagining the Modern City* (London: Athlone, 1999).

Claire Hancock, *Paris et Londres au XIXe siècle: répresentations dans les guides et récits de voyage* (Paris: Editions du CNRS, 2003).

Andrew Lees and Lynn Hollen Lees, *Cities and the Making of Modern Europe, 1750–1914* (Cambridge: Cambridge University Press, 2007).

Miles Ogborn, *Spaces of Modernity: London's Geographies, 1680–1780* (London: Guilford Press, 1998).

Donald J. Olsen, *The City as a Work of Art: London, Paris, Vienna* (New Haven: Yale University Press, 1986).

Michelle Perrot (ed.), *A History of Private Life: From the Fires of Revolution to the Great War* (Cambridge, Mass.: Belknap, 1990).

Richard Sennett, *The Fall of Public Man* (London: Penguin, 2002).

Karlheinz Stierle, *Der Mythos von Paris: Zeichen und Bewußtsein der Stadt* (Munich: DTV, 1998).

Robert and Isabelle Tombs, *That Sweet Enemy: The French and the British from the Sun King to the Present* (London: William Heinemann, 2006).

Introduction: Rough Crossings

Mercier's *Tableau de Paris* is available in a good modern French edition, and selections have been published in English translation, edited by Jeremy Popkin (as the *Panorama of Paris*, Penn State University Press, 1999). The present author and Laurent Turcot are currently preparing an English translation of Mercier's *Parallèle de Paris et de Londres*, which is already accessible to Francophone readers in the edition prepared by Claude Bruneteau and Bernard Cottret (Didier Erudition, 1982). For the political background to Anglo-French relations in this period, Tombs and Dziembowski are excellent. The Saint-Aubin *Livre de caricatures tant bonnes que mauvaises* is available online, thanks to Colin Jones's Saint-Aubin Project, via the website of Waddesdon Manor. It affords a rare glimpse into the imagination of an exceptionally creative family who were near contemporaries of Mercier.

Colin Bailey, Kim de Beaumont et al., *Gabriel de Saint-Aubin, 1725–1780* (Paris: Louvre, 2008).

Simon Burrows (ed.), *Cultural Transfers: France and Britain in the Long Eighteenth Century* (Oxford: SVEC, 2010).

Edmond Dziembowski, *Les Pitt. L'Angleterre face à la France, 1708–1806* (Paris: Perrin, 2006).

Edmond Dziembowski, 'The English political model in eighteenth-century France', *Historical Research*, 74 (2001), pp. 151–71.

David Garrioch, *The Making of Revolutionary Paris* (Berkeley: University of California Press, 2002).

Jean-Louis Harouel, *L'Embellissement des Villes: l'urbanisme française au XVIIIe siècle* (Paris: Picard, 1993).

Derek Jarrett, *The Begetters of Revolution: England's Involvement with France, 1759–1789* (Totowa, NJ: Rowman and Littlefield, 1973).

Raymonde Monnier, *Paris et Londres en miroir: extraits du Babillard de Jean-Jacques Rutlidge* (Saint-Étienne: Université de Saint-Étienne, 2010).

Chapter 1: The Restless House

Though Percy Pinkerton's *Piping Hot!* is hard to come by, Brian Nelson's translation of Zola's *Pot-Bouille* (as *Pot Luck*, Oxford World Classics, 1999) is a more than adequate replacement. For anyone seeking to uncover how apartment buildings were financed, designed, constructed and used in eighteenth-century Paris and London, Cabestan, and Burton and Cruickshank respectively offer fascinating, lavishly illustrated and thoughtful surveys. Equivalent studies for the nineteenth century are harder to find, although Dennis's work is a model of how to combine close analysis of floor plans with reading of fictional accounts, a model I have endeavoured to follow closely.

Neil Burton and Dan Cruickshank, *Life in the Georgian City* (London: Viking, 1990).

Jean-François Cabestan, *La Conquête du plain-pied: l'immeuble à Paris au XVIIIe siècle* (Paris: Picard, 2004).

Richard Dennis, 'Buildings, residences and mansions: George Gissing's "prejudice against flats"', in John Spiers (ed.), *Gissing and the City* (London: Palgrave, 2006), pp. 41–62.

Richard Dennis, *Cities in Modernity: Representations and Productions of Metropolitan Space, 1840–1930* (Cambridge: Cambridge University Press, 2008).

Sharon Marcus, *Apartment Stories: City and Home in Nineteenth-Century Paris and London* (Berkeley: University of California Press, 1999).

Ann-Louise Shapiro, *Housing the Poor of Paris, 1850–1902* (Madison: University of Wisconsin Press, 1985).

Anthony Sutcliffe (ed.), *Multi-Storey Living: The British Working-Class Experience* (London: Croom Helm, 1974).

J. A. Yelling, *Slums and Slum Clearance in Victorian London* (London: Allen and Unwin, 1986).

Chapter 2: The Street

There are several modern editions offering selections from *The Spectator* and *Tatler* (e.g. St Martin's, 1998). Benjamin is the starting point for any discussion of the *flâneur*, although the full text has yet to be made available in English. Rose combines an edition of key French and British texts on the nineteenth-century *flâneur* along with useful commentary. British and American scholars have become somewhat preoccupied with finding the *flâneur*'s female equivalent. The other works listed here give a less theoretical and possibly more compelling view of street life, particularly Roche and Hitchcock. Ménétra affords an exceptionally rare memoir of the eighteenth century by an artisan.

Walter Benjamin, *Das Passagen-werk*, ed. Rolf Tiedem, 2 vols (Frankfurt: Suhrkamp, 1983).

Clare Brant and Susan E. Whyman (eds), *Walking the Streets of Eighteenth-Century London: John Gay's* Trivia (Oxford: Oxford University Press, 2009).

Michel de Certeau, 'Walking in the city', in Certeau, *The Practice of Everyday Life*, trans. Steven Rendall (Berkeley: University of California Press, 1984), pp. 91–110.

Jonathan Conlin, '"At the expense of the public": the 1762 Signpainters Exhibition and the public sphere', *Eighteenth-Century Studies*, 36: 1 (2002).

Aruna D'Souza and Tom McDonough (eds), *The Invisible Flâneuse? Gender, Public Space and Visual Culture in Nineteenth-Century Paris* (Manchester: Manchester University Press, 2006).

Arlette Farge, *Vivre dans la rue à Paris au XVIIIe siècle* (Paris: Gallimard, 1979).

David Garrioch, 'House names, shop signs and social organization in Western European cities, 1500–1900', *Urban History*, 21 (1994), pp. 20–48.

Eric Hazan, *L'Invention du Paris: il n'y a pas des pas perdus* (Paris: Seuil, 2002).

Bernard Landau, Claire Monod and Evelyne Lohr (eds), *Les Grand Boulevards: un parcours d'innovation et de modernité* (Paris: AAVP [n.d.]).

Tim Hitchcock, *Down and Out in Eighteenth-Century London* (London: Continuum, 2007).

Tim Hitchcock and Heather Shore (eds), *The Streets of London: From the Great Fire to the Great Stink* (London: Rivers Oram, 2003).

Jacques-Louis Ménétra, *Journal of My Life* (New York: Columbia University Press, 1986).

Kathryn A. Morrison, *English Shops and Shopping: An Architectural History* (New Haven: Yale University Press, 2003).

Lynda Nead, *Victorian Babylon: People, Streets and Images in Nineteenth-Century London* (New Haven: Yale University Press, 2000).

Jane Rendell, *The Pursuit of Pleasure: Gender, Space and Architecture in Regency London* (London: Athlone, 2002).

Daniel Roche, *The People of Paris: An Essay in Popular Culture in the Eighteenth Century*, trans. Marie Evans (New York: Berg, 1987).

Margaret Rose, *Flaneurs and Idlers* (Bielefeld: Aisthesis, 2007).

Laurent Turcot, *Le Promeneur à Paris* (Paris: Gallimard, 2007).

Chapter 3: The Restaurant

There are several biographies of Grimod and Brillat-Savarin, as well as of Alexis Soyer, and editions/translations of works such as *La Physiologie du Goût* are easily accessible. Perhaps oddly, there is little scholarly writing in French on the history of gastronomy and dining out, though the works of food writers like Robert Courtine can be helpful. Mennell affords an excellent comparative introduction, both wide-ranging and thoughtful. Spang and Metzner are more tightly focussed, but also excellent.

Jean-Paul Aron, *The Art of Eating in France: Manners and Menus in the Nineteenth Century* (London: Peter Owen, 1975).

Alan Borg, *A History of the Worshipful Company of Cooks of London* (London: privately printed, 2011).

Thomas Brennan, *Public Drinking and Popular Culture in Eighteenth-Century Paris* (Princeton: Princeton University Press, 1988).

Alberto Capatti et al., *À Table au XIXe siècle* (Paris: Flammarion, 2001).

Robert Courtine, *La vie parisienne: Cafés et restaurants des boulevards (1814–1914)* (Paris: Perrin, 1984)

Edwina Ehrman et al., *London Eats Out: 500 Years of Capital Dining* (London: Museum of London, 1999).

Stephen Mennell, *All Manners of Food: Eating and Taste in England and France from the Middle Ages to the Present*, 2nd edn (Chicago: University of Illinois Press, 1996).

Paul Metzner, *Crescendo of the Virtuoso: Spectacle, Skill, and Self-Promotion in Paris during the Age of Revolution* (Berkeley: University of California Press, 1998).

Erika Rappaport, *Shopping for Pleasure: Women in the Making of London's West End* (Princeton: Princeton University Press, 2000).

Rachel Rich, *Bourgeois Consumption: Food, Space and Identity in London and Paris, 1850–1914* (Manchester: Manchester University Press, 2011).

[Ralph Rylance], *The Epicure's Almanack* [1815], ed. Janet Ing Freeman (London: British Library, 2012).

Rebecca Spang, *The Invention of the Restaurant: Paris and Modern Gastronomic Culture* (Cambridge, Mass.: Harvard University Press, 2000).

Chapter 4: The Dance

The V&A, the borough archives of Westminster and Lambeth, the Musée Carnavalet and the Bibliothèque Nationale de France's Arts du Spectacle division contain a wealth of posters, programmes and photographs of music halls and *bals publics*, as well as individual performers. Whereas the history of London's music halls is fairly well researched, good books on pleasure gardens, 'Wauxhalls', *guinguettes*, *bals publics* and Parisian music halls are very hard to find. Many wallow in nostalgia for this or that 'golden age'. Those listed below are more reliable; Gasnault, Langlois and Scott are excellent.

J. S. Bratton (ed.), *Music Hall: Performance and Style* (Milton Keynes: Open University, 1986).

Rae Beth Gordon, *Why the French Love Jerry Lewis: From Cabaret to Early Cinema* (Stanford: Stanford University Press, 2001).

François Brunet, *Théophile Gautier et la danse* (Paris: Honoré Champion, 2010).

François Caradec and Alain Weill, *Le Café Concert, 1848–1914* (Paris: Arhème Fayard, 2007).

Jean Castarede, *Le Moulin Rouge* (Paris: France-Empire, 2001).

Philippe Chauveau and André Sallé, *Music-hall et café-concert* (Paris: Bordas, 1985).

Rupert Christiansen, *The Visitors: Culture Shock in Nineteenth-Century Britain* (London: Chatto and Windus, 2000).

Jonathan Conlin, 'Vauxhall on the boulevard: pleasure gardens in Paris and London, 1759–89', *Urban History*, 35: 1 (May 2008).

Barry J. Faulk, *Music Hall and Modernity: The Late-Victorian Discovery of Popular Culture* (Athens: Ohio University Press, 2004).

Jacques Fescotte, *Histoire du Music-Hall* (Paris: PUF, 1965).

J. E. Crawford Flitch, *Modern Dancing and Dancers* (London: Grant Richards, 1912).

François Gasnault, *Guinguettes et Lorettes: bals publics et dans social à Paris entre 1830 et 1870* (Paris: Aubier, 1986).

Dagmar Kift, *The Victorian Music Hall: Culture, Class and Conflict,* trans. Roy Kift (Cambridge: Cambridge University Press, 1996).

Gilles-Antoine Langlois, *Folies, Tivolis et Attractions: les premiers parc de loisirs parisiens* (Paris: Action Artistique de la Ville de Paris, 1991).

Raoul Muriand, *Les Folies Bergères* (Sèvres: La Sirène, 1994).

Clare Parfitt, 'Capturing the cancan: body politics from the Enlightenment to postmodernity', (PhD diss., University of Surrey, 2008).

David Price, *Cancan!* (London: Cygnus Arts, 1998).

Derek B. Scott, *Sounds of the Metropolis: The Nineteenth-Century Popular Music Revolution in London, New York, Paris and Vienna* (Oxford: Oxford University Press, 2008).

Jerrold Seigel, *Bohemian Paris: Culture, Politics, and the Boundaries of Bourgeois Life, 1830–1930* (Baltimore: Johns Hopkins University Press, 1986).

Nicole Wild, *Dictionnaire des théatres Parisiens au XIX siècles* (Paris: Amateurs de Livres, 1989).

Chapter 5: The Underworld

The story of how the city night was colonized in the eighteenth and nineteenth centuries has yet to be told, and so accounts privileging the nineteenth century (like Schivelbusch) have gone largely unchallenged. Koslofsky and Cabantous offer useful models. Beattie and Emsley are the most authoritative historians of British crime and policing; some of the latter's work also makes comparisons between London and Paris. Biographies of Vidocq offer little more than commentary on his memoirs, which are, happily, available in English translation (Edinburgh: AK Press). The history of detective fiction is almost a cottage industry in itself, and there is room here to list only the most reliable and level-headed works.

John Beattie, *Policing and Punishment in London, 1660–1750: Urban Crime and the Limits of Terror* (Oxford: Oxford University Press, 2001).

T. J. Binyon, *Murder Will Out: The Detective in Fiction* (Oxford: Oxford University Press, 1989).

Roger Bonniot, *Émile Gaboriau ou la Naissance du Roman policier* (Paris: J. Vrin, 1985).

Alain Cabantous, *Histoire de la nuit: XVIIe-XVIIIe siècle* (Paris: Fayard, 2009).

Simone Delattre, *Les douze heures noires: la nuit à Paris au XIXe siècle* (Paris: Albin Michel, 2000).

Clive Emsley and Haia Shpayer-Makov, *Police Detectives in History, 1750–1950* (Aldershot: Ashgate, 2006).

Judith Flanders, *The Invention of Murder* (London: Harper, 2011).

Fayçal El Ghoul, *La Police Parisienne dans la second moitie du XVIIIe siècle (1760–1785)*, 2 vols (Tunis: Université de Tunis I, 1995).

Craig Koslofsky, *Evening's Empire: A History of the Night in Early Modern Europe* (Cambridge: Cambridge University Press, 2011).

Richard Maxwell, *The Mysteries of Paris and London* (Charlottesville: University of Virginia Press, 1992).

Régis Messac, *Le 'Detective Novel' et l'influence de la pensée scientifique* (Paris: Bibliothèque de la Révue de littérature comparé, 1929).

Michael Saler, '"Clap if you believe in Sherlock Holmes": mass culture and the re-enchantment of modernity, c. 1890–c. 1940', *Historical Journal*, 46: 3 (September 2003), pp. 599–622.

Wolfgang Schivelbusch, *Disenchanted Night: The Industrialization of Light in the Nineteenth Century* (Berkeley: University of California Press, 1988).

R. F. Stewart, . . . *And Always a Detective: Chapters on the History of Detective Fiction* (London: David & Charles, 1980).

Chapter 6: Dead and Buried

The pre-eminent scholar of cemeteries is James Stevens Curl, who has long ploughed a lonely furrow. His *The Victorian Celebration of Death* covers eighteenth-century French influences as well as the emergence of the great London cemeteries. French scholarship on cemeteries is almost non-existent. Where they exist, books or pamphlets on cemeteries tend to focus on a single cemetery, and can seem more interested in celebrity spotting than in documenting how cemeteries were financed, planned, designed and used. Much work remains to be done on how these enclaves relate to the city as a whole.

Philippe Ariès, *Western Attitudes towards Death, from the Middle Ages to the Present* (Baltimore: Johns Hopkins University Press, 1972).

Frédéric Bertrand, 'Cimetières, jardins et colonies', in Simon Texier (ed.), *Les Parcs et Jardins dans l'urbanisme Parisien: XIXe–XXe siècles* (Paris: Action Artistique de la Ville de Paris, 2001), pp. 125–30.

James Stevens Curl, *Death and Architecture* (Stroud: Sutton, 2002).

James Stevens Curl, *The Victorian Celebration of Death* (Stroud: Sutton, 2005).

James Stevens Curl (ed.), *Kensal Green Cemetery: The Origins and Development of the General Cemetery of All Souls, Kensal Green, London,*

1824–2001 (Chichester: Phillimore, 2001).

Richard A. Etlin, *The Architecture of Death: The Transformation of the Cemetery in Eighteenth-Century Paris* (Cambridge, Mass.: MIT, 1984).

Peter C. Jupp and Glennys Howarth (eds), *The Changing Face of Death: Historical Accounts of Death and Disposal* (Basingstoke: Macmillan, 1997).

Samantha Matthews, 'The London necropolis', in Lawrence Phillips (ed.), *A Mighty Mass of Brick and Smoke: Victorian and Edwardian Representations of London* (Amsterdam: Rodopi, 2008), pp. 257–82.

Ruth Richardson, *Death, Dissection and the Destitute* (London: Routledge and Kegan Paul, 1987).

Acknowledgments

In his 1632 book, *London and the countrey carbonadoed*, Donald Lupton wrote of his trepidation in addressing his home city. 'She is growne so Great, I am almost affraide to meddle with Her; she's certainly a great world, there are so many little worlds in her.' Lupton was certainly correct. Someone attempting to 'carbonado' (that is, slice and grill over coals) both London and Paris is highly likely to be raked over the coals himself. Before accounting some of my debts to others I must repeat a familiar proviso: responsibility for the errors that remain in this exploration of a few of Lupton's 'little worlds' is entirely my own.

My first forays into French history and first taste of Parisian archives resulted from an interest in the relationship between the Georgian rake and rabble-rouser John Wilkes and his French alter ego, the transvestite spy the Chevalier d'Eon. Simon Burrows, Edmond Dziembowski, Julian Swann and Robert Tombs were particularly welcoming as I took my first steps. They are partly to blame for encouraging me to continue working on Anglo-French history. So, too, are my agent, Andrew Lownie, and Ravi Mirchandani of Atlantic, who helped me develop the original idea, with a little help from Louis-Sébastien Mercier.

Research has required lengthy stays in Paris and London. Marine Bernier, Nigel and Phoebe Blackburn, Bob and Sylvie Mayo, Bernard and Pamela Soyer, and Alexandre Tessier all provided me with a roof and moral support at various points over the past ten years, for which I am very grateful. The Bibliothèque Historique de la Ville de Paris and the London Library both offered calm places to think and write.

At an early stage of the research I came into contact with Laurent

Turcot, historian of eighteenth-century Paris and much else besides. This book has benefited greatly from our discussions in Montreal and Paris, and particularly during a joint fellowship at the Lewis Walpole Library in the summer of 2011, which allowed us to prepare an English edition of Mercier's *Parallèle de Paris et de Londres*. The 2010 Quebec City conference on the history of Paris he convened with Thierry Belleguic provided the ideal opportunity for me to meet fellow scholars of Paris. I also gained much from other conferences, including the 'Paris/Londres' symposia (at the Institute for Historical Research and the Institut national d'histoire de l'art), the Waddesdon Manor Saint Aubin conference, as well as colloquia at the Sorbonne Nouvelle and Université de Bretagne Occidentale. My thanks go to Dana Arnold, Isabelle Bour, Jean-Louis Cohen, Annick Cossick, Norbert Col, Gillian Dow and Colin Jones for making these events possible. I am equally grateful to Lawrence Klein and Simon Kitson for opportunities to give papers on the *flâneur* at seminars in Cambridge and at the University of London in Paris (ULIP).

Richard Arnold, Brenda Assael, Peter Borsay, Wolfgang Cilleßen, John Clarke, Brian Cowan, Rachel Cowgill, James Stevens Curl, Hannah Greig, Gilles-Antoine Langlois, Simon Macdonald, Peter Mandler, Vanessa Schwartz, Derek Scott and Rebecca Spang all helped, whether by answering queries or provoking them. Among my colleagues at Southampton, Gillian Dow, Mark Everist, Joachim Schloer, François Soyer and Joan Tumblety were particularly supportive; I should also acknowledge veterans of my undergraduate course 'Cities of the Dead' for fuelling my interest in cemeteries. Jean-Baptiste Woloch of the Musée Carnavalet and Kate Heard both went beyond the call of duty in locating visual material. Rupert Christiansen, Alun Howard, Colin Jones and Lucia Ruprecht all read draft versions and offered useful comments, and, in Alun's case, bracingly trenchant criticism. At Atlantic Celia Levett, James Nightingale and Orlando Whitfield were very helpful as I prepared the manuscript for publication.

I dedicate this book to my friend Wim Weymans, in fond recollection of our many discussions of French history and theory in the Rue Mandar and the Rue de la Plaine.

Note on the Author

Jonathan Conlin was born in New York and later moved to Britain, where he studied history at Oxford. He went on to do graduate work at the Courtauld Institute and Cambridge, completing a PhD thesis on the early history of the National Gallery, London; his books include *The Nation's Mantelpiece* and *Civilisation*. He is regularly invited to comment on museums and broader questions of national heritage, on ITV's *South Bank Show*, *History Today* magazine and the *Today* programme.

Illustrations

Fig. 1:   Thomas Rowlandson, *The Paris Diligence*, watercolour with pen and black, gray and red-brown ink over graphite [n.d.] (Yale Center for British Art, Paul Mellon Collection, B1975.3.129.)

Fig. 2:   James Caldwell after John Collet, *The Englishman in Paris*, etching and engraving, 1770. (Courtesy of the Lewis Walpole Library, Yale University, LWL770.05.10.01+.)

Fig. 3:   Charles White after John Collet, *The Frenchman in London*, etching and engraving, hand-coloured, 1770. (Courtesy of the Lewis Walpole Library, Yale University, LWL770.11.10.01+.)

Fig. 4:   Unknown artist after John Donowell, *A view of Marylebone Gardens*, engraving, 1761. (© Guildhall Library, City of London, Collage 19385.)

Fig. 5:   Unknown photographer, view of Katherine Buildings, Cartwright Street, rear elevation, 1970. (© London Metropolitan Archives, City of London, Collage 118115.)

Fig. 6:   Nicolas Toussaint Charlet, 'Ces petites gens du second...', lithograph, 1826. (© The Trustees of the British Museum, 1880,0508.267.)

Fig. 7:   Unknown artist after Robert Dighton, *A pleasant way to lose an eye*, 1820–5. (© The Trustees of the British Museum, 1853,0112.315.)

Fig. 8:   Detail of Nicholas Yeates after Robert Thacker, *View of St Mary le Bow*, engraving, *c*. 1680. (© Guildhall Library, City of London, Collage 21697.)

Fig. 9:   Detail of Unknown artist after Antoine Hublot, *Abbildung des auf der Straße Quincampoix in Paris entstandenen so berühmten Actien-Handels*, engraving, 1720. (© The Trustees of the British Museum, 1882,0812.461.)

Fig. 10: Pierre Aveline after Jean Antoine Watteau, *The shop sign of Gersaint*, *c*. 1732, engraving. (© Bibliotheque Nationale, Paris, France/Giraudon/The Bridgeman Art Library.)

Fig. 11: Charles-Germain de Saint-Aubin, 'Bâtir Est beau, mais detruire est Sublime', 1761, in *Livre de Caricatures tant bonnes que mauvaises*, *c.* 1740–1775. Watercolour, ink and graphite on paper, 187 x 132 mm. (Waddesdon, The Rothschild Collection (The National Trust), acc. no. 675.358. Photo: Imaging Services Bodleian Library. © The National Trust, Waddesdon Manor.)

Fig. 12: William Hogarth, *Beer Street*, engraving, 1751. (Yale Center for British Art, B1994.4.514.)

Fig. 13: Unknown artist, '*Flâneur* hit by *volet*', from Louis Huart, *La Physiologie du Flâneur*, 1841.

Fig. 14: George Scharf, Blacking tin men, graphite, 1834–8. (© The Trustees of the British Museum, 1862.0614.1090.)

Fig. 15: Gault de Saint Germain after Unknown artist, *Entrez Messieurs et Dames, C'est le moment ou les Animaux prennent leur Nourriture!*, hand-coloured etching, 1817. (© The Trustees of the British Museum, 1992,0516.30.)

Fig. 16: Jean-Baptiste Lesueur, *Famille allant à la guinguette*, gouache, 1790s. (© Musée Carnavalet/Roger Viollet/Topham Picturepoint, 27122-20.)

Fig. 17: William Hogarth, *Cookshop*, drawing, 1746–7. (© The Trustees of the British Museum, 1896,0710.29.)

Fig. 18: James Gillray, *Hero's recruiting at Kelsey's*, hand-coloured etching, 1797. (© The Trustees of the British Museum, 1868,0808.6640.)

Fig. 19: Unknown artist, *Mr Horton's Soup Room*, engraving, 1770. (© Guildhall Library, City of London, Collage 1825.)

Fig. 20: G. B. Moore after William Radclyffe, *Reform Club. The Kitchen*, engraving 1840s. (Courtesy of the Reform Club.)

Fig. 21: Henri de Toulouse-Lautrec, *The Englishman at the Moulin Rouge*, colour lithograph, 1892. (© Musée Toulouse-Lautrec, Albi/Giraudon/Bridgeman Art Library.)

Fig. 22: George Cruikshank, *'Life' on Tip-toe, or Dick Wildfire Quadrilling it, in the Salon de Mars in the Champs Elysées*, hand-coloured etching and aquatint, 1822. (© The Trustees of the British Museum 1865,1111.2237.)

Fig. 23: Unknown artist, *National Education*, engraving from *The Censor*, 20 June 1868. (© Westminster Borough Archives, Alhambra/Royal Aquarium Box.)

Fig. 24: William Downey, Kate Vaughan as Lalla Rookh at the Novelty Theatre, photograph, 1884. (© Victoria and Albert Museum, 2006AP4762-01.)

Fig. 25: Unknown artist, Nini Pattes-en-l'air, la Sauterelle, Grille d'Egout and La Goulue at the Moulin Rouge, photolithograph, 1900. (© Roger Viollet/Topham Picturepoint, 1577-10.)

Fig. 26: Unknown photographer, *Quai des Orfèvres/Rue de Jérusalem, c.* 1900. (© Roger Viollet/Topham Picturepoint, 24641-8.)

Fig. 27: Anonymous artist, frontis. to Rétif de la Bretonne, *Les Nuits de Paris,* 1789. (© Roger Viollet/Topham Picturepoint, 768-4.)

Fig. 28: William Hogarth, *Night* from *The Times of Day,* engraving, 1738. (© Guildhall Library, City of London, Collage 25079.)

Fig. 29: Henri Joseph van Blarenberghe, *Descente de police la nuit,* graphite, pen and gouache, *c.* 1780. (© RMN/Musée du Louvre, Département des Arts graphiques, RF3487.)

Fig. 30: Henri Joseph van Blarenberghe, *Scène de rue*, graphite, pen and gouache, *c.* 1780. (© RMN/Musée du Louvre, Département des Arts graphiques, RF3490.)

Fig. 31: Gillot, *Émile Gaboriau*, engraving, 1873. (© Roger Viollet/Topham Picturepoint, 8961-7.)

Fig. 32: Cover of Vizetelly edition of Émile Gaboriau, *In Peril of His Life*, 1884. (Private Collection.)

Fig. 33: Charles Heath after A. C. Pugin, 'General View of Paris', frontis. to vol. 2 of *Paris and Environs* (London: Jennings and Chaplin, 1830). (© British Library.)

Fig. 34: Lesueur after Louis Carrogis [Carmontelle], 'Bois des Tombeaux' from *Jardin de Monceau, près de Paris appartenant à son altesse sérénissime monseigneur le Duc de Chartres* (Paris: Delafosse [et] Née & Masquelier, 1779). (© Dumbarton Oaks Research Library and Collection, Rare Book Collection, Washington, DC.)

Fig. 35: A. W. N. Pugin, 'New General Cemetery for All Denominations', *Apology for Christian Architecture* (London: John Weale, 1843), plate 4. (© RIBA Library Photograph Collections.)

Index